I LOVE YOU SO MUCH AL,
YOU DON'T EVEN KNOW,
LOVE,
MIKE

Social Mobility in Canada

MCGRAW-HILL RYERSON SERIES IN CANADIAN SOCIOLOGY

GENERAL EDITOR: LORNE TEPPERMAN
Department of Sociology
University of Toronto

THE CANADIAN CLASS STRUCTURE
Dennis Forcese

DEMOGRAPHIC BASES OF CANADIAN SOCIETY
Warren Kalbach and Wayne McVey

A STATISTICAL PROFILE OF CANADIAN SOCIETY
Daniel Kubat and David Thornton

IDEOLOGICAL PERSPECTIVES ON CANADA
Patricia Marchak

SOCIAL MOBILITY IN CANADA
Lorne Tepperman

Forthcoming:
CANADIAN SOCIETY IN HISTORICAL PERSPECTIVE
S.D. Clark

DEVIANCE: THE SOCIOLOGY OF DISREPUTABLE PLEASURES
John Hagan

ETHNIC GROUP RELATIONS IN CANADA
Wsevolod Isajiw

SOCIAL CHANGE IN CANADA
Lorna Marsden

FAMILY LIFE IN CANADA
Benjamin Schlesinger

Social Mobility in Canada

Lorne Tepperman
University of Toronto

McGraw-Hill Ryerson Limited
Toronto   Montreal   New York   London   Sydney
Johannesburg   Mexico   Panama   Düsseldorf
Singapore   São Paulo   Kuala Lumpur   New Delhi

Social Mobility in Canada

ISBN 0-07-082257-3

12345678910HR4321098765

Printed and bound in Canada

INTRODUCTION AND ACKNOWLEDGEMENTS

❧

This book attempts several different things and has something of a split personality as a result. It contains a *mélange* of observations on formal and informal organization, demography, and the Canadian stratification system as thrown into perspective by the central question: what determines who succeeds and who fails in Canada? The book is both about Canada and about social mobility but, on balance, more about the latter than the former. Material is presented in Chapters Two and Three to re-orient the way we think about social mobility, and these two chapters are more abstract and more demanding than the others. A student may gain most by reading these chapters last of all, or perhaps by skimming them the first time through and rereading them after having received a more concrete introduction to social mobility in the other chapters.

The reader who is already familiar with the topic of social mobility will find that most of the standard issues are discussed here, as well as some of the less usual ones. This book is concerned, on the one hand, with the study of careers inside and outside formal organizations; and, on the other hand, with the study of intergenerational mobility from a comparative, cross-national perspective. The focus on careers will lead us into a discussion of work and occupations, while the concern with intergenerational mobility will direct our attention toward large-scale societal processes such as industrialization, toward cultural values and aspirations, and toward the impediments to achieving success.

Because this book has been designed to cover many distinct aspects of social mobility, most of the chapters are self-contained, and can be read in a variety of orderings and combinations. This will increase the utility of this book in teaching undergraduates about mobility, stratification, Canadian society, or even the aims and methods of sociology. I have been using this book in lectures to an introductory sociology class because it displays the "sociological imagination" in regard to a particular broad problem, and the cultivation of such a style of thinking is, for me, the purpose of an introductory course. But the reader is warned that what follows is not a mainstream approach to social mobility; I have emphasized certain issues and played down others, so it is conceivable that another instructor in sociology will want to shift the emphasis of this book to accord with his or her own approach.

This book has debts, some more visible than others, to a large number of people. Most obviously, my approach to the study of social mobility has been shaped by Harrison White and, somewhat less so, by Seymour Martin Lipset. When all has been said, my general approach to sociology has a kinship to the work of Talcott Parsons; yet if my native predisposition is Parsonian, I have given the greatest part of my attention to rethinking sociology in light of the approaches of George Homans and Harrison White. Indeed the mark of all my teachers and peers at Harvard's Department of Social Relations will be found throughout this book. Such demographic skills as I have been able to acquire and use in this book are the result of more recent studies with Ansley Coale and the people at the Office of Population Research. I am fortunate in having been exposed to the kinds of stimulation available at Harvard and Princeton; however well or badly I have used these opportunities, they have helped me—even made me—write this book in the way I have.

Chapters Four and Five were written under my supervision by Sandra Wain, the most capable student I have encountered at the University of Toronto. Her collaboration is acknowledged in each of these chapters and I am grateful for it. My colleagues Raymond Breton, Nancy Howell and Jeff Reitz have provided encouragement and commented at length upon the manuscript. Their criticism and help made it easier for me to revise my own thinking and push through to the end of this book, although I may have rejected too many sound suggestions for improvement my friends have offered. Finally, I have found the editors of the *Canadian Review of Sociology and Anthropology*, first Frank Jones and then Raymond Breton, always enlightening and sympathetic; this receptivity contributed to my undertaking this book, and some of the material presented here has already been published in the *Review*.

Anna De Luca and Elaine Du Wors, among others, typed parts of this book in its earliest incarnations; I have Sandra Abraham to thank for the final draft. Gordon van Tighem and, lately, Herb Hilderley and Josefa Kropp at McGraw-Hill Ryerson have seen the book through at their end of the line with kindness and good humour for which I am grateful.

Last, my wife Ruth secured copyright permissions for reprinted material and, more important, sacrificed her time so that I could concentrate on writing. I thank Ruth and my sons Andrew and Charles for having tried their best to bear up under the strains associated with the writing of this book.

TABLE OF CONTENTS

∾

LIST OF CHARTS

∽

LIST OF TABLES

∾

1

AN INTRODUCTION TO SOCIAL MOBILITY

∾

Let me introduce myself. I am a man who at the precocious age of thirty-five experienced an astonishing revelation: it is better to be a success than a failure. Having been penetrated by this great truth concerning the nature of things, my mind was now open for the first time to a series of corollary perceptions, each one as dizzying in its impact as the Original Revelation itself. Money, I now saw ... was important: it was better to be rich than to be poor. Power, I now saw (moving on to higher subtleties), was desirable: it was better to give orders than to take them. Fame, I now saw (how courageous of me not to flinch), was unqualifiedly delicious: it was better to be recognized than to be anonymous.

Norman Podhoretz, Making It

Why Study Social Mobility?

What is usually meant by (vertical) *social mobility* is the movement of people from one social stratum or level into another. Inversely, however, we can think of social mobility in terms of the movement not of people but of property, authority, and prestige ... what I shall call "power resources" below. As such, social mobility is change in the *relative* amount of power resources held by a person or group of people, over the course of time.

Mobility is an important social process, especially today. Modern societies are unusual in having recognized the arbitrariness and malleability of social arrangements and the usefulness of planning for change. Thus, recent centuries have seen attempts to remake societies (and their stratification systems), and, where inequality has remained, to stimulate upward mobility. People probably find inequality less tolerable today than they did when inequality was thought natural and vertical mobility was rare (Laslett, 1965). For this reason, the prospect of upward mobility makes inequality somewhat more palatable to modern people. "Success", viewed as movement up the hierarchy, and "failure", either a lack of upward movement or a movement downward, have become the focus of much human anxiety and enterprise.[1] This both distracts from the unpleasantness of inequality (and even poverty) and provides for those who "fail" a transcendent goal in planning for the success of their children. This topic will be discussed at greater length in Chapter Seven; for the time being, it should be noted that social mobility has become an important sociological topic because it has become important to people and societies.

There is one other respect in which mobility is important. Modern people regard mobility as a normal means of filling important positions in society with "competent" people. Modern citizens measure the performance of social institutions against their cultural values and economic and political goals. The perceived failure of these institutions to work properly is often attributed to an improper allocation of people to positions. This perception has contributed to the recent expansion and change in educational institutions. Formal education is one means of training and selecting talented people for mobility; and we have feared the consequences of failing to bring talented people into the most important social positions.

Most generally, many feel that if social inequality must be endured, we should at least attempt to prevent dynastic rule by a powerful few. This can be achieved in large part by opening all positions in society to all who are qualified. Under these circumstances, a measurement of social mobility becomes a measurement of social openness or democracy.

In the first systematic study of social mobility, Sorokin (1964) put forward five propositions that may provide a starting point for our discussion, a point of departure. Sorokin hypothesized that 1) there has almost never been a society in which mobility (economic, political and occupational) was not present; 2) there has never been a society in which mobility among all social strata was free or unimpeded; 3) the "amount" of mobility varies from society to society; 4) the "amount" of mobility within a given society fluctuates over the course of time; and 5) there is no evidence—either for a particular country or group, or for mankind in general—to suggest that the "amount" of mobility increases or decreases forever. What I have called "amount" of mobility, Sorokin referred to as "intensiveness" and "generality", or as we might say, the average distance (in strata) a mobile person might move, and the probability a person would leave his original stratum at all. Sorokin's propositions 1 and 2 seem acceptable enough today, but propositions 3, 4 and 5 do not, for they imply an almost random unpredictable variation in "amount" of mobility. They explicitly reject the view of the social evolutionist that social mobility is increasing all the time, alongside modernization. Chapter Two will be particularly concerned with reviewing this trio of hypotheses; more generally, this book will be concerned with the factors which cause mobility to vary predictably from one society to another.

The amount of social mobility in a society varies over time and varies from one locale to another; in addition, the amount of mobility varies from one society to another. As a result, the analysis of social mobility, which is relatively easy to measure in comparison with other social phenomena, points up differences between societies and changes in social organization over the course of time. Social mobility is a reasonably clearcut process as it is most commonly studied, and sociologists with leanings to mathematics have often found the study of mobility an area where formal mathematical representations are feasible and fruitful. It is often more difficult to fully explain a change or difference in social mobility than to discover it; but the ease of discovery and measurement certainly aid in finding an explanation. ˒

Some sociologists believe that social mobility is less worthy of study than social stratification, to which mobility is related in ways to be discussed shortly. They view social mobility as no more than a subtopic of social stratification. Moreover, social mobility is seen as a process that distracts people from the injustice of social inequality, reducing their willingness and ability to attack the system of inequality within which mobility takes place. This point of view has justification: an exclusive concern with success or failure makes those who succeed unwilling to criticize society, and those who fail organizationally or psychologically incapable of promoting change. Yet this observation does not lessen the sociological (and social) importance of mobility; rather, the reverse is true.

Mobility and Stratification

Social stratification and mobility are closely connected topics in sociology; the former is often concerned with describing and explaining the form of a hierarchy and the latter with movement through that hierarchy. At the extremes, these two topics merge into one. If every day (or even every year or decade) all the power resources in society were reassigned to members of society on a random basis, inequality would remain. But one would deny there was stratification, or stratification of consequence, in this society. The term stratification implies not only inequality of power resources and a correlation among power resources, but also continued membership in social strata, and behaviour aimed at maintaining (or bettering) power resources. A frequent change of stratum membership would prevent the formation of class consciousness or class awareness, and a random allocation of people to strata would make behaviour based on class interests unprofitable. If power resources continuously changed hands over time, or were "perfectly mobile", there would be no social stratification as we know it.

Conversely, if one's power resources throughout life were precisely those available at birth, there would by definition be no social mobility. In such circumstances we would be concerned with social inequalities however slight and power resources however poorly correlated, because these were permanent fixtures of everyone's life and the basis for strong class interests. In such a society, the degree to which strata were conscious of their advantage or disadvantage and willing to act to protect or better their relative position would occupy our whole attention.

Ignoring these extreme cases, stratification and mobility can be seen to influence each other in ways that are not yet fully understood. We are led to wonder whether the amount of mobility in a society varies with the degree of inequality in that society, and if so, why.

In a society in which the range of inequality from top to bottom is very great, there will necessarily be great potential for distant upward or downward mobility; but it is unclear whether such mobility will occur. In the Near East and China, close personal servants and ministers of the ruler were occasionally chosen from among slaves or other outcast groups because such selection gave no advantage to any of the noble families over any others, caused no resentment, and reduced the personal risk run by a ruler who was always endangered by noblemen eager for the crown (Levy, 1965; Mitamura, 1970). However, the frequency of such elevation to high office was not great; this kind of mobility was always possible, but not to be expected by a slave or outcast person.

In very unequal societies such as late medieval England, there was a lot of mobility within particular occupational categories. Town tradesmen and artisans became wealthy and rose to positions of authority in their community; occasionally they acquired enough money to purchase a country estate and become gentlemen (Thrupp, 1962). However, this mobility was usually across few strata, and moreover, a majority of people continued to live on the land, where there was little vertical mobility.

It appears that societies with great inequality, as measured by the Gini index of inequality, for example, have relatively little mobility. Conversely, industrial societies have both less inequality and more mobility than pre-industrial societies; this relationship will be discussed at length in the next chapter. One cannot say for certain, in view of our limited knowledge of pre-industrial societies, whether or not the apparent relationship between inequality and mobility is real, i.e., whether both inequality and mobility vary simultaneously as the result of industrialization. Nevertheless, some theorize that industrialization increases inequality. "Commercial expansion, money, usury, landed property and mortgage were thus accompanied by the rapid concentration and centralization of wealth in the hands of a small class, on the one hand, and by the increasing impoverishment of the masses and a growing mass of paupers, on the other," reported Engels in his survey of human history. Private property, the division of labour and a greater surplus productivity changed social organization from essentially communal and egalitarian to state-run and inegalitarian in character. Indeed, Engels held that the state came into being to maintain the interests of the great property owners, and depended for its own maintenance on the continued production of a surplus.

Lenski (1966) has followed this same line of reasoning, arguing that differential power and privilege have arisen with the division of labour and production of a material surplus. Yet paradoxically Lenski found, in carrying his study one hundred years beyond Engels, that the evolutionary trend has tended to reverse itself: further industrialization did not further increase inequality, but decreased it. This forces us to conclude either that Engels and Lenski were wrong in their analysis of social evolution prior to industrialization, or at least that the relationship between division of labour and inequality is curvilinear, not linear as Marx and Engels have assumed in all their works predicting pauperization of the masses, and ultimately revolution (cf. The Communist Manifesto).

The production and the distribution of power resources are somewhat independent processes, it is true. Industrialization produces more power resources by increasing national wealth, the division of labour (and hence positions of authority) and the dissemination of information necessary for prestige attribution. The distribution of power resources is a political phenomenon, and for this reason industrial nations subscribing to different political ideologies have not produced identical social structures as some sociologists had expected. Mobility is a function of the distributive process, and so is stratification. An explanation of the correlation between reduced inequality and increased mobility must finally be found in the politics of resource distribution.

Perhaps there are characteristic features of industrialism which influence the politics of resource distribution under any form of government or formally espoused ideology. Industrial nations are typically large, diverse in ethnic and economic composition, pluralistic in their mix of interest groups, and as a result hard to govern dictatorially. The state may be unable under such circumstances to attend to the interests of only one group, let alone control the allocation of all resources in favour of that group. Efficiency, as well as social protest, may require that the state and ruling class exercise less dominance over the distribution of power resources than they may desire or than may have been practicable in an earlier stage of social evolution.

Also, since industrialism generates the greatest surplus of any economic order where capable people of whatever origins are fitted into the most important productive roles, a ruling class may profit more from taking a smaller percentage of large surplus production than a larger percentage of less surplus production. The former strategy implies relinquishing a monopoly over resource allocation to a class-blind labour market mechanism—that is, to equality of opportunity—and thus relinquishment of total control over social mobility.

To close, social stratification and social mobility are closely related, but their relation to each other is as often spurious as real. Many concerns in the study of stratification are irrelevant to social mobility, and some aspects of social mobility discussed in this book—for example, career mobility—are of minor interest to students of social stratification. In some instances, social mobility is more readily understandable within the context of formal organization analysis or the sociology of occupations than in the perspective of social stratification. If a study of social mobility does not teach us everything of interest about stratification, this should come as no surprise.

"Amount" of Mobility Defined

I have referred, vaguely thus far, to the amount of mobility as something worth explaining. But what is an "amount" of mobility? Research on social mobility answers this question differently at different times (Miller, 1960). Most commonly the amount (or rate) of mobility to be explained is the proportion of a specified population that is mobile, or the *probability* of moving. In some contexts, one seeks to explain all movement, up and down, or the excess of upward movement over downward movement (i.e., net upward mobility). A study of intergenerational mobility may measure and explain the proportion of sons of farmers who enter a white collar occupation, for example. Lipset and Bendix (1959) argued that the proportion of sons of blue collar workers who became white collar workers was a critical measure of mobility in industrial societies. This was so, they argued, both because the blue collar–white collar line is the major class distinction in modern societies, and because movement across this line each generation is roughly the same in all industrial societies.

If the probability of upward movement were 100%, one would want to know something about the amount of mobility other than its likelihood. This is particularly salient in studies of career (or intragenerational) mobility, but also in some studies of intergenerational mobility. Almost everyone with a career in a formal organization will move up in the course of time. A career officer in the armed services will almost certainly move up in rank and pay after receiving his first commission; similarly, a college-educated junior executive at Shell Oil will usually improve his position and salary after entering the company. For this reason, one is less interested in the probability of upward movement than in the *distance* of upward movement over an individual's lifetime. In some cases of intergenerational mobility we are likewise uninterested in the probability of movement, because the theoretical probabilities are well known and relatively fixed. If the sons of peasants and artisans never became noblemen—and this probably describes most of human history—we need to know something more about what these sons did become in order to distinguish one pre-industrial society from another, and to distinguish the relative mobility of peasants and artisans. A close analysis often uncovers "hidden hierarchies", in this case different types of peasant, and perhaps as much inequality among such types as between white collar and blue collar workers in our own society (Belshaw, 1965). We will do best to ignore probabilities entirely and simply describe how far peasants move upward within the peasant status or outside it, unless we are prepared to formulate our questions in terms of the existing social structure.

In some instances we may not want to ask how far people move *in a lifetime*, because lifetimes vary considerably in duration. Instead we might investigate how fast average "movers" move in the system: how many ranks or strata they pass through in some specified period of time. A study of officers' careers in the Coldstream Guard (Tepperman, 1975a) showed that the distance an officer moved upward depended on how long he remained in the Guard. Sons of noblemen moved through the ranks somewhat more quickly than other officers. It was most interesting to note the average number of years it took men to move from any one rank to any other, and the difference in number of years taken by noblemen's sons and commoners' sons to move between specified ranks. However, all officers moved up the ranks and of those who attained lower ranks than others, many had simply died or retired before reaching the highest ranks.

Finally, a study of mobility may be unconcerned with the probability of movement out of or into any particular stratum, or the average distance or speed of movement, but concerned rather with the direction of movement, and the proportion of all movement that is upward. A higher proportion of movement is upward in noncompetitive than in competitive mobility systems (Tepperman and Tepperman, 1971) and this will be elaborated on in a later chapter. Thus the direction of movement says less about the openness or permeability of a society than about the way people are selected for positions; but it also points to a particular problem that will receive attention in the last chapter of this book. In most industrial societies, children are urged to succeed, to move upward at all costs (McClelland, 1961). Yet in most industrial societies, except those that are changing very rapidly, there is about as much downward mobility as there is upward mobility. Thus in most industrial societies widespread aspirations for success must be thwarted for a great number, perhaps a majority, of the population.

This is a social problem which is just being recognized as such, and our society has not come anywhere near solving it.

The Units of Analysis

Not only are individual people socially mobile, but families, tribes, castes, ethnic groups, organizations, cities and nations are also mobile. In respect to each size of unit, there is a different order of hierarchy and a different time perspective; the mobility of cities must be studied in reference to the power resources of other cities, over decades or centuries and not over single years, for example. Yet in each instance, a unit with power resources is capable of changing its relative position in respect to other similar units. In 1820 it was unclear whether Kingston or York (Toronto) would become the pre-eminent city in Ontario, and most contemporaries would have bet on Kingston. A sociologist might explain the upward mobility of Toronto since 1820, and hope to derive from this explanation insight into the processes of mobility characterizing other (smaller) social units.

It is easiest to think of social mobility in terms of individual people realizing an improvement in status during their own lifetimes. Careers contain all the positions or resources held from first entry into adulthood (and typically, into the labour force) until death or retirement from the labour force. *Career mobility* (or intragenerational mobility) is accordingly the change in position one experiences from the beginning to the end of adult (work) life.

Families are mobile too, although we more readily think of intergenerational social mobility as an achievement of individuals. Thus, one may record the *intergenerational mobility* of an individual from birth into a working class family until retirement or death as a prominent judge. If this person had trained as a lawyer, as one supposes, his career mobility would appear unremarkable—a movement from articling law student to junior partner in a law firm to senior partner in a law firm to judgeship (cf. Klein, 1975). What is dramatic here is the jump from a working class birth to legal training. We always inherit the social stratum of our parents at birth, but movement into another stratum is rarely to our credit alone. Support is received from our families that may be financial or emotional or both, and this support facilitates movement beyond the status our parents had achieved. A parent invests some of his or her own resources in the careers of his or her children, but unlike other investments of power resources, the children and not the parent are the prime beneficiaries. After the parents have died, the family will exist only in its children. Whether or not the family as a whole shares in a son's or daughter's success, the family has moved upward as a whole.

This sounds metaphorical only because families have become more loosely organized in the last century than ever before. In previous times families commonly acted as long-term cooperative social, residential and economic units. In these circumstances, the achievement of success by any individual had direct consequences for the other family members—parents and siblings included. Where families acted as units, marriages were planned by the family to satisfy familial as well as individual desires and marriages were viewed as alliances or economic exchanges between families (Morton, 1963).

The French sociologist Dumont (1890) was so firmly convinced that the mobility of children depended on parental planning and resource investment that he linked mobility and family (size) planning in the concept "social capillarity". Using the metaphor of a liquid rising in glass tubes of various widths, and noting that it rose higher in narrow than in wide tubes, Dumont argued that children from smaller families would rise higher than children from larger families of the same social class. Parents could use their resources more effectively to educate and set up their children in life if there were fewer children requiring such assistance. A similar concern beset Victorian parents and may account in part for the decline in fertility in late nineteenth century England (Banks, 1954). This idea has not disappeared with time, and a population economist has recently compared childbearing to a family investment in consumer durables (Schultz, 1972). Such evidence as we have of the effect of family size on the well-being and "success" of children seems to give Dumont's thesis continued credibility (Wray, 1972).[2]

Thus the reference to family mobility in a discussion of the movement of individuals from status at birth to status at death is not at all metaphorical in respect to social life before 1900. In more recent years, the commitment among family members to provide mutual support has been less obvious but perhaps not less important for the social mobility of all family members.

Just as the fluctuation in family fortunes can affect the life chances of family members, so the fluctuation in resources of larger units can affect the life chances of both families and individuals. If, for example, Canadian Indians as a group can gain better treaty rights from the government than they presently enjoy, and if they are able to overcome the prejudices held against Indians by white people, the position in Canadian society of every Indian family and individual will automatically improve. The change in Indian status, like the change in women's status vis-à-vis men, or the surpassing of Kingston by Toronto, is a case of mobility by units larger than the family or individual. The hierarchy in terms of which we evaluate the Indian's position and observe its relative change over time comprises all ethnic and racial groups in Canada. Such a change in position will not be measured in less than lifetimes, although occasional dramatic improvements in conditions may give the impression that group mobility is sudden or rapid.[3]

If there is any trend in the changing importance of units of analysis, this trend is towards the greater importance in mobility analysis of large units. Our work careers and income depend increasingly on the fates of large corporate bodies, and as an organization flourishes or declines, its employees and associates do likewise, although those at the bottom of the corporate hierarchy are likely to suffer more than those at the top. Such corporate dependency is nowhere clearer than in company towns, where all aspects of the local economy rest on a single enterprise (Lucas, 1972). Less dramatic but more often well documented is the dependency of employees within cultural and mass media organizations. Many high circulation magazines and newspapers have failed recently, and one such decline and fall—that of the *Saturday Evening Post*—has been described by Friedrich (1971). The transition from small to large corporations and the increasing dependency of individual careers on corporate activity are indicated by the trends in Canadian retail marketing over the last forty years. Individual proprietorships have declined in number while corporate proprietorships have increased considerably and now dominate retail sales in Canada (Moyer and Synder, 1967).

What Influences Social Mobility?

A full answer to this question will take the rest of this book, but it is now worthwhile to examine the framework of an answer and follow up with greater detail in the chapters below. At least two main dimensions affect the level of mobility in a society and I have elsewhere (Tepperman, 1973) called them the *absorbing* and *control* dimensions of a social structure. The absorbing dimension of mobility is that set of forces affecting the supply of power resources in relation to the number of competitors demanding these resources. The control dimension is that set of forces which, given any absorbing condition, allocates resources to people in a systematic manner. These forces correspond loosely to the production and distribution functions of a society discussed earlier in considering the relationship between stratification and mobility.

The Absorbing Dimension

A story in the *Toronto Globe and Mail* of October 11, 1974:(B1) carried the headline, "Vacancies for top jobs at record", and noted that job openings for executives, accountants, engineers, and scientists had soared to record levels, thirty-six per cent above the previous year's level. Vacancies at the top are the most likely of all vacancies to increase upward social mobility, for they necessitate both promotions and new recruitment. The 1974 vacancies were primarily created by $31.6 billion in corporate capital spending in that year, which was in turn promoted by high levels of consumer spending. An "upturn in the economy" produced these jobs.

With a shortage of persons to fill vacancies, industry responds in a number of predictable ways. High starting salaries are offered; forty-six per cent of them in 1974 were in the $15,000 to $20,000 range. Some engineers and accountants with appropriate levels of experience were able to make job changes at increases in salary of fifteen to twenty per cent. Large employers ensure that their professional staff does professional work, rather than routine work that could be done by more available types of employees. However, the shortage remains because employers desire specialists with five to fifteen years of experience; after such people become rarer, employers will consider workers with much less experience for these jobs. In 1974 the competition for experienced workers had become so great that some companies began to recruit workers in Britain.

In such a situation, of continuing worker shortage and unfilled vacancies, we can expect an intensification of these tactics: higher monetary inducements, lower standards (e.g., less experience) required of candidates, and more concerted recruitment efforts abroad. As we shall see later, a similar process characterized the staffing of Canadian universities in the late 1960s. In general it is fair to say that a shortage of qualified workers relative to the number of "good jobs" is the strongest promoter of upward mobility. Stated otherwise, mobility increases with an increase in the ratio of power resources to competitors for these power resources: this is the absorbing dimension of social mobility.

The absorbing dimension comprises two main kinds of effect: structural and demographic. Under such circumstances as industrialization there is a rapid and continuing increase in power resources (wealth or property, authority, and prestige) per capita. The association between industrialization and wealth can be seen in cross-tabulations of gross national product per capita by other measures of "modernity" for any selection of countries (Russett et al., 1964). The national increase in amount of authority is reflected in the larger proportion of managerial occupations in modern than in pre-industrial nations. The increase in prestige is less easily measured but has been discussed by Boorstin (1964) under the rubric of "celebrity making". These are typically called structural changes (and the resulting mobility, structural mobility) because they result from large-scale changes of the social structure that, lumped together, are termed "modernization" (Weiner, 1966).

However, the ratio of power resources to competitors can change demographically as well as structurally, through fluctuations in the

number of competitors. These fluctuations are somewhat more characteristic of pre-industrial than industrial societies, and result mainly
from epidemics, famines and wars. Far from being unexpected, these
disasters were frequent prior to 1750 (Sauvy, 1963; Wrigley, 1969) and
largely account for the failure of the human race to increase at rates
anywhere near present levels of increase, despite very high levels of
fertility.[4] But such disasters, while frequent, were not spread smoothly
across human history, and some had much greater impact than others.
Thus, for example, the Black Plague epidemics of the mid-fourteenth
century killed between one-quarter and one-half of the European
population wherever they struck (Ziegler, 1970); between 1348 and 1400
England's population dropped from about four million to slightly over
two million people (Wrigley, 1969).

Outside the Third World, which has continued to suffer sporadic
famines and epidemics to the present date (e.g., Biafra, Bangladesh, and
Ethiopia in recent years), the only comparable disasters in the past two
centuries have been wars. Like other forms of organized social life,
wars have grown larger over the course of time, employing more
soldiers and equipment to kill more effectively. In addition, the strategies and technology of modern warfare have claimed many more civilian victims than did pre-industrial wars. Great demographic changes
have resulted; World War I killed vast numbers of Frenchmen, and
World War II a vast number of Soviet males. One result of such depletion of young men was a reduction in marriages, increased spinster-
hood, and a reduction in the number of male competitors for (civilian)
power resources. Females in countries at war commonly assumed the
economic roles formerly held by men, and in those countries which
suffered great losses of men at war, women continued to participate in
the work force in large numbers. Thus, to the extent that wars claimed
large numbers of males, females in the population experienced upward
mobility as a group.

Demographic fluctuation has resulted from sudden shifts in fertility as well as mortality. In most industrial countries of the world there
were major or minor "baby booms" after World War II, which resulted
from an increase in marriages and rapid procreation by veterans and
non-veterans alike. Coming after very low fertility in the late 1930s and
moderate fertility in the early 1940s, this increased childbearing of the
late 1940s and early 1950s produced large cohorts of children entering
primary school in the 1950s and universities in the 1960s.

The implications of this demographic force in the institutions of
Canada may be instructive. Large birth cohorts strained existing
educational facilities, forcing an increase in teacher training and school
construction, and leading also to pressures for change in the ways these
institutions operated. Foreign-born academics were hired to teach in
newly created university positions, as neither the existing supply of

Canadian scholars nor the rate of training additional Canadian scholars was adequate to the needs of school expansion. Such an impact of high fertility on social institutions is common in pre-industrial nations, which find it difficult to maintain, much less decrease, their teacher-pupil ratios in the face of rapid population growth (Gavin Jones, 1972). Thus, increased fertility acts either to cause structural expansion or to increase the value of skills that are in short supply; in both cases, the mobility of some is likely to increase.

The mobility of others is likely to decrease at the same time, if they possess no skills of particular value. High fertility eventually pours many unskilled young people into the labour market, and if that labour market is stagnant or expanding slowly, the supply of labour will exceed the demand, and many people will be unemployed or underemployed (Myrdal, 1968).

Although the influence of structural and demographic change on mobility is complicated, it is safe to generalize that when the ratio of power resources to competitors increases over time, either through industrialization, other expansion, or sudden mortality, the mobility of people in that society also increases. If the ratio of power resources to competitors decreases over time, either through economic stagnation or levels of fertility which exceed the rate of structural expansion, the mobility of that population will typically decrease.

Exchange Mobility as a Renewal Process

Where the ratio of resources to competitors is in rough balance, there is mobility of the type commonly called *exchange mobility* [or, following Rogoff (1953: chapter 2), social distance mobility]. Exchange mobility is characteristic of many kinds of systems having a one-to-one relationship between people and positions, and mathematicians call something like it a *renewal process*. What is "exchanged" and what is "renewed" in this type of mobility will become more apparent with some examples. Marriage and divorce form an extremely simple exchange process, since the law makes it impossible for a woman to become the second Mrs. Richard Burton before the first Mrs. Richard Burton has been dislodged. In a restaurant with a legal seating capacity of seventy-five people, a newly arrived customer cannot eat unless or until one of seventy-five seats has been vacated; in the course of a busy evening, the clientele is "renewed" several times.

There is no one-to-one fit between person and position in many areas of social life. If it is illegal for Richard Burton to have two wives simultaneously, he can still have two daughters without one displacing the other; while restaurants may strictly limit the number of customers to be served at a given moment, buses and trains do so less strictly; and finally, although there can only be one monarch at a time in England, there may be any number of vice-presidents of Canadian Pacific. People who are self-employed create a role and fill it as long as they can afford to, especially if they need not be licensed to do so. Thus, there is no fixed number of doctors, lawyers, or pharmacists in Canada, in the sense that the entry of a new person in each profession need not await the death of a present member. The existing number of professionals is limited primarily by the ability of schools to train new professionals and the willingness of provincial associations to license them. More dramatically, nothing but market conditions affects the number of candy stores there are or can be in Canada; the flow of such proprietorships is very far from a renewal process.

As a model for exchange mobility the renewal process is quite informative in some instances and wholly inappropriate in others. The reasons for trying to think in terms of a renewal process are several. First, this is a simplifying or heuristic device, like the concept of social strata, which allows us to grasp an idea and move along from there more easily. Second, renewal processes are good approximations of mobility in formal organizations (White, 1970), if not in professional or entrepreneurial occupations, and many careers are found within formal organizations. Finally, if more occupations are becoming integrated in large organizations, then the renewal process will become an increasingly useful model for studying occupational mobility.

But will the renewal process metaphor be adequate for studying the mobility of people through strata in general, and not merely through occupations? The answer is a qualified yes. An occupation is the primary means by which most people obtain power resources and therefore occupational mobility will imply power mobility to a large degree. Second, since the ratio of power resources to competitors is fixed in all exchange mobility, the wealth, authority, or prestige one person gets must by definition reduce the amount that remains for others. This is not the only characteristic of a renewal process, but it is an important one. It reminds us that, at bottom, exchange mobility is a zero-sum game played by many competitors for a single position.

The Control Dimension

Who controls the control dimension, in the sense of creating and enforcing rules of access to desired resources, is a difficult question. One may suppose that those who hold the *most* power resources and have the most interest in maintaining this situation will do so; we are reminded of Michel's "iron law of oligarchy" (*cf.* Clement, 1975). Yet this is not always the case, for trade unions are often the most ardent protectors of promotion by seniority, for example, and by specifying this rule in labour contracts they are partially controlling the control dimension. Further, many criteria by which rewards are distributed in our society are so thoroughly accepted as equitable that those who do not succeed are as likely to blame themselves as blame the system. Marx called this "false consciousness" and it may be "false" in that it accepts arbitrary inequities as reasonable and fair. Yet it cannot be denied that false consciousness makes for as strong conformity and maintenance of existing rules as conscious manipulation. In this sense we all control the control dimension. One example of general cultural control over mobility is found in age-grading and mobility with the passage of time.

Life is age-graded in many if not all societies, meaning that certain activities are thought proper for those of some ages and not others; this is largely the meaning of the term "life cycle". Age-grading is not a natural phenomenon but a social one, as Ariès has shown in his brilliant study of childhood in many societies (1962), and it is obvious that age-grading is very important in our society. One cannot become a juvenile delinquent at the age of 40 or a school drop-out at the age of 10 or an old-age pensioner at the age of 21: each of these is an age-specific legal status we cannot violate with impunity. Similarly, our norms and values discourage us from retiring from the work force at the age of 25, marrying a person 30 years older, or dressing like a teenager at the age of 55, although these are perfectly legal activities in which some people indulge.

Equally, it is uncommon for someone to become a company president or full professor at the age of 35; neither is against the law or improper but each is nonetheless uncommon. This is due to the belief that many roles require experience or maturity gained mainly through the passage of time. In many organizations a seniority rule of promotion specifies that vacancies must be filled by people next in line for promotion on the basis of time spent at a lower position. This rule may hold the status of a custom, or it may be written into a union contract with management. In any event, if it is breached a "crisis of succession" may occur (Gouldner, 1954) in which legitimacy is denied the person who has leap-frogged into the vacancy from inside or outside the organization.[5]

Age-grading does not always work against young people, because seniority is not favoured in all occupations. Sometimes "juniority" may be the key to success. If length of experience is the justification for promotion by seniority, jobs that do not require experience as much as some other quality may reward people on the basis of their juniority. All things being equal, an employer might well prefer a young, newly drafted hockey player to one who has seen his fortieth birthday, or a young stripper to an old one. Where the qualities a job requires are precisely youth, energy and vitality, the juniority rule may be invoked so that increasing age brings a decrease rather than an increase in rewards. Some have asserted that knowledge in the physical and applied sciences and mathematics is outdated very quickly, and that a scientist's best work is done before the age of thirty. This view would justify promotion based on the juniority principle in organizations employing scientists, inasmuch as the value of a scientist decreases steadily with time spent out of school. While young full professors may be more common in the sciences than in the humanities for this reason, there has been little other application of the juniority principle in the university, or indeed in any other fields outside of sports and entertainment.

The other part of mobility control revolves around the importance of merit for promotion. Societies differ in the importance they attach to good past performance as a criterion for promotion, and while our society pays great service to the ideal of promotion based on merit, we are far from what Michael Young has called a "meritocracy" (1967), for many reasons. First, it is often difficult to evaluate merit. Second, in many activities, mere adequacy may suffice; great merit may prove unnecessary. Third, demonstrated merit at one level may predict performance at a higher level rather badly. Fourth, evaluating merit and regularly rewarding on the basis of it would upset many people, and perhaps organizations in general. Fifth, those who hold power would not wish in most instances to allow a re-allocation of resources.

Many of these points are straightforward, but it is worthwhile taking each a little further. Merit is hard to evaluate because what many workers produce is intangible. And, where a tangible product is turned out, there is no absolute standard of goodness with which to compare it; in the twentieth century, we have all become cultural relativists. Second, in some or many activities, the difference between a fair, good, or excellent performance is inconsequential because each is *adequate*. Mere adequacy is least satisfactory for concert violinists or quarterbacks; it seems that arts and sports are the only areas where we are reasonably certain of merit and competitive advantage. Adequacy is sufficient for the mass production of automobiles and the processing of insurance claims, however. Third, merit in one activity may or may not predict meritorious performance at the next higher level; the Peter Principle (Peter and Hull, 1970) goes so far as to predict that promotion on the basis of merit ensures incompetence at all levels. We shall take up this amusing and complicated idea again in Chapter Seven.

Fourth and fifth, rewarding on the basis of merit will not be pleasant or beneficial for many, and they may seek to prevent it. The disruption caused by such changes and the resistance to them have been documented in many places, but two cases describing the scientific establishment are particularly interesting (Koestler, 1973; Medvedev, 1971). In particular, Medvedev's history of the rise and fall of the geneticist Lysenko in the U.S.S.R. is informative because we usually think of scientific truth and political power as basically unrelated or even antagonistic; but this is not always so. Science is a vocation and hence a source of power resources just like any other occupation. Every worker wants to assume the stability of his own tenure and that of his colleagues. Our own work is affected not only by uncertainties about our permanence but also by the transiency of our colleagues, superiors and subordinates.

Thus merit based on past performance may or may not guide promotion, but this is only partly explained by the reasons given above. In traditional societies, merit was occasionally ascribed as well as achieved. Nobility was an inherited status, although it might have no cash value for younger sons and daughters who had to make their way in a world based on (male) primogeniture. Yet social institutions still ascribed merit to those of noble blood regardless of their material circumstances. We may err at times in imagining noble blood to have been more important than it really was in traditional societies, but there is little doubt it counted for a lot more in the past than today. The significance of blood-line, while diminished today, is not wholly forgotten and this accounts for the continued interest in genealogy construction, heraldry, and the maintenance of traditional associations based on blood-line.

The combination of merit ascription and the irrelevance of merit in performance produces what Ralph Turner (1970) has called "sponsored" mobility. Under conditions of sponsored mobility, a young person is selected for an adult role on the basis of some ascribed characteristic, and trained for that role until he is either ready or obliged by circumstances to enter it. He then performs as well or badly as he can, and that has to suffice. This is how kings and queens, the nobility, and perhaps all upper class people come into their status. Under conditions of what Turner has called "contest" mobility, the selection for training is based on competitive merit in performance, as is the continuance of training, adult performance of the role, and promotion to higher related roles. Ideally, this is how people enter and leave universities. Careers in some occupations approximate contest mobility more than careers in others.

We shall be interested in considering how the amount of mobility in a system is affected by the control dimension. Less is known about the control dimension than the absorbing dimension, but the following assertions enjoy some credibility. An adherence to the seniority (or juniority) principle appears to maximize mobility. In a renewal process, mobility is influenced by such demographic factors as life span and age at retirement; but given some set of demographic conditions, a controlled selection procedure moves more people than a random one.

Mobility based on performance merit is probably greater than mobility based on ascription, but for a different reason. The correlation is likely spurious, like that we discussed earlier relating stratification and mobility. Where mobility is unrelated to success in the creation and investment of power resources, there is less incentive to undertake these activities, and hence less likelihood of industrialization, which stimulates mobility. There is also a direct relationship between the amount of mobility and criteria for promotion: where eligibility for selection or promotion is ascribed at birth, most people will be ineligible for most forms of mobility, and hence mobility will be infrequent. But these arguments require much more specification, and they will receive it below.

To close, the amount of mobility in society is influenced by the absorbing dimension of that society, or what we shall call social mobility as an economic process; and by the control dimension of society, defining social mobility as a renewal process. The "economics" of social mobility balance available power resources and competitors for these resources; while the "renewal" of a stable system is determined by rules about the selection and orderly progression of people through positions. In succeeding chapters, I will deal with each of these dimensions at length and then apply the insights they have provided to an analysis of the mobility of various units. The book will close with a consideration of the dilemmas posed by success and failure.

Chapter 1 Notes

[1] The shifting of attention from social justice to personal improvement may result from a recognition that equality of condition is at best an uncertain and more probably an impossible goal, inasmuch as no known society has achieved such equality. Personal success is attainable for many, and its societal equivalent, equality of opportunity, is a goal that can be regarded as attainable in theory, if difficult to attain in practice.

[2] Recent Canadian research has also shown that upward occupational mobility is less among men and women with many rather than few siblings (Cuneo and Curtis, 1975). Notwithstanding the decline of the family as a cooperative economic institution in industrial societies, we continue to find verification of Dumont's hypothesis about social capillarity.

[3] Hutton (1946) has discussed the ways in which Indian subcastes (in India, not Canada) seek and achieve collective mobility by establishing a claim to higher status, changing the subcaste name, and finally, denying any connection with their caste of origin.

[4] "Birth rate" is one particular way of measuring fertility level, which is properly the reproductive behaviour of an individual woman or a collection of individual women. Fertility is typically defined by age, often by marital status; birth rate is a societal property which does not take into account the age or marital status of reproducing women.

[5] This denial of legitimacy may result in non-compliance or deviant behaviour which, in turn, may call forth tough, coercive rules. Perhaps, as Gouldner has implied, the origin of highly specific "bureaucratic" rules may be found in the breakdown of conformity based on custom where custom has been breached initially by the "illegitimate" promotion of a person without proper seniority or similar credentials.

2
SOCIAL MOBILITY AS AN ECONOMIC PROCESS

ϾϿ

A despondent Hindustani god, one afflicted by his celibacy, solicited of another god the loan of one of his 14,516 wives. The husband consented with these words: "Take the one you find unoccupied." The needy god went visiting each of the 14,516 palaces. In each one, the lady of the house was with her lord. The latter had increased himself 14,515 times and each wife thought herself the only one to enjoy his favours.

Simon Pereyra, *Cuaranta anos
en el lecho del Ganges* (1708)

Power Resources

Some Definitions

In every society there is a distribution of power, in the sense that each person has a greater or lesser chance of prevailing in a conflict of interests. Societies differ in how unequally power is distributed, but there are no known societies in which everyone has equal power. A person's power affects the conditions under which life will be lived—his or her life chances—and ultimately that person's survival. At the very least, a more powerful person will enjoy a life of more satisfactions than a less powerful person.

The distribution of power is based upon a distribution of *power resources*; one can have one's own way only by possessing special commodities or attributes. Such power resources can be used to bargain for or purchase the compliance of others; for this reason, they have been called by Parsons (1966) *generalized media of exchange*. Or they can be used to force compliance by those who would not voluntarily give way in a conflict. Power resources are of three main kinds: property, authority and prestige, and each will be described in turn (*cf.* Gerth and Mills, 1964: chapter VII).

Property (or private property) is not a thing but an exclusive right to use things in ways not prevented by law. In some societies, selected types of people have been considered potential or actual property; slave-holding is the best illustration of this depersonalization of people.

In many patriarchal societies, women and children have been nearly, if not completely, the property of their male family heads (Maine, 1963). One important aspect of property is its alienability, the right of an owner to dispose of a thing he owns. In slave societies, people were commonly bought and sold, and in many patriarchal societies, daughters were exchanged for a bride-price. However, human beings are not generally bought and sold, and most property is non-human. According to some, the course of human history has witnessed a progressive reduction in the variety of things that may be held as property, and a reduction in the number of legal uses to which property may be put (Renner, 1949). Others, especially anthropologists, remind us that preliterate tribal people can own very little in comparison with ourselves.

Authority is the right to expect or command specific actions of specifiable types of people, and to enforce these commands with defined sanctions. Some authority is equally available to large segments but not all of the population—for example, the right to vote for a change of government, to sign a contract, or to demand payment for services rendered. Those parts of the population eligible for such authority are often defined by their age (e.g., adulthood) or birthplace (e.g., citizenship).[1]

Frequently, authority is gathered up within an organized many-person entity and delegated to individuals to use on behalf of the organization. The nation-state is one such entity, and within it a tax collector has the authority to collect taxes, and a policeman authority to arrest. A business organization, given certain types of authority by the nation-state to employ, buy and sell, delegates its authority to personnel acting for the organization. Some employees will have the authority to hire or fire others, a very important type of authority in a society whose work force is largely composed of wage and salary earners. A university, in the same way, is granted the authority to hire faculty to teach courses; and individual teachers are granted the authority to grade students in these courses.

Prestige, the third power resource, is defined by the dictionary as "prominence or influential status achieved through success, renown, or wealth." A person's prestige is judged by the voluntary deference he receives from others, who may also report having esteem or admiration for that person. However, prestige is accorded to sets or categories of people, as well as to individuals. For example, physicians enjoy higher prestige than shoe salesmen or news vendors in most countries of the world (Hodge *et al.*, 1966); any person will receive more deference and esteem as a doctor than as a shoe salesman. People are able to accord prestige to such an abstract category as an occupation because occupations vary in the formal education they demand and the remuneration they bring. Since our society holds those who are well educated and prosperous in highest regard, prosperity being a major life's goal for most in our society, people therefore attribute most prestige to those social categories likely to contain highly educated and prosperous people. For similar reasons, some ethnic origins are more prestigious than others.

Property, authority and prestige are intrinsically valuable and valuable in exchange. All three resources are desirable because they are scarce; conversely, they are scarce because they are desirable and much in demand. They are distributed unequally among people, and in any given society some people are wealthy and many are poor; some can command and enforce compliance and many must comply and cannot command. There are, finally, some people who are much admired and many who receive little admiration or deference.

The Mobility of Power Resources

What is particularly interesting about these resources is their mobility. Power resources can be (1) transferred, (2) exchanged for one another, (3) exchanged for something else, and (4) increased or decreased through investment. To begin with transferral, power resources (and especially property) can be inherited. Children can inherit the property and prestige of their parents, and under some circumstances, they can assume the positions of authority their parents once held. Second, these resources are exchangeable one for another. As the dictionary definition has indicated, prestige may be achieved through the acquisition and show of property or authority. There is an apparent eagerness to admire and defer to people who are wealthy and in command of the lives of others (Homans, 1974). Likewise, positions of high authority are often well paid and help their incumbents to acquire property in other ways. Wealth allows one to assume positions of authority, or to spend effort capturing positions of authority that are not reserved for wealthy people. For example, American presidents have often been wealthy men before entering the Presidency, and both Prime Minister Trudeau and his main rival, Robert Stanfield, are independently wealthy.

Third, power resources are exchangeable for commodities and services that are not primarily power resources. Possessors of many power resources are more likely than others to achieve long life, for they can best afford vacations, good diet, hygienic living conditions, and medical treatment (Kitagawa and Hauser, 1973). They can be "beautiful people" and mingle with other "beautiful people", both because they are able to cultivate high fashion and the arts, and because less powerful people admire and are drawn to them. Power resources, then, can be used for what Veblen (1912) called "conspicuous consumption", a style of life that does more to symbolize inequalities of power than to create them (Goffman, 1968).

Finally, power resources can be increased through investment or risk. Property in the form of money can be invested at known rates of annual increase so that unless the investor takes action to prevent it, property will increase in amount with the passage of time. This is one main reason why the rich remain rich (or become richer) and rarely become poor. Investments of authority are somewhat less obvious but not less frequent. A person may "risk" his usually well paid time as a corporation lawyer, for example, to act as a $1 a year consultant to the government or as a campaign organizer for a major political candidate. If this investment pays off, he may end up in the Senate, in a ministry, or an ambassador to a foreign country. Those who already hold much property or authority can afford to invest these to gain more authority. In like manner, prestige too may be invested. An esteemed Albert Einstein or Bertrand Russell may risk his prestige by supporting an unpopular political cause, pacifism during a period of world war, for example. If his cause wins popular sympathy, he becomes doubly prestigious as a great scholar and a great humanitarian.

Summarizing to this point, there is an unequal distribution of power and power resources in all societies. These power resources— property, authority and prestige—are notably valuable in exchange for one another and for other desirable goods and services.

Because power resources are exchangeable one for another, they are found associated with one another; a small number of people are wealthy, prestigious, possessors of much authority, while the majority are not wealthy and have little authority or prestige. It is true that cases are observed of what has been called "status inconsistency" (Lenski, 1954), when a person possessing much of one power resource is poor in the other resources. Such status inconsistency sometimes affects an individual's psychological state and behaviour (e.g., voting patterns). However, it is important to note that status inconsistency is much rarer than status consistency, and social strata exist as a result of this.[2]

A *social stratum* is a set of people with roughly equal (or homogeneous) power; they have more or fewer power resources than people in any other social stratum. Although a society is heterogeneous in respect to the amount of power resources its members hold, such heterogeneity is due mainly to differences *between* social strata, not to differences among people *within* social strata.

To simplify, imagine that society is comprised of a pile of social strata, one atop another, producing what is called a social hierarchy. At the top of the hierarchy is that stratum containing people with the most property, authority, and prestige. Sociologists have sometimes doubted that this hierarchical metaphor represents social inequality adequately, for two reasons. First, individual power resources are distributed in a continuous, not a discrete, manner; however, the idea of a hierarchy made of piled up social strata implies (discrete) breaks at the boundaries between one stratum and another. Second, the discoveries of status inconsistency imply less than perfect homogeneity *within* any social stratum. Yet the hierarchical model of inequality maintains itself because it is a simple and powerful representation of reality, and because the correlations among property, authority, and prestige are generally strong. For these reasons, the hierarchical model of inequality will be used in this presentation.

The Malthusian Problem

The preceding chapter noted that social mobility may be viewed as an economic process, in that the amount of mobility in a society is determined by a balance between available power resources and the number of competitors for resources. To the extent that economics deals with the supply and demand of goods, the production of power resources in a society and the changes in allocation over time may be better understood through the use of an economic metaphor.

Since mobility can be regarded as the flow of power resources from person to person or group to group over the course of time, it should follow that upward mobility, which is analogous to an improvement in the standard of living—since it is an individual or group increase in power resources—will be influenced by the total number or amount of power resources in society and the total number of competitors for such power resources. At any given moment the distribution of power resources among people is affected as much by the distributive process as by the supply and demand (or economic) process, and I shall discuss this distributive process in the next chapter. However, in the present chapter, we shall confine ourselves to the economics of social mobility, and these are best understood from a dynamic analysis comparing the rates of change in power resources and competitors.

Some popular discussion of resource allocation has followed from a mistaken notion of what Thomas Malthus was arguing in his nineteenth-century essays on population. Malthus asserted that population always increases in geometric progression, while resources, especially those deriving from the land (i.e., agricultural products), can only increase arithmetically or additively.[3] He deduced that the annual rate of increase in a population would generally be greater than the annual rate of increase in resources necessary for the support of that population, unless strong measures—so-called preventive and positive checks—controlled and minimized population increase. Even if we allow that Malthus' estimates of nineteenth-century population increase are too high to have meaning in the analysis of contemporary industrial societies, and allow that the potential for large and even geometric annual increase in resource productivity was underestimated, there remains a basic insight upon which this chapter will be built.

Malthus was less concerned with what is today called "overpopulation", an excess of people in proportion to available resources, than with the inevitability of overpopulation, despite schemes propounded in his time and since for a more equitable distribution of the resources of a society. Malthus noted that virtually any process of *geometric* increase, however small the annual increment, would ultimately overtake a process of additive increase. For example, if the amount of resources available to society (e.g., acres of fertile land or productivity per acre) were increasing at a rate of 1% per year and population were increasing geometrically only half as fast at 1/2% per year, the ratio of resources to population would fall below its original level after about 260 years and would continue to decline thereafter. The same rate of resource increase by addition, coupled with a higher rate of population increase, would yield an even faster decline in *per capita* resources. Malthus pointed out that these were mathematical facts of life.

The overpopulation problem is really much more complicated than this, for one reason that supports Malthus and one reason that does not. To take the latter first, as industrialization has led societies away from a land-based economy and hence away from primarily additive or arithmetic increases in productivity, developed economies have achieved geometric growth, not arithmetic growth, in gross national product and hence in *per capita* income. As regards the former complication, there are many societies even today where population is increasing geometrically at a faster annual rate than is the economy, even though the economy may also be increasing geometrically. Wherever this imbalance in rates of geometric increase exists, Malthus' concerns continue to hold importance.

Further, it has been argued that there are limits to growth imposed by a finite world supply of natural resources (e.g., fuel and minerals) needed for industrial expansion, and also limits to the human tolerance for the pollution resulting from industrial development. Whether these limits will lead first to a decline in population increase or to a decline in industrial expansion is something that cannot be predicted, although the authors of *The Limits to Growth* (Meadows et al., 1972) imply that readers of this book will live far enough into the twenty-first century to find out which will decline first. Allowing that changes in the ratio of resources to people are problematic, as Malthus has suggested, the relative rates of increase and the process of increase in population and resources—whether geometric or arithmetic—suggest a set of scenarios for the future that are useful in the analysis of human survival as a whole.

If population increases geometrically and resources increase additively, population will *always* overtake resources in the long run, regardless of the differential in rates of annual increase between population and resources. The size of this differential will only determine the time needed for population to overtake resources. In the example given earlier, it took only 260 years; given other differentials, it might take 10 years or 1,000,000 years. Thus the size of the differential should influence how seriously those living today take the problem Malthus posed.

If, however, population increases geometrically and resources also increase geometrically, the ratio of resources to population, or what we might call "standard of living", will rise continuously if the annual resource increase is greater than the annual population increase, and will decline continuously if the reverse is true. The speed of rise or decline will be proportional to the difference in rates of population and resource increase. To take an example, if resources are increasing geometrically at a rate of 1% per year and population is increasing geometrically at 2% per year, it will take just under 70 years for the standard of living (or resources *per capita*) to decline by 50%. If, conversely, resources are increasing geometrically at the higher of these two rates and population at the lower of the two rates, in about 70 years the standard of living will have doubled.

Those convinced of the existence of "limits to growth" would hasten to add that in the long run the rate of industrial expansion must decline, because of an increasing shortage of raw materials. Ultimately, unless the rate of population increase declines through voluntary birth control or the effects of war, famine or atmospheric pollution, everyone's standard of living must certainly decline. What is again important is the magnitude of difference between industrial growth rate and population growth rate. Where Meadows *et al.* (1972) would argue that the cataclysm will come within the next 150 years, they are basing their estimate upon questionable assumptions and problematic data; the cataclysm may in fact come in 20 years or in 20,000 years. What is striking is the immutability of the eventual result; we are still the victims of intractable arithmetic.

The preceding discussion has shown that, all things being equal, if population or the number of competitors for resources increases *geometrically* and the amount of resources *additively*, the average (or *per capita*) resources received by competitors will decline over time. This is to say, downward mobility will be more frequent than upward mobility. Similarly, if both resources and competitors are increasing geometrically, but competitors are increasing in number more rapidly than resources, *per capita* resources and hence the amount of upward mobility will decline over time and downward mobility will increase.

Two Types of Structural Mobility

We can take as given that population will always—unless and until births are controlled by the state—increase or decrease geometrically, if the number of children each woman bears is reasonably constant over time. For all intents and purposes, population has increased geometrically throughout human history and will likely continue to do so unless there is a major shift in human fertility norms, or state intervention in support of zero population growth. Hence, the "number of competitors", which is the work force of a population if our units of analysis are individuals, will increase geometrically, except for two complicating factors related to labour force participation. First, women have been adding themselves into the work force and hence into the ranks of competitors over the past fifty years, and are likely to continue doing so. Thus the growth in number of competitors will have this additive aspect to it, as well as the geometric type of increase considered to this point. Second, young people and old people have been subtracting themselves from the work force for the last fifty to one hundred years, and are likely to continue doing so for some time to come. Entry into the labour force has come progressively later in life, and exit from the work force through retirement is becoming increasingly early. This process of age-specific subtraction from the number of competitors, like the sex-specific addition of competitors, is arithmetic in nature; it merely complicates an otherwise geometric increase in number of competitors for power resources.

Thus the number of competitors for power resources will increase over time at some annual rate that will reflect geometric increase in population through reproduction, arithmetic increase through the addition of women, and arithmetic decrease through the subtraction of young and old people. Immigration and emigration are further arithmetic influences one might consider. This all makes the prediction of future work force composition and size rather risky. But conceptually we are close to where Malthus left us; namely, faced with a primarily geometric increase in the number of competitors for (scarce) power resources.

The more difficult problems are at the other end, where Malthus also ran into difficulty; they lie in analyzing the character of change in power resources. I shall specify the problems in some haste and try to deal with them at greater leisure throughout this chapter. The first question is: do power resources—property, authority and prestige—tend to increase geometrically or arithmetically? Second, whatever the nature of their increase, is there any reasonable way of estimating the annual rate of increase of power resources? Third, whatever their type or rate of increase, is there any conceivable limit to their continuing increase in the long run?

To summarize to this point, mobility is in part a process of supply and demand, and some mobility is directly attributable to changes in the ratio of power resources to competitors for these resources. This type of mobility is generally called *structural mobility*. What is called "standard of living" or perhaps "quality of life" depends on the ratio of resources to competitors, and other factors we shall not consider at this point. The amount of structural mobility in a population is primarily the change in standard of living or quality of life enjoyed by an average person (or members of a particular group) in society. Even if this were brought about through a proportional increase in everyone's power resources, involving no change in relative ranking, it might still be considered a type of mobility. The largest part of intergenerational mobility is precisely of this type.[4]

We can now set out a paradigm for thinking about social mobility that draws upon the metaphor used to this point. This paradigm, presented in Chart 2.1, defines four types of social mobility among which we will wish to distinguish. I have called these four types, in keeping with at least some current conventions, exchange mobility, pure demographic mobility, pure resource mobility, and mixed structural mobility.[5]

Exchange mobility is found where a constant relationship or equilibrium is maintained between resources and competitors. This constancy may result either from a lack of change in either the number of competitors or the amount of resources, or from equivalent increases or decreases in resources and competitors. Pure demographic mobility is a subtype of structural mobility and results from a changing ratio of resources to competitors mainly attributable to a change in the number of competitors. This may derive from an increase or decrease in mortality or fertility, or a combination of these, such that annual population growth is faster or slower than annual resource growth, which is assumed to be unchanging. Pure resource mobility, also a subtype of structural mobility, is the result of a change in available power resources, given (relatively) fixed levels of mortality and fertility. An increase in the ratio of resources to competitors under these circumstances is wholly attributable to an increased rate of resource production. Mixed structural mobility, a third subtype of structural mobility, is that mobility resulting from some combination of uneven changes in population and resource creation. It is probably the most common type of structural mobility in real societies but the least useful for heuristic purposes.

The discussion that follows in this chapter will be confined to so-called pure forms of structural mobility—demographic and resource mobility. Exchange mobility will be discussed in the next chapter.

How Power Resources Change: Property

Is dR, the change in power resources, an arithmetic or geometric series? Is the change generally positive (i.e., an increase over time) or negative;

Chart 2.1

A paradigm of social mobility

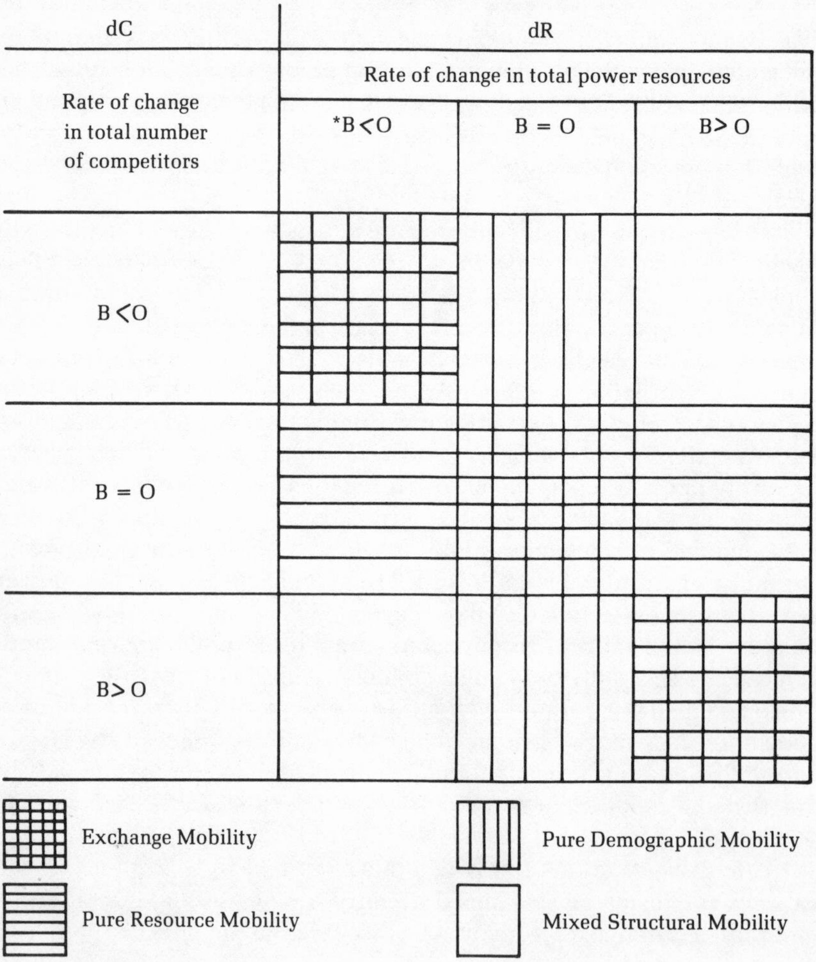

dC	dR		
	Rate of change in total power resources		
Rate of change in total number of competitors	*B < O	B = O	B > O
B < O	Exchange Mobility	Pure Demographic Mobility	
B = O	Pure Resource Mobility	Pure Resource Mobility	Pure Resource Mobility
B > O			Exchange Mobility

Exchange Mobility   Pure Demographic Mobility

Pure Resource Mobility   Mixed Structural Mobility

* B is any real number

and whatever the direction of change, have we any idea of the annual rate of change? Finally, are there definite limits to the increase or decrease of power resources?

These questions are easiest to answer with respect to the power resource of property, and most difficult to answer in respect to prestige. Using incomes—whether *per capita* income, average wage, or real disposable income—to measure property, we can chart the course of changes in property reasonably well over time. The trend in incomes is upward in most modernizing and modern countries, although rates of increase vary from country to country and from one measurement of income to another, and vary somewhat unevenly over time. Incomes represent the creation and sale of goods and services. With industrialization, those with money are more likely to save or invest their money than spend it in conspicuous consumption. These savings become capital for economic expansion and thus the producer of additional power resources. Because goods and services increase in volume with industrialization, industrialization brings an increase in incomes, even taking inflation into account.

Another measure of property that gives a firmer fix on the magnitude of annual growth is the rate of interest received on investments and savings. Money put out at risk in one or another kind of speculation—whether in bonds, mortgages, stocks, or savings accounts—is likely to bring the investor at least 5% interest *per annum* (e.g., in a savings account) and possible 10% interest *per annum* or more in mortgages or other high risk investment. Gross National Product (GNP) is increasing at a slower rate than this—on the average, 3.5% per year in the period 1960-65 in Canada, for example. Since population is simultaneously increasing at about 1.8% per year (Canada, 1963-69), the increase in Gross National Product *per capita* is much less than 3.5%. However, it is clear that GNP *per capita*, or what is sometimes called per capita income, is rising.

The GNP increases geometrically, just as population does. Thus as long as GNP is increasing at 3.5% and population is increasing at 1.8% (or at any annual rate less than 3.5%), the *per capita* income will be rising and in this sense available property will be increasing relative to competitors. This would lead to the prediction that social mobility is likewise increasing over time.

However, property is not merely "income". A previous section defined property as all types of exclusive rights to make use of things. We need ask not only whether material things are multiplying in number, but also whether, independently of this, the rights to existing things are becoming more or less numerous. In principle, rights to material things are infinitely expansible. For example, the state can immediately accomplish a twenty-four-fold increase of property rights in typewriters if, for each existing typewriter, only one person has

Table 2.1

Selected indicators of growth in power resources,
Canada: 1921–1961*

Year	Average wages and salaries of male wage earners, in constant dollars†	Per capita income (gross national product per capita), in constant dollars	Percentage of all workers in establishments employing 500 or more workers	Approximate number of establishments with 100 or more employees
1921	1,486	—	19.9	1,000
1931	1,649	729	25.7	1,300
1941	1,915	1,085	30.2	1,500
1951	2,563	1,324	33.4	2,100
1961	3,679	1,452	33.3	2,500

*For columns 3 and 4 the actual years are 1922, 1930, 1940, 1950 and 1959
†Constant dollars for column 1 based on 1961 dollar value; for column 2, based on
1949 dollar value

Sources: Column 1, Podoluk (1968: 242); Column 2, Porter (1967: 91); Columns 3 and
4, Urquhart (1965: 489).

control over that typewriter for only one hour of each day. It is certain that some property rights have been multiplied in this way in the last century, although we more commonly think of such rights as "communal" than "sequential" (or rotating) private property. A related and rather more important form of this is the limited liability stock company; stock shares may be dispersed among thousands or millions of people. This allows a holder of as little as 10% of all stock—whether an individual or a group formed for this purpose—to effectively dictate corporate policy unless opposed by a larger shareholder. Such fragmentation of property rights has therefore made possible what is called a "holding company", a company which purchases small portions of stock, but portions large enough to effectively control the policies of companies whose assets are many times larger than those of the holding company itself.

Thus, to the extent that property can be subdivided into many parts, to that extent property is multiplied, although not equally dispersed among all shareholders. Each time additional stock shares are printed, or for that matter, dollar bills are printed by the government, property rights increase in number. Whether this merely produces inflation and no net increase in *real* advantage—what the critics of Social Credit call "funny money"—depends on whether other nations accept the additional supply of dollars at prevailing exchange rates; and whether or not the prices of all commodities are driven up by such an increase in money supply. Limits to the increase in property are imposed by the unwillingness of other nations to accept an additional quantity of currency at the old prevailing value. Similar regulation on property increase within nations is imposed upon security exchange. This serves to maintain trust in the value of existing stocks by, among other things, assuring that increases in the number of extant shares are somehow justified. Not only available material resources and products limit the supply of property, then.

Thus some property—especially property that can be valued in dollars—increases geometrically at a rate in excess of population growth. The limits to property expansion depend less on productivity or the continued increase in a tangible commodity, such as gold bullion, than on trust between people and between countries that obligations can and will be fulfilled on demand. The presence of such trust is what Durkheim (1964) referred to as the non-contractual elements of contract; where trust in the eventual fulfillment of obligations is lacking, exchange of property is reduced to barter and the rate of property growth is exactly proportional to the rate of growth in material commodities.

A rather more difficult question is whether the means by which virtually indefinite expansion of property is promoted, notably state regulation (e.g., legislation and monitoring of security exchange) and state redistribution (e.g., taxes, transfer payments), represents an expansion of private property and hence more property mobility, or communalization of property ownership. Renner (1949) seems to believe the latter, and there is no doubt Western societies have moved a great distance from *laissez faire* trade in private property in the two hundred years since the industrial revolution began. This complicates estimating how much (private) property mobility is actually occurring in a society, for the concept "property" includes both the idea of exclusive use (under specified conditions) *and* the right to sell or dispose of something (under specified conditions). In the shared typewriter example given above, we may have increased mobility into the "typewriter-using class" by granting exclusive rights of use for one specified hour a day to each of twenty-four people. Yet presumably the right to sell the typewriter will reside with the group as a whole, and mobility into the "typewriter-owning class" will not have increased by our having distributed control among twenty-four people. This implies that the analysis of property mobility in a true communist society would be impossible, or at best trivial.

How Power Resources Change: Authority and Prestige

Much of the authority and prestige in our society derives from occupational roles. Thus the growth in these two power resources will be indicated by changes in the occupational structure. In the past two centuries, most of the labour force has left farming and other forms of private entrepreneurship, such as craft occupations, to work for others in large organizational units. In most societies, whatever their level of industrialization, only a small part of the population controls the means of production. Modernization has increased the proportion of workers who, while not their own bosses, are nonetheless the bosses of other people, and in this limited sense the amount of authority in society has increased with industrialization. More orders are given by more people.

The proliferation of large organizations containing many authoritative and prestigious ranks has therefore *upgraded* the occupational structure in terms of authority resources, because industrialization has increased the amount and mobility of authority resources. It is extremely difficult to judge the rate at which this increase has taken place. The increase in number of large organizations and managerial or administrative positions does denote the development of additional authority positions. Often the movement out of farming and into white collar occupations is used to measure the extent of the industrial and managerial revolutions, and hence the expansion of authority in a society.

Table 2.2

Labour force by occupational groups, Canada, 1931–1971 (percentages)

Occupational Group	1931	1941	1951	1961	1971
			Percentages		
White Collar	24.4	25.2	32.5	38.6	45.1
Managerial and Proprietary	5.6	5.4	7.5	7.9	9.6
Professional	6.1	6.7	7.4	10.0	14.1
Clerical	6.6	7.2	10.9	12.9	14.6
Commercial and Financial	6.1	5.9	6.7	7.8	6.8
Manual	33.8	33.4	37.6	34.9	34.3
Manufacturing and Mechanical	11.5	16.0	17.4	16.4 ⎫	24.8
Construction	4.7	4.7	5.6	5.3 ⎬	
Labourers	11.3	6.3	6.7	5.4	4.1
Transportation and Communication	6.3	6.4	7.9	7.8	5.4
Service	9.3	10.5	8.6	10.8	12.0
Personal	8.3	9.3	7.3	9.3 ⎫	12.0
Protective	1.0	1.2	1.3	1.5 ⎬	
Primary	32.5	30.6	20.1	13.1	8.7
Agriculture	28.8	25.8	15.9	10.2	7.0
Fishing, Hunting and Trapping	1.2	1.2	1.0	0.6	0.3
Logging	1.0	1.9	1.9	1.3	0.7
Mining and Quarrying	1.5	1.7	1.3	1.0	0.7
Not Stated in Census	–	0.3	1.2	2.6	–
	100.0	100.0	100.0	100.0	100.0
All Occupations, Number (000s)	3,922	4,196	5,215	6,342	8,188

Source: Porter (1967: 93); Kubat and Thornton (1974: 153)

In principle, there cannot be any limits to the ultimate amount of authority in a social system. The greater the pluralism in society and the less state intervention, the more positions of authority and authoritative types of control are possible. As industrialization acted to increase the amount of power resources in society, the state acted to limit further increases by restricting and redistributing property and by limiting, not the number of authority positions, but the things people had the authority to do to other people. This limitation on authority in private hands, or gathering up of new authority in the hands of the government, has resulted from movements of social protest. The labour union movement has acted systematically in the last hundred years to limit the corporate use of authority and to stimulate the state to do similarly. As with the restrictions placed on "private" property, the restrictions placed on "private" authority may ultimately bring authority to rest in the hands of the citizenry as a whole, and thus authority may prove as ambiguous as the twenty-four-person ownership of a typewriter. We are far from seeing that everyone who gives orders is equally receiving orders, but our society seems to be moving in this direction, however slowly.

To conclude then, power resources are all capable of increase and they all seem to increase geometrically. It is more difficult to ascertain whether they increase at an annual rate that is higher or lower than the rate of population growth, and therefore whether all *per capita* power resources are increasing over time or not. Finally, there are probably limits to the increase of power resources, but these limits are quite high, and are less dependent upon natural resources or environment than upon political factors, such as legislation to control or redistribute resources, and the technological abilities to "devise" resources—the mass media creation of prestigious celebrities being a case in point (Boorstin, 1964).

How Power Resources Change: Effects of Industrialization

The preceding section has made repeated reference to the last one or two hundred years as a period within which power resources increased, and suggested that much or all of this increase is a result of industrialization. The industrialization process has several features worth noting here: it has brought manual labour into mass production in factory contexts; has increased the need for non-manual labour (in the form of managerial and clerical work) to supervise and coordinate mass production and sales; and has both received surplus labour from the farms and made much farm labour superfluous, thus creating a "surplus" labour force in agriculture (Moore, 1965).

Industrialization had the effect of increasing power resources in society and of "upgrading" the occupational structure. In this respect at least, industrial societies are similar despite many other differences (Goldthorpe, 1966). We shall now determine with some greater precision the effect of this process on social mobility. What follows will provide a neat illustration of pure resource mobility, as this type of mobility was defined in relation to Chart 2.1.

The sociologists Seymour Martin Lipset and Reinhard Bendix (1959) asserted that industrialization has affected intergenerational occupational mobility similarly wherever it has occurred in the world. This statement is based on both an empirical analysis of occupational mobility in a variety of industrial countries, and on a theory of why industrialization affects mobility. Table 2.3 provides a recapitulation of the data used by Lipset and Bendix (and some additional data) to show the essential similarity of intergenerational mobility in industrial countries.

Table 2.3

Probabilities of upward, downward and net upward* intergenerational social mobility in selected industrial countries

Sample	Type of mobility		
	Upward	Downward	Net Upward
	(Blue Collar to White)	(White Collar to Blue)	
Aarhus 1949	.260	.424	-.048
Belgium 1953	.309	.234	.080
Finland (postwar)	.110	.241	.036
France 1950	.350	.180	.012
France 1964	.274	.363	-.007
Germany (1950s)	.300	.199	.045
Germany (1950s)	.258	.279	.005
Germany Prot. 1953	.353	.333	.182
Germany Cath. 1953	.328	.266	.167
W. Germany 1955	.211	.305	.025
Germany 1956	.271	.380	-.117
Indianapolis 1910	.210	.400	.020
Indianapolis 1940	.270	.376	.045
Japan 1956	.330	.210	.003
Norway 1957	.220	.307	.070
Puerto Rico 1960	.142	.428	.013
Quebec 1954	.224	.456	.082
Quebec 1964	.375	.351	.232
Rome 1908	.220	.270	.022
Russian emigres (postwar)	.280	.102	.124
Sweden (postwar)	.594	.316	.271
Sweden 1957	.291	.232	.109
Switzerland (1950s)	.435	.131	.035
USA 1947 (unadj.)	.351	.251	.099
USA 1947 (adj.)	.241	.371	.011
USA 1952	.309	.344	.060
USA 1952	.311	.340	.082
USA 1957	.300	.301	.077
USA 1962	.361	.291	.141
Mean	.293	.299	.056
Median	.291	.307	.045

*Net upward mobility is calculated as (the number of blue collar sons who enter white collar jobs *minus* the number of white collar sons who enter blue collar jobs) *divided by* the total number of white collar and blue collar sons who hold a white or blue collar job.

Source: Primarily, Lipset and Bendix (1959: Chapter 1). See Tepperman (1975b: Appendix) for a specification of samples.

These data indicate that the average likelihood that the son of a blue collar (skilled or unskilled manual) worker will enter a white collar (non-manual) occupation is about 29%, and the average likelihood that the son of a white collar worker will enter a blue collar occupation is about 30%. The immediate impression that there is slightly more downward movement from white collar status to blue collar status than the reverse is illusory, since the blue collar category always contains more people than the white collar category. In fact, the average probability of *net* upward movement from blue collar to white collar occupations is 4½-6½% in a given generation. This means that although sons of white collar and blue collar workers have roughly the same probabilities of moving out of their class of origin, in industrial societies there is slightly more upward than downward movement. This conclusion is opposite to that reached by Miller (1960) on the basis of similar data but a different way of comparing rates of upward and downward movement. There is variation among countries and, within countries, variation from year to year; but what is most striking is the relative uniformity of these mobility rates.

Bendix and Lipset explain their findings by asserting that the *aspirations* for mobility in industrial societies are uniform: there are no marked differences in aspiration between different cultural or religious groups, for example. Only differences in the occupational structure itself explain the observed variation among countries, for some countries are more industrialized than others, and some countries are industrializing more quickly than others. Industrialization level and rate determine the character of the occupation structure: the proportion of jobs that are white collar, blue collar, or farming at any given moment. Hence the structure of opportunity for upward mobility is determined by these aspects of industrialization. Since aspirations are assumed to be the same in every industrial country (whatever its level or speed of industrialization), we would need only to make the occupational structures identical to have identical patterns of mobility in all industrial countries.

An attempt was made to verify this conclusion by simulating or creating imaginary industrial societies using the computer (Tepperman, 1975b). Using a statistical technique called normalization by iteration (Mosteller, 1968), a "basic nucleus of association" was extracted from the data summarized in Table 2.3, which represented the aspirations for mobility Lipset and Bendix believed were shared by people in all industrial countries.[6] This basic nucleus of association was then combined with hypothetical societies having various levels of industrialization (i.e., different proportions of the work force in white collar, blue collar and farming occupations). Arbitrarily designated as 15 in number, these levels or stages of industrialization were developed after an examination of the industrialization process in countries that had already industrialized (Kuznets, 1966; Soares, 1966).

One could then estimate the amount of mobility that would hypothetically result from combining the common "basic nucleus of association" with different levels of industrialization in father's and son's generations, and different rates of industrialization. A rate of industrialization was deemed faster if father's generation entered the labour force at industrial level 3 and son's generation entered it at level 10,

Chart 2.2

*Economic development and the class structure:
international comparisons, 1950*

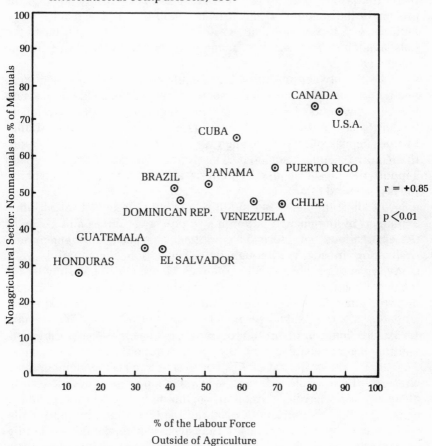

Source: Soares (1966: Figure 1)

than if father's generation entered the labour force at stage 3 and son's generation entered it at level 6, for example.

This simulation showed there is a higher probability of upward mobility (and lower probability of downward mobility) where industrialization is fast than where it is slow. There is also a higher probability of upward mobility (and lower probability of downward mobility) where the society in question is highly industrialized than where it is little industrialized, even if there is no change in the occupational structure over time. There is more upward than downward mobility in industrialized societies, and the more industrialized the society, the greater is the amount of *net* upward mobility. These results agree entirely with Lipset and Bendix's theory, and are quite similar to the data available from surveys of mobility in relatively highly industrialized societies.

The fit between observed and simulated data and between data and theory finally implies that if sociologists had been able to measure mobility continuously throughout the process of industrialization of modern societies, they would have found changes in mobility similar to the changes observed through a computer examination of hypothetical or imaginary societies. The present findings serve at least to support the Lipset-Bendix hypothesis against criticisms brought by Jones (1969) and others.[7]

Not all of the increased mobility attributed to industrialization is explained by the change in volume of power resources and shape of the occupational structure. The political changes that attend industrialization are many, although industrialization is compatible with many types of political organization, as Moore (1966) has shown. Yet it has not been uncommon for industrialization to substantially undermine the numerical, economic and moral dominance of a pre-industrial landed aristocracy, such as Canada's "Family Compact" (Tepperman, 1972). This "natural disruption of dynasties" has the effect of creating additional élite positions to be filled by persons of lower social origins.

Finally, industrialization has been related to certain demographic changes, which we shall discuss below. One of these is the instigation of society-wide fertility reduction, beginning typically with members of the social élite and finally reaching families at the bottom of the social hierarchy. Whereas in pre-industrial society, completed family size was often *positively* correlated with social class (Wrigley, 1969; Laslett, 1965), in industrial society, completed family size is *negatively* correlated with social class. Thus as industrialization adds new occupational positions at the middle and top of the job hierarchy, low fertility at the top diminishes the likelihood that sufficient candidates for such positions will be found in families in the top social classes.[8] Stated otherwise, the ratio of higher born children to higher status jobs declines with industrialization; this means that the likelihood that

Chart 2.3

Simulated mean* probabilities of upward, downward, and net upward intergenerational mobility, by stage of industrialization at time of hypothetical survey

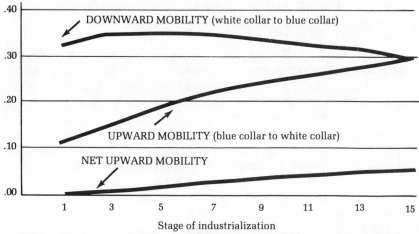

*Mean values are calculated because there is variation between these hypothetical societies, due to different rates of industrialization in the generation preceding the survey.

Source: Tepperman (1975: Tables 5,6) and unpublished data

higher status jobs will be filled by children from lower classes will increase. This phenomenon illustrates the working of a combination of resource mobility—an upgrading of the occupational structure—and demographic mobility—a change from too many to too few higher class children. Either alone would increase upward mobility, and in combination they increase it more; industrialization is ultimately responsible for both processes (cf. Blau and Duncan, 1967: 420 et passim).

How Power Competitors Change: Demographic Mobility

The ratio of resources to competitors can change through an increase or decrease in the number of competitors, as well as through change in the amount of power resources in a society. This section will discuss pure demographic mobility, mobility attributable to change in the number of competitors, given constant power resources. The arguments will be somewhat abstract, because in the last several centuries important demographic changes have taken place alongside industrialization, and indeed the two processes are linked together by what is called the "theory of demographic transition" (Davis, 1945).

The labour force constitutes the primary set of competitors for power resources, and between 1901 and 1971 the Canadian labour force increased from about 1,885,000 to 8,188,000 persons. In part, this increase resulted from the addition of new provinces to Canada. The magnitude and pattern of change is much more ascribable to other factors, notably (1) population growth, (2) change in labour force participation rates, and (3) changes in the age structure of Canadian society.

Population growth was achieved by both natural increase, the excess of births over deaths, and immigration. Kalbach and McVey (1971: 34) assert that, "At no time since 1867 has the contribution of net migration comprised more than half of the decade's change in population." This indicates that natural increase has been the main source of population growth in Canadian history, but also that immigration has supplied a very substantial proportion of population growth. Maximum and minimum estimates of immigration provided by these same authors suggest that the excess of immigrants over emigrants between 1851 and 1961 was no fewer than 1,840,000 and possibly as many as 1,926,000 persons (op. cit.: 41). Kubat and Thornton (1974: 18) estimate the net migration into Canada between 1871 and 1971 as 2.6 million persons.

Yet changes in fertility and mortality, by changing the rates of natural increase, have had the greater impact on Canadian population growth and hence on the growth of the work force. There is difficulty in determining very precisely how much mortality has changed since Confederation. Between 1931 and 1961 the life expectancy at birth of Canadian males increased from 60.0 years to 68.4 years, and that of Canadian females from 62.1 years to 74.2 years, increases of roughly 14% and 19% respectively in a period of only 30 years.[9] Life expectancy at birth in late 19th-century England and the Eastern United States was about 45.0 years for males and females. From this we can estimate that Canadian life expectancy has increased in the past century about 62% for males and 65% for females at the minimum. These increased life expectancies, implying as they do increased rates of survival in infancy and old age especially, have contributed greatly to population growth: more infants now survive to become parents, and more people of all ages survive to be counted in censuses.

Yet just as mortality has declined, thereby increasing population growth, so too has fertility declined, with the opposite effect. Between 1921 and 1968, total fertility rates declined from a hypothetical 3.5 births per woman who survives the childbearing period (given prevailing age-specific fertility rates) to 2.4 births per woman, a decline of about 30%. This decline has been by no means smooth. It was interrupted by very low fertility during the Depression, and very high fertility in the postwar "baby boom". Generally fertility in Canada has remained much higher than fertility in most developed nations, due to the large-scale immigration to Canada of young men and women from high-fertility countries—the Mediterranean European countries chief among these. However, the main trend in fertility has been downward and will probably continue in that direction, as in other developed nations over the last 100 years or more.

Participation in the Labour Force

The size of the labour force has been affected not only by population growth, but also by patterns of labour force participation. All societies are to some degree age-graded and sex-graded, in the sense that certain activities are thought proper only at certain ages or proper for only one sex or the other. This maintenance of proprieties has the effect of keeping some categories of people out of the labour force, temporarily or permanently. The last 50 to 100 years have witnessed a change in age-grading, in that a higher proportion of young people are kept in school for a longer part of their lives, and a higher proportion of old people than in the past are made to retire from the work force around age 65. Thus, in 1961, it was not until age 18 that one-half or more of all males of that age were in the work force, and not until age 23 were 90% or more of all males of that age or higher in the work force. Conversely, by age 67 and thereafter, more than half of all males had left the work force. This is a contrast with 1921, when over half of Canadian males aged 15 and over and 90% of males aged 21 or more were already in the work force, and not until age 72 were half or more men that age or older out of the work force (Denton and Ostry, 1969: 24, 25, 51).

Although this change has tended to reduce the years an average worker spends in the work force, the number of person-years spent by the Canadian male population in the work force has not declined. With the reduction in mortality noted earlier, a higher proportion of people survive through their work years than in 1921 or before. Thus the decline in male labour force participation in 1901 from 87.8% (for all males 14 years of age and over) to 81.1% in 1961 has been almost perfectly counterbalanced by the decline in mortality, so that an increase in the size of the labour force cannot be attributed to changes in age-grading (Denton and Ostry, op. cit.: 54).

The change in female labour force participation has been much more dramatic, increasing from 16.1% to 39.9% of all females 14 years of age and over between 1901 and 1971; this represents more than a doubling of the female participation rate, and hence a large contribution to the number of competitors for power resources. The increase has come about through changes in attitude to females working outside the home, legislation to prevent discrimination in hiring, an increase in jobs which are thought of as "female work" (e.g., secretarial jobs), and a reduction in childbearing that has freed women from the need to stay home with infants throughout their adult years. There is little doubt that female labour force participation rates will continue to increase in the future, adding greatly to the size of the work force.

The decline in fertility and mortality noted above has produced a change in the age composition of Canadian society. Our society has become older, in the sense that the average age of Canadians has increased and the proportion of people over age 65 has risen from 5.0% of the total Canadian population in 1901 to 7.8% in 1969. The population will age even more as Canadian fertility continues to decline; in countries such as France and Sweden the proportion of the population over age 65 is about double that of Canada, because of continuous fertility decline. This aging process has meant that a higher proportion of the Canadian population is the "right age" for working, somewhere between 15 and 65. Accordingly, the "dependency ratio" has declined between 1881 and 1966, in that today there are fewer persons than in 1881 under age 15, per person aged 15 through 65. It is a common characteristic of industrialized nations that the dependency ratio is low, about 1 young person per 2 work-age adults. Non-industrial countries with a high rate of population increase very often have a dependency ratio 50% to 100% higher.

The aging of the Canadian population has not increased the size of the labour force directly, but indirectly. As Canada's population has grown, a higher proportion of that growing population has been of work age, 15 to 65, and fewer have been young dependents. However, some of the effect of this aging has been offset by the reduction in work force participation among young adults and old people.

Let us consider how the number of male competitors for power resources would increase annually under various levels of constant mortality and fertility, excluding immigration, and without changes in labour force participation patterns. From presently prevailing levels of Canadian fertility and mortality, namely a Gross Reproduction Rate of 1.27 and a male life expectancy at birth of 68.9 years (Canada, 1966–68, excluding Newfoundland), we would deduce a stable male increase of 0.44% per year. Mortality and fertility have not been constant in the recent past; but assuming they are constant hereafter, the stable rate of male increase in Canadian society would be 0.74% per annum (Keyfitz and Flieger, 1971: 327). The actual rates of increase of the male population are just under 1% per annum and are expected to rise to almost 1.3% per annum by 1982 as Canada's postwar immigration and the baby boom work their way through the age structure (ibid.: 327).

It is certain that under virtually any foreseeable conditions of fertility and mortality, the annual growth in number of male competitors for power resources will be less than the growth rate in power resources. What will most affect the competition for power resources

Table 2.4

Annual percentage rate of change in number of male competitors, under stable demographic conditions

Life expectancy at birth (years)	Gross reproduction rate*		
	1.00	2.00	3.00
51	-0.93	1.50	2.96
61	-0.50	1.94	3.69
71	-0.14	2.28	3.75

*The number of daughters born to women subject to the prevailing age-specific fertility rates, in this case having a mean reproductive age of 29 years.
Source: Extrapolated from United Nations (1967: 114, 116, 118), Model Stable Populations (males) West 15, 19 and 23 respectively.

will be the participation of females, and the annual rate of increase in this is quite unpredictable. Female participation rates have been rising with increasing speed, in a roughly geometric pattern between 1901 and 1971, and are already increasing at more than 1% per annum. While this may or may not lead growth in the work force to outstrip the rate of growth in power resources, it helps to explain the reluctance of men to see women enter the labour force as equals. The consequence of equality is a markedly higher level of competition for jobs and hence for all power resources, with men (as a sex) the losers.

Inequality in Competition

Growth in the work force is not by itself an adequate measure of changes in the intensity of competition for power resources. This is because differential advantages are enjoyed in the competition by males and females, people of different ages, people residing in different regions of Canada, and people of different education levels, to name some relevant bases of variation. The competition among members of the work force is not competition among equals, and this inequality will be discussed further in Chapter Six. Even allowing for inequality, the number of people in the work force and the rate of increase in this number are somewhat misleading unless unemployment and underemployment are taken into account. Many who are nominally in the work force are actually unemployed for some part of the year, perhaps with regularity and for long stretches of time. Others are underemployed, in the sense that they are working part-time involuntarily, preferring full-time work. Ostry (1968: 26) has shown that Canadian unemployment has varied over time from a low of 2.6% of the work force in 1947 to a high of 7.1% in 1961; and that it varies markedly by region, with the Atlantic Provinces having unemployment rates 2 or 3 times as high as those of Ontario in any given year between 1946 and 1966. Educational attainment and occupation or industry worked in are also important influences on the probability of being unemployed at any given moment, while for women, age is an extremely important determinant of unemployment likelihood, older women being more often unemployed than younger women (ibid.: 81).

Between 1953 and 1964, 40 to 60% of men who were employed part-time were working part-time involuntarily, while only 10 to 15% of part-time female workers were involuntarily part-time. There is some question about the voluntariness of part-time work even where the respondent declares himself or herself to have chosen part-time work. Ostry has estimated that as much as 7% of the male labour force capacity and 21% of the female labour force capacity were underemployed in Canada in 1964. The largest part of female under-utilization was due to withdrawal from work between part-time jobs, and involuntary withdrawal characterized from 0% to 21% of the female work force capacity (op. cit.: 40).

Thus in discussing changes in number of competitors for power resources, if we are to use the size of the work force at all, we should properly adjust it to take into account regular unemployment and underemployment. These factors effectively reduce the size of the work force by 13% for males and 25% for females even in a year such as 1964, which witnessed a decline in total unemployment from rates one and one half times as high in 1961. While the size of the effective work force continues to grow at about the same rate as the total work force under conditions of relatively invariant unemployment, a precise estimate of the changes in the ratio of resources to (effective) competitors would require an adjustment for unemployment and underemployment.

The competition for power resources is likely to change more noticeably through sudden demographic upheavals than through such regular annual changes as we have considered to this point. For example, wars have in the twentieth century almost universally brought women into the labour force to substitute for men fighting and dying abroad. This has occurred in Canada as elsewhere, although the levels of male mortality were not sufficient to allow women to gain the same degree of labour force participation as in France or the Soviet Union, for example. Canadian women entered jobs in wartime they had not held previously, but with war's end they were largely driven out of these jobs once more. For example, Ontario and Quebec saw a rapid increase in female participation in the legal profession and government positions between 1911 and 1921, followed by a decline in further growth between 1921 and 1931. Although in the long run the World Wars stimulated higher female participation in the work force, this has not been a smooth upward trend, especially in high status occupations.

The same can probably be said of other groups in society which have typically had limited opportunities for entry into the labour force at all (e.g., the young and the old) or at higher occupational levels in particular (e.g., French Canadians, immigrants). Since the social and occupational élite is relatively small, any disaster which affects the population of that élite to the same degree or more than the rest of the population will create vacancies to be filled by people otherwise denied the opportunity to enter such positions. The two World Wars, and perhaps especially the First, appear to have drawn a large number of middle class Anglo-Saxon Ontario males out of the work force, creating new opportunities for women, as I have mentioned, and for immigrant males.

The sudden expansion of particular sectors of the work force as a result of natural increase has created new opportunities hitherto unavailable to certain types of people. The postwar baby boom caused a rapid expansion of the educational system, the teen-age merchandising market, and the social services. These sectors drew women and young people into the work force in greater numbers than before, and probably created new opportunities for upward mobility. As the impact of the baby boom recedes, a monopoly over educational and social services may conceivably return to those who held it before the baby boom. It was the suddenness of impact that opened opportunities which otherwise, even under conditions of constant population growth, would have continued in the hands of those who customarily held these roles.

The impact of sudden demographic change helps disadvantaged groups because they are awaiting the opportunity to enter the work force on more favourable terms, cannot plan careers in traditionally high-status pursuits, and therefore have the flexibility to move into any part of the occupational structure they may be permitted to enter. Wars, other disasters, and sudden population growth in many instances both increase the production of power resources and open desirable positions to those who had heretofore been kept out. Demographic variation, as Chamberlain (1970) has argued, takes advantage of institutional unpreparedness and inflexibility in developed societies. While this rigidity and lack of preparedness may be to the disadvantage of society as a whole, it is typically to the advantage of particular segments of society at particular moments. Chamberlain implies that rapid population growth generally works against those who hold dominant authority in society, by shifting the numerical balance of powerful and powerless, and by keeping institutions in constant flux and hence vulnerability to new ideas and personnel.

Summary

This chapter has considered two pure types of structural mobility: resource and demographic mobility. The extent of structural mobility depends upon the relative rates of increase in power resources and competitors for these resources. Despite difficulties in measuring these rates of increase, it seems likely that in contemporary Canadian society, as in other industrial societies, there is net upward occupational mobility of about 5%, due to industrialization. Other data introduced above suggested that power resources, and particularly property, were increasing more rapidly than population, again implying some degree of upward mobility due to structural expansion and ultimately due to industrialization.

Gross national product *per capita* has risen steadily in this century, even as measured in constant dollar values. Positions of authority have been increasing and there is reason to believe that the total amount of prestige in society has been boosted by the celebrity-making processes of the mass media.

The number of competitors for power resources, if measured by the work force size, is increasing at a relatively slow rate through natural increase. Immigration and a rise in the labour force participation of women afford greater prospects for future increase in the work force. However, it was argued that demographic cataclysms, more than gradual growth, shift the balance between power resources and competitors for these resources. This assertion was illustrated with examples from the wartime experience of women and the effect of the postwar baby boom.

The next chapter will discuss social mobility as a renewal process under hypothetical conditions of pure exchange mobility. We shall consider how mobility varies where there is no significant difference between the rates of change of power resources and of competitors.

Chapter 2 Notes

[1] The progressive broadening of categories of people who can share in public authority or "citizenship" has been discussed at some length by Weber (1958) and Marshall (1950).

[2] Status inconsistency may be created and maintained by a multiplication of criteria for ranking people. This is practised in communities that wish to avoid the appearance of structured inequality, so that people may act toward one another as equals. In such cases, moral and material bases of ranking are invoked in ways that counterbalance one another; one finds such characterizations as "poor but honest", "wealthy but crude", and so on. Yet this kind of purposeful maintenance of status inconsistency is apparently unstable; it seems to require isolation from the outside world, a high degree of moral consensus, and little social change (Hutson, 1971). Such cases are instructive primarily because they suggest that status consistency is the norm in human societies. They also show that where status inconsistency prevails, it is difficult to demonstrate that there is a social hierarchy and, therefore, difficult to demonstrate that there is social mobility.

[3] An amount increasing geometrically gets larger by a fixed *proportion* each year, while an amount increasing arithmetically gets larger by a fixed *amount* each year. Under geometric increase, the absolute amount of increase gets larger each year; under arithmetic increase, the proportional amount of increase usually declines each year. If we let A be the original amount, r the annual rate of increase and t the years that have elapsed, the

amount produced after t years will be $A(1 + r)^t$ in a geometric progression; while if R represents the annual amount of increase, the amount produced after t years will be $(A + tR)$ in an arithmetic progression.

[4]Mathematical representation can be employed to make this set of relationships explicit. I have simply asserted that:

$$S = k\left(\frac{R}{C}\right)$$

and $\qquad M = dS = k\left(\frac{dR}{dC}\right)$

where S = standard of living
k = variables and constants left undefined at present
R = total amount of power resources in society
C = total number of competitors for power resources
M = amount of structural mobility over a specified period of time
d = a rate of change (in S, R or C as the case may be)

The preceding discussion has noted that there is difficulty predicting M (mobility) over a given period of time because we do not know (1) whether dR and dC are both geometric or not; (2) whether $\left(\frac{dR}{dC}\right)$ is always or after some particular period of time greater than, less than, or equal to, 1; and (3) whether k includes a term that sets limits to either dR or dC or both.

For these reasons, it is not appropriate to act as though we knew more about structural mobility than we do, or to use the mathematics of economic demography to reach an apparently precise formula for predicting mobility.

[5]This formulation corresponds relatively well to that by Kahl (1957) in which pure resource mobility is called "technological mobility"; pure demographic mobility is called "reproductive mobility" and "immigration mobility"; and exchange mobility is called "individual mobility".

[6] Reitz (1974) has recently argued that this method of adjusting mobility tables to new marginals is invalid. Its underlying assumption—that odds ratios are preserved as the occupational structure changes—is arbitrary, as it is not based upon substantive considerations of what preserving the odds ratio (as opposed to some other feature in the table) actually means. It is therefore purely a computational convenience and, as such, one of many possible.

[7] While one is forced to agree with S.M. Miller (1960) that industrial societies vary considerably, especially in the ways they combine high or low rates of *upward* mobility with high or low rates of *downward* mobility, there is as yet little predictability or explanation of this variation, and I have largely neglected it here. The similarities may prove more interesting than the differences among industrial societies, at least at this point in our understanding. If nothing else, the similarities are both noticeable and explainable by a simple, powerful theory generally attributed to Lipset and Bendix.

[8] *cf.* Sorokin (1964): 346, 359
"In the course of time (sterility, lower differential birthrate, or higher mortality of the upper classes) cause either an extinction of the aristocratic families or a decrease of their proportion in the total increased population of a society. In both cases, such a situation creates a kind of "social vacuum" within the upper strata ... which must be filled by the climbers from the lower strata. ... *And the greater the difference in the number of surviving children of the upper and lower strata, the more intensive the vertical circulation caused by this factor will be.*"

[9] Here and elsewhere in this section the primary source of demographic data is Kalbach and McVey (1971).

3
SOCIAL MOBILITY AS A RENEWAL PROCESS

∾

What man, however rare his talents, however excellent his quali-
ties, cannot but be convinced of his uselessness, on considering
that in the world he must leave at death his loss will pass
unnoticed, and a host of others will be ready to take his place.

Jean de la Bruyère, *Characters*

Mobility as a Rate of Renewal

The term "renewal process" is used here in reference to a social system
with (1) constant or nearly constant size; (2) two or more separate states
of existence; (3) recurring events, such as the arrival of people in states;
and (4) a turnover of people resulting from "wastage" (leaving) and
"recruitment" (entering) (Bartholomew, 1967; Bhat, 1972). Exchange
mobility—that mobility which takes place in the absence of a changing
ratio of resources to competitors—is essentially a renewal process.

In order to visualize the renewal process by which mobility is
maximized in an organization or society of constant size, we can begin
with several examples of other renewal processes. If we are running
water into a sink and want the water never to rise above or fall below
a certain level, the rate at which the water enters must come to be
identical to the rate at which water leaves the sink. If we are adding
people to a population and want to ensure zero population growth (or
"stationarity"), the annual birth rate must neither exceed nor fall short
of the annual death rate. And finally, if cars are being manufactured
on an assembly line of fixed size and we wish to ensure that car parts
should not have to line up for assembly for more than a specified time,
nor should workers await the parts more than a specified time, we are
supposing a waiting line, or queue for assembly, of a relatively fixed
size. Maintaining this queue at a fixed size requires that the rate at
which units are added at one end of the line must be equal to the rate
at which they leave at the other end of the line. In each of these cases,
the overall rate of renewal may be restricted primarily by either the
entry rate or the departure rate.

The rate of renewal is maximized by maximizing the rates of both
entry *and* departure, since these must be identical to maintain an

unchanging system size. A population with a birth and death rate of 3% per annum—having a female life expectancy of about 30 years and a completed family size of roughly 4½ children—will have a greater turnover than a population with a birth and death rate of 1½% per annum—having a female life expectancy of 65 years and a completed family size of about 2½ children. The mobility, renewal, or turnover rate in the former population will be greater than that in the latter, in that a greater proportion of the population will be "newcomers". The average age in the first population is about 29 years and in the second population, about 38 years (United Nations, 1967: 97, 104).

It would seem that the factor limiting mobility, in a working population or in an organization, is not the rate of entry but the rate of departure. To achieve high mobility it would be necessary to increase both the entry and departure rates; and of these it would be easier to increase the entry rate than the departure rate. In the long run, the maximum entry rate could not exceed the birth rate in society at large (assuming no immigration), which is rather low in most industrial countries, although in the short run the entry rate could be much higher than this. Theoretically, the departure rate, which is presently low, could be increased to very high levels, but only if society were willing to tolerate high levels of emigration, unemployment, or underemployment. It is because we are unwilling to accept these that the departure rate remains lower than could be readily matched by a higher entry rate; and because the departure rate is relatively low, to achieve population stationarity it is necessary to control the entry rate. The progressive lengthening of the period for educational certification, and the impediments to easy entry into the work force by women serve the end of maintaining stationarity at a relatively low level of mobility.

In general then, a high rate of mobility or turnover of any kind would require high rates of entering and leaving. But a high rate of upward mobility would, in a system where people start at the bottom of a hierarchy, require that leaving take place toward the top. In an organization with many low level jobs that are frequently vacated while the incumbency of top positions is of longer duration, there can be little upward mobility. Thus we must begin by assuming that the rate of upward mobility in a system of fixed size is dependent upon the rate of entry into and departure from top positions. The higher the correlation between rank and the annual rate of departure (and entry), the higher the upward mobility rate in a system of unchanging size.

Three Methods of Maximizing Renewal Rates

The question then becomes how to achieve a high rate of departure from the top positions of an organization or society in order to maximize upward mobility. Many ways to achieve this suggest themselves. The first is by maximizing downward mobility from top positions; however, this option is rarely used, and downward mobility in careers is infrequent. It is especially infrequent in formal organizations because it creates uncertainty at all levels of the organization and demoralizes those at the bottom as well as at the top. Those at the top are least willing to establish the precedent of downward mobility, which might eventually be used against them. To resist downward mobility is to maintain some measure of certainty for all and to guarantee oligarchic control by those who have reached the top.

Thus downward mobility (or demotion) is rarely used to vacate top positions in order to maximize upward mobility. Sideward movement or "simotion" is used somewhat more frequently for this purpose, because it has the result of freeing top line positions, by moving people into essentially powerless staff positions, without unambiguously degrading the person moved. The ways demotion and simotion are used in formal organizations will be discussed in the next chapter; it is important to note at this point that neither demotion or simotion are particularly frequent, and that they are used delicately. These methods cannot be used as the mainspring for organizational mobility: they are too demoralizing.

Retirement is a better method by which an organization can guarantee the vacating of top positions. Retirement is universal, and the chief merit of specifying a mandatory retirement age is that it establishes a clear standard that is used universalistically to vacate top positions. Since the age of retirement is relatively fixed over long periods of time, it provides certainty for all in the organization and is less demoralizing to the organizational employees than downward mobility. The retirement age can be lowered in order to achieve a great increase in the rate of departures, and hence in the rate of upward mobility in the organization.

Yet these are not the only means by which the rate of departures from the top positions can be regulated; at least three other methods can be imagined. The first we shall call the method of *gradual attrition*; the second, the method of *sudden attrition*; and the third, the method of *actuarial selectivity*.

By the method of gradual attrition, the process by which people enter the top positions is made so long and hard as to give a high likelihood of early departure from the top positions. For example, a study of the Coldstream Guard officers corps between 1690 and 1830 (Tepperman, 1975a) revealed that most men entered as Ensigns, at the bottom of the officer hierarchy, and moved up the hierarchy very much as though there had been promotion by seniority. It would take an average of 20 to 25 years to reach the top positions in the regiment—Major and Lieutenant-Colonel—and once these positions were been achieved, they were occupied for only 2 to 4 years, after which the officer departed. The men who achieved these top positions were so old and physically unprepared for command in battle that they rarely stayed to execute the command they had sought so long. In order to provide continuity of command in this organization, the regimental commanding officer, the Colonel, was always brought into his position from outside the organization. He was often younger than the senior officers assisting him, and retained command for an average of 7 to 8 years.

Although the Colonel was more a symbolic than an actual commander, he could more readily have endured battle conditions than his older assistants; in any event, his youth and exemption from past or present battle conditions helped him stay on for a longer time than other senior officers. This provided continuity in an organization that had an extremely high rate of population turnover—an entry and departure rate of about 147/1000 *per annum*, or over 6 new officers per year in a group of 44 officers.

Less distant examples of the gradual attrition method can be found to illustrate this same idea. A prime example is the prize fighter: very few professional fighters will win a title before they have had thirty or forty professional fights. These figures must take their toll of the champion, who quickly begins to go into decline and rarely keeps the championship for more than a few years. It is equally common for popular entertainers and jazz musicians to die in youth or middle age; early death is much more common for such people than it is for those in other professions. The physical and emotional effort expended to achieve prominence in these fields—illustrated by the case study of jazz musician Ornette Coleman in Chapter Five—and the use of drugs or alcohol, in part to ease the hardship, hasten departure from these top entertainment positions and their filling by others of less eminence. The early deaths of jazz musicians Charlie Parker, Lester Young, Clifford Brown and John Coltrane, as well as of rock stars Janis Joplin, Jimi Hendrix and Mama Cass, could serve to start a list of such eminent departures.

The method of *sudden attrition* is perhaps misnamed, for departure is not exactly sudden and it is, further, not readily distinguished in practice from the method of gradual attrition. Someone has named the shuttle airplane flights between Boston, New York and Washington, and Montreal, Toronto and Ottawa, "cardiac club" flights. These morning and evening flights are taken largely by senior executives who travel a great deal on behalf of their organizations. The strain of frequent travelling and great corporate responsibility is reflected in high rates of cardiovascular disorder and death among top executives. While in some hierarchies reaching the top allows a reduction in work, travelling, and physical-emotional strain—the university, government and the military may have this characteristic in common—high positions in private enterprise tend to demand more rather than less of their highly placed personnel, and therefore to increase the likelihood of early departure. This is not to say the intent of an organization is to achieve high mobility by killing off its senior officers; yet such is the pattern occasionally observed.

A final method of achieving high turnover I have called *actuarial selectivity*: the selection of persons for top jobs who have a high actuarial risk of early departure. This "method" is related to the method of gradual attrition in some respects, as it is to retirement. If early departure is desired, one of the best types of person to promote to a high position is an old person. The older a person is, the more likely that person is to retire or die in any given year. Yet there are other types of people who might also be selected actuarially to provide a high risk of departure.

People depart from organizations for various reasons, and in order to employ the method of actuarial selectivity we must know these reasons. Some people die, some retire, some leave for another job, some leave the country, and some drop out of the labour force for a longer or shorter time. The probability of dying or retiring in any given year is primarily dependent upon an employee's age; thus, to maximize the rate of departure from top positions by death or retirement, we should ensure that the holders of top jobs are old rather than young. This suggests that an age-dependent system of selection and promotion, such as promotion by seniority, will be effective in vacating top positions, and hence in increasing upward mobility in the system.

The probability of leaving a job for another job, or indeed leaving for another country, is very largely dependent upon the skill or merit level, and hence the "marketability", of a given individual. This would suggest that top positions ought to be filled by the most meritorious, among other things, for they will be the soonest to leave. We are reminded of the "brain drain" of Canadians to the United States in the 1950s and 1960s, as described by Parai (1965). Yet the occurrence of such a brain drain is dependent upon various other factors: upon an expanding market for labour in another country, or perhaps another part of Canada, or even in another sector of industry, for example. It requires easy transportability of skills—easy acquisition of work papers in another place, for example—and an orientation to work and residence that ignores national boundaries or even local differences in culture, such as these may be.

It may be supposed that with the development of "professional subcultures" that transcend local or national boundaries, all movement among jobs, including emigration, may depend primarily upon the opening of opportunities elsewhere, through economic expansion. It is typically in periods of economic recession that opportunities for movement decline. Fewer new jobs develop; nations become more reluctant to allow the entry of foreigners for purposes of work; and individual workers become less willing to risk moving to another job they are not certain to like or retain, especially if they suppose that returning to a job like their original one will be made difficult.

The probability that a worker will drop out of the work force is also unpredictable, although there is some information on the types of people more likely than others to drop out. Two particular categories of people with this characteristic are sick people and young women. Sick people may drop out temporarily or permanently in order to convalesce; young women drop out temporarily or permanently in order to raise a family. The actuarial risk in each case is probably lower than it once was; today people with physical or mental disorders, for example, can more readily receive supportive medical treatment while continuing to work than they could in the past. Young married women today are more likely to remain childless than in the past, and also more likely to bear their children in a short period of time, making their absence from the work force brief. They are also more likely to utilize child care facilities today, and therefore less likely to interrupt their careers for child-rearing at all.

However, both sickly people and young women provide a higher actuarial risk of dropping out than do healthy young men. This has customarily worked against their achieving important positions; organizations appear unwilling to put the goal of upward mobility above all else. If achieving a high rate of upward mobility were the paramount goal in formal organizations, young women would customarily be given the top organizational positions. But organizations also wish to achieve predictability and reasonable stability over time. Moreover they would find it difficult to rationalize the actuarial selection of sick people and young women on grounds related to organizational efficiency. They can so rationalize the selection of old people and meritorious people, who are likely both to leave soon and to dispatch their duties capably by virtue of experience or talent.

Thus in practice, promotion in formal organizations is based upon seniority and talent; these are rational bases for promotion from the standpoint of the organization and they also have the consequence— perhaps unanticipated—of increasing upward mobility. Of these two, promotion by seniority, or age-dependent promotion, is the more common and, perhaps unintentionally, produces the greater and more predictably high levels of upward mobility. Death and retirement are more predictable mechanisms for vacating top positions than emigration or job-changing: neither death nor retirement depends upon fluctuations in the national or international economy, as do emigration and job-changing; nor do they depend upon governmental decisions to maintain open or closed boundaries; nor upon the sentiments of individuals towards leaving. Death is universalistic and inexorable.

Death is also relatively common at greater ages. In a population such as our own, with a male life expectancy at birth of 65 to 70 years, the death rate for males aged 55 to 65 is about 2% *per annum*, and the male probability of surviving through ages 55 to 65 is only about 80% (United Nations, *op. cit.*: 91, 94). The mandatory retirement age in many organizations is 65, but workers often retire before this. Indeed as Denton and Ostry have shown in Table 3.1, the departure rate of male workers from the Canadian labour force was in 1961 about 3% *per annum* for those aged 55 to 59 and 9% *per annum* for those aged 60 to 65.

Table 3.1

Annual rates of separation of males from the Canadian work force, by age of worker and cause of separation, 1961

| Age | Separations per 1,000 labour force | | |
	All causes	Death	Retirement
35-39	3.0	2.3	0.7
40-44	4.7	3.6	1.1
45-49	9.0	6.1	2.9
50-54	15.6	10.0	5.6
55-59	32.3	16.0	16.3
60-64	93.3	23.8	69.5
65-69	140.6	34.6	106.0
70-74	173.1	51.9	121.2
75-79	201.4	77.6	123.8
80-84	232.7	117.6	115.1

Source: Denton and Ostry (1969: Table 1, Part B)

These rates of departure are higher and more predictable than rates of emigration. Even at their highest, as during the brain drain period, emigration rates were rarely higher than 2% *per annum* of those in a given occupation in a given year. Parai shows in Table 3.2. that, with the exception of "other engineers", during the decade 1953–1963, the maximum total emigration of professional people was about 20% of the total membership of a given occupation (e.g., chemists, all engineers, graduate nurses). This decade rate leads us to expect an average annual rate of no more than 2% emigration per occupation, and even so we cannot assume that *all* who emigrated were the most highly placed in their occupation. The actual rate at which top positions was vacated may, therefore, have fallen far short of 2% *per annum*.

The Best Method of Maximizing Renewal Rates

It would seem that the maximization of upward mobility could best be achieved by age-dependent promotion or by its approximation, promo-

Table 3.2

Decade rates* of separation of professional and skilled workers from the Canadian work force by emigration to United States; by occupation

Occupations A. Professional	Emigration to U.S. 1953–63 Labour force 1961
Accountants and auditors	9.4
Architects	12.4
Chemists	19.5
Dentists	0.2
Draughtsmen and designers	12.7
Engineering, Chemical	15.1
Mining	5.3
Electrical	13.9
Mechanical ⎱ Aeronautical ⎰	14.0
Other	34.4
All Engineers	21.6
Laboratory technicians and assistants	6.3
Graduate nurses	22.6
Physicians and surgeons	12.3
Teachers and professors	3.0
Total, all professional	**8.9**

Occupations B. Skilled	Emigration to U.S. 1956–63 Labour force 1961
Airplane mechanics and repairmen	4.7
Automobile mechanics and repairmen	1.5
Bakers	5.5
Barbers, hairdressers, manicurists	4.6
Brick and stonemasons	7.0
Cabinet and furniture makers	5.6
Carpenters	3.8
Dressmakers and seamstresses	6.4
Electricians and wiremen	5.1
Machinists	7.8
Mechanics and repairmen	5.1
Painters, decorators and glaziers	3.3
Plasterers and lathers	4.1
Plumbers and pipefitters	3.4
Sheet metal workers and tinsmiths	2.9
Shoemakers and repairers	3.1
Tailors	11.1
Toolmakers, diemakers and setters	26.0
Upholsterers	4.7

*Ratio expressed as a percentage.
Source: Parai (1965: Tables 27, 29)

tion by seniority. This method can be relied upon to provide the highest levels of departure under present conditions, and it is justifiable on the grounds that age gives experience and experience is needed in the top positions. We can take this idea one step further by asserting that age-dependent promotion maximizes upward mobility under all conditions, and that upward mobility declines as a system of promotion becomes more indifferent to age or seniority. One might reasonably treat organizational promotion systems as though they were arrayed along a single continuum ranging from wholly *age-dependent*, and therefore completely "controlled" in the sense that mobility is maximally predictable and maximally high, to wholly *age-independent* and therefore effectively random or uncontrolled.

Ralph Turner (1970) has distinguished between what he calls *sponsored* mobility and *contest* mobility, and offers the following definition of these ideal types of mobility:

> *Contest* mobility is a system in which elite status is the prize in an open contest and is taken by the aspirants' own efforts ... Since the "prize" of upward mobility is not in the hands of an established elite to give out, the latter cannot determine who shall attain it and who shall not. Under *sponsored* mobility recruits are chosen by the established elite or their agents, and elite status is *given* on the basis of some criterion of supposed merit and cannot be *taken* by any amount of effort or strategy. ... Ultimately the members grant or deny upward mobility on the basis of whether they judge the candidate to have those qualities they wish to see in fellow members (1970: 353).

Turner emphasizes that these are only ideal types intended to clarify the observed differences between English (sponsored) and American (contest) stratification and educational systems.

The concept of a control dimension in mobility was discussed in Chapter One. I have elsewhere provided a formal proof that where "control" is defined to mean promotion by age or seniority, a high degree of control ensures that the *likelihood* of upward mobility is at its greatest (Tepperman, 1973). What Turner has called "sponsored" and "contest" mobility are shown to be two types of mobility representing polar extremes on the control dimension, holding the level of absorption constant.

Since I have become rather abstract in describing why age-dependent promotion acts to maximize upward mobility, it may be worthwhile to turn to a simple illustration of how age-dependent mobility works in a particular organization.

The Renewal of University Faculties: An Illustration

Holmes (1974) has asserted that the "future for an ambitious 25-year-old is far less bright than it was in the heady 60s. Prospects for academic

Chart 3.1   *An opportunity paradigm*

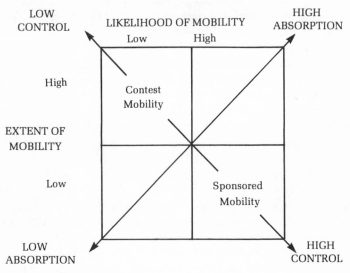

Source: Tepperman (1973: Figure 1)

promotion will grow dimmer ... " (*ibid.*: 2). A young faculty member will have to wait much longer to become a full professor or associate professor, and a smaller proportion of young faculty members will get tenure than in the past.

University faculties will get older, Holmes predicts, because they will contain a higher proportion of aging young and middle-aged people with tenure who will remain in their positions for another 20 to 30 years, until retirement. Holmes believes that:

aging is generally accompanied by increased conservatism. . . .
Most would agree that universities should have a steady turn-over in staff to stimulate the flow of new ideas and attitudes. . . .
A problem here is that the professors more likely to take opportunities to retire early, or to move to government or industry, are the ones the university least wishes to lose. In a state of slow growth it is frequently the dynamic members of the community who emigrate.

He concludes by suggesting that these changes may have an adverse effect on university curricula, research, and campus life, and that young people would less likely be attracted to university faculties because of the difficulty of advancement. We will have an opportunity in the next 5 to 10 years to judge whether these guesses are correct.

The bleak future of careers (and studies) in universities can be traced to at least four factors. First, promotion in a university is largely by seniority rather than merit. Second, future promotion will take place in a stationary or non-growing structure. Third, this absence of growth follows upon the heels of rapid growth, the "heady 60s". Fourth, there is a relatively fixed amount of power resources—in this case, senior positions, tenure, and money for salary raises—in the university system. These coldly impersonal factors will shape academic careers in both their objective and subjective aspects for the next ten years at least. It is worth following the line of Holmes's reasoning to see how career patterns can be analyzed in terms of the restrictions imposed upon mobility by external or "structural" forces.

Holmes asks us to suppose a renewal process—a one-to-one replacement of retired professors in the period 1973–1983 which maintains the present number of Canadian university teachers (27,800 in 1972–1973). We are further to suppose that there will be mandatory retirement at age 65, roughly as at present, making for about 230 retirements a year for the 10-year period, or 8 retirements per 1000 faculty members a year. One-to-one replacement would mean hiring only about 230 new faculty members each year. If the salaries of retiring faculty members were used to hire new junior professors, it would be possible to hire double this number per year. This would still be a small number of hirings in comparison with the growth period of the 1960s in Canadian universities. Besides offering fewer job opportunities for graduate students hoping to enter jobs in the universities, how would this limitation of hiring affect those already there?

Chart 3.2 compares the age profiles of faculty in Canadian universities in 1972–73 and (projected) in 1982–83. The 1972–73 age distribution is "fir-tree shaped", and is characteristic of all human populations with a high annual birth rate (Wrigley, 1969: 23–28). With the exception of the 21 to 30 age group, which already shows the signs of decreased hiring, the younger an age group is, the larger its number in the population. Because there are so many young faculty members, half of the professors in 1972–73 are under 38.4 years of age; thus the *median* age is 38.4 years. The projected age distribution for 1982–83 is very different, having a majority of professors in the age group 41 to 50, and very small numbers under age 40. In these circumstances the median age of full-time faculty is 46.7 years, more than 8 years older than the median faculty age in 1972–73.

The only two ways the faculty in 1982–83 would be kept from aging as much as projected would be through earlier retirement, e.g., at age 60 rather than 65, or through continued high rates of growth equivalent to those in the 1960s. If the first alternative is chosen, the present size of university faculties can be held to 27,800 but the median age will rise to about 45.0 years. Under the second option, the median age of 38.7 years can be maintained, but to do so an additional 16,000 professors under age 40 must be hired in the decade 1973–1983. This amount of hiring would represent 58% growth in university faculties in the decade,

Chart 3.2

The changing age structure of Canadian university faculties

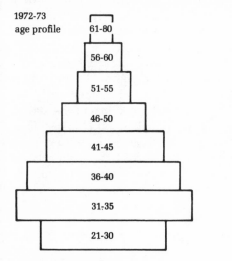

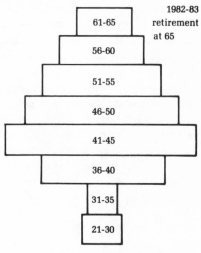

Growth of the sixties is reflected in the 1972-73 age profile of full-time Canadian university faculty. Half the professors are under 38.4 years of age.

One-for-one replacement of retiring professors would give this profile by 1982-83. To restore the fir-tree shape, i.e., maintain the earlier growth trend, would require an additional 16,000 professors under age 40. This would mean a total faculty of some 44,000, with a median age of just under 40.

Source: Holmes (1974)

or just over 4½% growth in universities *per annum.* To maintain the present age structure, hiring will have to proceed at a rate almost five times as high as the rate under one-to-one replacement of faculty.

If, as seems likely, there will be little or no increase in university resources in the next decade, all mobility within the universities will take place only through the renewal of present faculty members, that is, through one-to-one replacement of professors who die or resign. Universities tend to promote faculty members largely on the basis of seniority; as we saw in the preceding chapter, this procedure would *normally* produce the greatest mobility for the greatest number. However, two factors are operating to make prospects for future mobility unattractive. First, much mobility in the late 1960s was structural mobility and provided more rapid ascent than could be expected from exchange mobility (or renewal). Faculty members must now adjust to new expectations which are appropriate to exchange rather than structural mobility.

Second, the next several decades will see even slower than normal exchange mobility because of the peculiar age structure that has developed: age and rank became less correlated in the 1960s and early 1970s than would be expected in a seniority system. As we shall note shortly, the worse the correlation between age and rank within an organization, the more a system approaches age-independent mobility, and the less mobility there is in that organization.

In this particular case, we see future academic careers being structured by economics (e.g., government spending policy), by historical tradition (e.g., promotion by seniority) and historical accident (e.g., the baby boom, which led to a growth of university faculties in the 1960s) and by the structure of the hierarchy within which mobility takes place (e.g., a four or five level pyramid within which a distinction is made between tenured and non-tenured faculty). Each of these aspects of career mobility will be discussed in more general terms in Chapter Four.

Some General Observations on Seniority Systems

In seniority systems, almost everyone has some success; only those who leave the organization very soon after entering it will be unlikely to have moved upward some distance. Of course, the greater successes—attainment of the higher ranks—are achieved only after a much more substantial investment of time than a first change of rank requires; this is because there are many fewer upper ranks, and so many contenders for these positions.

One finds the greatest turnover of personnel in the lowest ranks, where people decide they really hadn't wanted a career in that organization after all. Once five or ten years of service have been invested, employees become less likely to sacrifice their seniority by leaving or risking discharge. They become locked into the renewal of the total system, in which their own mobility is dependent largely upon the retirements of persons at much higher levels in the organization. Each time a retirement occurs, a string of promotions follows in consequence; that White (1970) has called a "vacancy chain" is set in motion by such retirements at the top.

The average person in such a system can move upward a great distance. In theory everyone can ultimately move to the top ranks, although this rarely occurs in practice. Movement to the top in a seniority system takes a very long time; for this reason, the Coldstream Guard's top officer, the Colonel, was never installed in his position through seniority, as I noted earlier in this chapter. It is similarly rare for prospective top managers in large corporations to have their careers begun on the lowest levels of management; they will typically enter an organization in middle management, so that the organization can plan to utilize these men in top management when they are entering their forties rather than their sixties.

Not everyone moves to the top, for various reasons. Some die or retire before the time comes for entry into the top position; others leave the organization too soon. Some must wait a longer time than usual before a vacancy occurs at the top. If a corporation has installed a 45-year-old at the top after previously allowing only people 55 years and over to hold that position, this change of policy will slow down the mobility of everyone in the line of succession by about ten years. A man who is 50 and next in line for the post, according to seniority, may be forced to retire before his younger superior has vacated the top position.

A seniority system differs from a strict age-graded system in that aging is both necessary and sufficient for promotion in the latter, but only necessary and not sufficient for promotion in the former. In many and perhaps most organizations basing promotion on seniority, no amount of seniority will bring a recognized incompetent the top job. This factor too will reduce the average distance people actually move upward in an organization with essentially age-graded promotion, despite the theoretical possibility that anyone could move to the top by simply enduring the passage of time.

Age-Dependent Power Resources: Three Examples

In the Coldstream Guard (Tepperman, 1975a) the average length of time it took to move upward to a specified position in a stationary (or non-growing) organization varied with such *demographic factors* as the age structure and prevailing retirement patterns. Moving time to any position is predicted by matching the age structure to the rank structure (assuming all entries are at the bottom, and all movement is age-dependent).

An officer's rank in the Guard was largely dependent on the time he had already spent as an officer of any rank. Most men, about 72% of all 796 officers between 1690 and 1830, had entered the Officer's Corps at the (bottom) rank of Ensign, while 89% had entered at the rank of Ensign or Lieutenant; very few ever entered above the rank of Captain. Officers generally moved up in rank as time passed, and none moved down. As a consequence, little more than 20% left the Guard at the rank of Ensign, and those who did were primarily men leaving in their first year or two of service; just under one-half of all departing officers held a rank of Captain or higher.

A man's mobility in the Scots Guard (a regiment similar in structure to the Coldstream Guard) over the period 1690–1930 is strongly correlated with the death rate in his own cohort ($r = .374$), and with the death rate in the cohort preceding his own ($r = .161$). (It should be noted that these two death rates are closely interlinked, and therefore are not two separate tests of the hypothesis that death produces mobility.) His mobility is also correlated with the wound rate (and presumably with the increased retirement rate induced by wounding) in his own cohort ($r = .373$) and in the cohort preceding his own ($r = .127$).

Despite fortuitous elements, men's careers in the Guard were chiefly age-dependent: as officers got older, they almost invariably moved up the ranks. The age at which an officer reached any given rank depended upon two features of the organization: (1) the relative scarcity of that rank in the organization; and (2) the age distribution of the organization relative to the age of the individual. If, for example, 26% of all officers were at or above the rank of Captain and 74% below it, an average Ensign would have to wait until that age Y above which 26% of all officers in the organization were age Y or older, in order to attain the rank of Captain. More simply, the percentile at which a rank was located in the organizational hierarchy determined the percentile to be attained in the age structure before an officer attained a given rank. Thus the final rank an officer attained in the Guard was *almost* perfectly predicted ($r = .95$) by the rank at which he had entered the Guard and the years he subsequently served. There is very little individual variation in career mobility within such an organization.

Perhaps the single most important aspect of age-graded systems, pure or hybrid, is that all mobility is upward and none is downward; the amount of stagnation or immobility in a system depends on how far the organization in question deviates from a pure age-graded system.

Age-graded mobility is to be found in some form in a wide range of social milieux, even outside formal organizations. This is illustrated by data in Table 3.3. and Chart 3.3. The first shows income mobility in a late medieval clothmaking town, Coventry, England; the second infers careers from cross-sectional income data for Canada, 1961. In each case, income tends to increase with age, which implies age-grading, but neither was a pure age-graded system. The top income class in Coventry could be entered by younger men: there, aging or seniority may have been sufficient for the attainment of top incomes but was not necessary if, for example, a father were especially propserous and left his sons his fortune or business enterprise (Tepperman, 1973).

In contemporary Canada, incomes tend to increase with age, but as Chart 3.3 indicates, the amount of increase depends upon the particular occupation, and some occupations show declines in income after middle age while other occupations simply level off. These apparent aberrations from strict age-grading may be misleading, the result of using cross-sectional data to infer longitudinal (i.e., career) changes in income. If we were to follow a particular cohort of workers from their entry into the work force until their exit from it, we might instead find

Table 3.3

Highest class ever occupied, by age: Coventry, England, 1449

Highest class* ever occupied	Age†					
	16	20	30	35	40	45 and over
bottom	34.1	0.0	6.3	0.0	0.0	0.0
second	25.1	10.8	18.0	1.7	0.8	0.0
third	26.8	43.9	30.6	17.2	18.3	0.0
fourth	10.1	27.7	23.9	32.8	23.3	0.0
top	3.9	17.6	21.2	48.3	57.5	100.0
N	358	148	222	58	120	30

*The term "class" is used interchangeably with "income quintile", because of the high correlation between income, authority and prestige in this population.

†As measured by the number of years on Coventry tax rolls, 1420–1450, and assuming tax payment began at age 15.

Source: Tepperman (1973: Table 2)

a pattern of continually rising income; however, such data are not available. At this time one can only conclude that career mobility in Canada, as indicated by the data in Chart 3.3, is largely but not wholly age-graded. Or, stated otherwise, the relationship between age and

Chart 3.3

Average Income from employment by age groups for selected broad occupations, year ended May 31, 1961

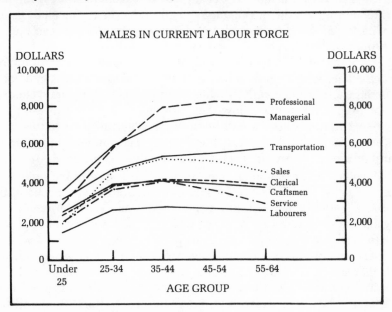

Source: Podoluk (1968: Chart 4.1)

income is not linear, as we would expect, but curvilinear; it may also vary from one structure to another, depending on how strongly age and competence are correlated, for example.

Promotion based on seniority is a hybrid of promotion by age and promotion by merit. According to the principle of seniority, the most qualified person is chosen from among a number of people at roughly the same rank, implying roughly the same age, to fill a vacancy at a higher rank. Thus, promotion by seniority implies a competition restricted to those within a limited age range, but selection for promotion may be based on any performance or characteristic (other than age or rank), and may include chance selection. To most readily understand the difference between promotion by seniority and promotion by competition, we shall examine the extremes of each: ranking determined wholly by age; and ranking determined independently of age, or by processes that are random with respect to age.

Merits of an Age-Dependent System

Where there is ranking and promotion by age—as in the Coldstream Guard—everyone moves upward who lives long enough. Mobility is perfectly predictable in that sense, but it is slow, and its speed depends upon such things as organizational growth or stationarity, and average span of control in the organization. It also depends upon prevailing rates of retirement and mortality: the higher these annual rates of "leaving", the faster is mobility, or the shorter is moving time from one rank to another. As this was demonstrated in the preceding analysis of the Guard, we can now consider mobility as it would proceed under conditions of perfectly random selection to fill vacancies.

Suppose the Coldstream Guard had selected men for promotion by chance alone, so that all men below the rank in which a vacancy had occurred were automatically eligible for promotion. Men would choose not to compete for ranks below their present rank, and as a result all movement in the system would be upward. We shall refer to this as a "lottery" system. Table 3.4 indicates the average "moving times" that would be required to attain each rank under these conditions.

We shall define "moving time" as the years required for sufficient chance contests to take place for any individual to have a probability of 50% or better of moving into a specified vacant rank. Moving time may also be considered an expected waiting time for entry into a given rank through lottery competition. A formal proof is provided elsewhere (Tepperman, 1975a) to show that average moving time grows longer with increase in span of control, the distance between a man and the rank he is seeking, and the average number of years spent in a space by a man whose departure is awaited by competitors for mobility. Moving time shortens with an increase in the number of spaces within a desired rank, that is, with structural expansion.

Table 3.4

Mobility in the Coldstream Guard under a hypothetical lottery contest system

Rank	number of spaces	probability of entry from below in 1 contest: $p =$	mean required contests[*]: $n =$	mean years in rank[†]	mean contests per year for rank[‡]	mean years to attain rank[°]
Lieutenant	16	.06250	11	6.307	2.537	4.3
Captain	8	.03125	22	7.961	1.005	21.9
Jr. Major	1	.02500	28	2.707	0.369	75.9
Sr. Major	1	.02439	29	3.395	0.295	98.3
Lt. Colonel	1	.02381	29	5.571	0.180	161.1

[*]Calculated with the binomial theorem: $[1 - P \{0|n\} \cong .5$, or $[1 - (1-p)^n] \cong .5$.
[†]Observed in the Coldstream Guard.
[‡]Calculated as the number of spaces in rank, divided by the mean years spent in a rank.
[°]Calculated as mean required contests, divided by mean contests per year for rank.
Source: Tepperman (1975a: Table 10)

The average number of years spent in a space depends on age-specific mortality and retirement rates. Where these rates are high, the average number of years is low; thus moving time is low where deaths and retirements are frequent. In a contest system as in an age-dependent system, higher mortality and retirement rates at each age will increase mobility. It would seem then that in both a contest and an age-dependent or seniority mobility system, the rate of mobility is affected by organizational size and growth, and by staff retirement and mortality.

The data in Table 3.4 suggest that on the average one hundred and sixty years of waiting would be needed to reach the Lieutenant-Colonel's position from Ensign under a lottery contest system, as compared with less than thirty years under a seniority system. It would be futile to plan a career in a contest system, for one would have no control over one's future and no certainty of reaching any specified rank within one's work life.

It would be equally foolish to organize a hierarchical system along the lines of a lottery contest, for several reasons. First, such a system would take no advantage of experience gained by officers at lower levels in the hierarchy. Second, highly capable people would be reluctant to enter such an organization with the foreknowledge that they had no control over, or certainty about, their own future. Third, great variations in age of entry into various ranks would produce great variations in the length of time served by incumbents of the same rank. One's moving time would be largely determined by the ages of people in front. If by chance they were old, one's chances for mobility would be good; if young, one's own chances would be bad. In this respect, the randomization of ages in a hierarchy would work against people in the lower ranks: a man would be at the mercy of his superiors' ages. In a random lottery system, such problems would occur frequently and, more important, unpredictably.

However, such random selection would have its advantages. Like a lottery, it could bring sudden improvement in a man's condition; the age-dependent system could never do this. The chance of winning in such a lottery would motivate people who were predisposed to risk-taking to enter the organization. Random selection would, more often than promotion by seniority, bring officers to high command at early ages; this could benefit the organization. By virtue of their youth, such officers would be physically fit, whether or not adequately experienced, to command in battle, and their troops would have a longer average time to adjust to new leaders, thus increasing battlefield efficiency.

Mobility in an age-dependent system is typically slow but certain, for each individual and in the aggregate. In the aggregate, mobility in a lottery system is also slow and certain since all vacancies always get filled (hence, certainty) and the same demographic and structural factors determine the creation of vacancies in a lottery as in an age-dependent system (thus, slowness). But for any given individual, a lottery system is very uncertain and may bring fast or slow mobility, or none at all, depending entirely on luck.

Because age-dependent and purely random mobility have their special advantages and disadvantages, we never find a purely age-dependent system: instead we find a seniority system, which combines age and competition. Nor do we ever find a pure lottery system: rather, we find competitive systems that are random with respect to some characteristics but not others, and are rarely random with respect to age and experience. Thus, what is most usual in social organization is some hybrid of age-dependency and age-independence. Such hybrids vary in the ways in which a competition is conducted, and in the criteria considered important for promotion.

Some General Observations on Chance Systems

Is Individual Mobility Predictable?

It was earlier asserted that all systems of promotion are predictable or controlled in the aggregate, and variably controlled or predictable from the standpoint of individuals whose careers are at risk. This is true only in the trivial sense that all renewal processes renew the membership of fixed structures, and therefore such structures, predictably, continue to exist with all vacancies filled. In fact, the amount of control an organization exercises over the *precise* selection of staff for promotion can vary, depending on the selection rules it has decided to employ. An age-graded system is deterministic, or perfectly predictable, for both the organization and the individuals involved, and so is a sponsored mobility system, as Turner has defined it. In each case, there is full knowledge of who shall succeed to higher positions, and all that remains in question is when the succession will take place. Such a predictability within a system is found wherever an organization has decided to tolerate the amounts of ability or inability "sponsored" individuals bring with them. A boss's son-in-law, for example, will be allowed to stumble to the top if his performance is minimally satisfactory and he is agreeable to receiving training and a lot of advice from more capable employees.

At the other end of the continuum, a "random walk system" is completely probabilistic, or *stochastic*. Neither the organization nor the individuals involved can predict who shall reach the higher positions, or when. This type of promotion system is probably non-existent in practice, or may be found only where the aim is to select among equally good (or bad) candidates with equal claims on any vacant position, whether that position be higher or lower than their own. In the middle range, there is a band of promotion systems that are partially determined and partially stochastic: here any individual has no more than moderate certainty about his or her future, and the organization has degrees of certainty that may range from high to low.

Of these, the seniority system offers the organization an opportunity to select candidates for promotion from a narrow range of people with equal seniority (or experience) and some variety of talent. The organization can and does define the type of talent that is most relevant, and promotes the person who has more of that talent than the others. Turner's contest system is next most predictable: in a lottery system an organization can define the types of talent it wishes to reward, but this talented person must be sought in a wider range of ranks than is necessary where promotion is by seniority. Promotions through open examination, as in the civil service for example, would illustrate such a contest: the organization can be reasonably certain of the type of person who will be promoted—namely, a high scorer on the examination—but it has little certainty who the precise winner will be, since the contest is open to many contenders. Finally, the pure ladder[1] and lottery systems afford the least organizational control: selection is wholly by chance, and the organization can predict neither who the winner will be nor what talents he or she will have.

It is somewhat more difficult to generalize about mobility in partly or wholly stochastic systems than about deterministic systems such as the age-graded system or sponsored system. Yet the general principles are reasonably straightforward. The probability of success in a stochastic system is dependent upon 1) the probability of success in a single chance trial, and 2) the number of trials. The probability of success in a single trial can be deduced from the rank structure of any given organization, and the selection rule (i.e., lottery, ladder, etc.). The opening of a vacancy in a higher position presumably constitutes one trial, if an individual is willing and allowed to compete for that position.

The proportion of people who will have some upward mobility during a career in a ladder or lottery system can be predicted using matrix algebra. The greater the number of trials, the greater the amount of upward career mobility; and the greater the likelihood of success in any given trial, the greater the amount of upward mobility. The likelihood of success in a given trial is determined by the organizational structure, which we shall treat as fixed; however, the *number of trials* is determined by the rate of creation of vacancies—by death, retirement, and leaving—and therefore can vary widely over time.

If a twenty-five-year-old is selected in a lottery to enter the top position, the next trial to fill the position will presumably not take place for forty years; this will reduce the chances for upward mobility of everyone else in the organization, however slightly. When we apply this same insight to all of the positions in the organization, it becomes clear that promotion by chance will produce fewer vacancies than promotion by seniority, and hence less average upward mobility. To generalize, anything that reduces the likelihood of people leaving the top positions makes for less upward mobility for all. Stating the case even more strongly, the amount of upward mobility in an organization declines more the further promotion rules deviate from a strict age-graded system. This will be as true of promotion systems that ignore age and systematically reward any age-independent quality, as it will be of wholly stochastic systems such as the random walk.

The principle is identical in both cases. Any age-independent promotion system will randomize the ages of people holding various ranks. Yet the rate of creation of vacancies (or trials) is dependent upon death and retirement rates, and these rates are age-dependent: that is, they increase with age. The annual number of high-level vacancies produced is greatest when age and rank are highly correlated, as in an age-graded system, and least when age and rank are uncorrelated. Thus arises the paradox that a gerontocracy produces maximum career mobility. Conversely, a mobility system that bases promotion on achievement or ability rather than on age, which is an ascribed rather than an achieved status, may be equitable and rational, but nonetheless reduces the upward mobility of everyone in the organization. It is undoubtedly this fact that has made age-grading, seniority and geron-tocracy such common bases for the allocation of power resources. In its own way a gerontocracy is equitable, for everyone has an equal and certain likelihood of acquiring the prerequisite for high status—namely old age—if he or she lives long enough.

Because the age of a lottery winner is always unpredictable, it is impossible to generalize about the distance average people move in a stochastic system. In certain periods there will be extremely few trials (and hence little average mobility), and in other periods many more trials, and more mobility. On the average, a person of modal age will win any given contest. Therefore, the higher ranks will typically be occupied by people of modal age, and these people will be young in all organizations that are growing, tree-shaped, or both. As before, this suggests that the distance an average person will travel upward in an age-independent career system will be less than in an age-dependent system.

Merits of an Age-Independent System

The likelihood of reaching the top during one's career is also less in an age-independent or stochastic system than in an age-dependent system.

In the former as in the latter, the likelihood is dependent upon the rank structure of the organization. However, in the latter the number of trials or vacancies is maximized by the correlation between age and rank; in the former the number of trials is less, and so the likelihood of reaching the top during a normal career span is less. In this way we can explain why it would have taken an average of one hundred and sixty years to attain the rank of Lieutenant-Colonel in the Guard had a lottery system prevailed, instead of the thirty years needed under the seniority system.

Yet any age-independent system has one particular virtue that makes it appealing: as in a lottery, men can go from rags to riches overnight. To the question, "How long would it take to reach the top?" the answer given is, "Anywhere from 0 years to infinity." There is by definition no instant progression from bottom to top rank in an age-dependent system, nor is there any possibility that an infinite number of years would be needed: there is simply *less variation* among career patterns in an age-dependent than in an age-independent system. This is another sense in which mobility is more controlled in the former than in the latter. However, one who was young, inclined to risk-taking, and confident of his own worth—and these characteristics are probably related—would probably prefer an open contest system to an age-dependent system of promotion. Such a person would have nothing to lose and everything to gain by an open contest, at least at the beginning of a career. How many young people would trade a chance of instant success for the guarantee of success very much later? Few, I think.

It is this difference between young and older people that underlies much of the belief that aging increases conservatism, and more generally, that there is a generation gap. There is little direct evidence that biological aging has any effect whatever on beliefs, attitudes and perceptions. People become more conservative and less prone to risk-taking as they age because they have more responsibilities to shoulder and therefore a greater fear of failure. They have also invested a great amount of their identity in their work, and failure in their work would imply failure as a human being. Aging as an economic and social-psychological process may proceed more quickly or slowly than biological aging; it is the former that would trade an open contest for the security of slow advancement by seniority.

The proportion of mobility that is upward in a stochastic or age-independent system will depend on the rules of the specific system. The lottery and random walk systems are essentially the same, except that contest losers in the former stay at their original rank and in the latter move down any number of ranks. Downward mobility is more plausible in an age-independent than in an age-dependent system, for there are more grounds for demotion possible in the former and none but excessive age possible in the latter system. Of course, age-dependent systems may operate on the juniority rather than seniority principle, as we noted in Chapter One; this would make downward mobility predominate. As downward mobility is less common than upward mobility in most organizations, we would suppose that promotion by juniority is relatively rare. And conversely, because we know that promotion by seniority is a common form of organizational mobility, we would suppose that such downward mobility as is found in organizations is attributable to the age-independence of promotion in such organizations. Demotion is discussed further in the next chapter.

To conclude, there is little doubt that upward career mobility, however defined, is greater in age-dependent than in stochastic or age-independent systems of promotion, for reasons that have been specified at some length. The contest system, as defined by Turner, has as its chief merits the appearance of greater rationality and equity, and the possibility of instant or rapid success. However, the more controlled systems—whether age-graded or sponsored—are more predictable, hence more secure; and they move larger numbers of people longer average distances in their careers. While most systems in actual use are a hybrid of control and looseness, age-dependence and independence, most lean more to the former than to the latter pole.

Control implies both predictability *and* maximum mobility. There is some evidence that this is true of intergenerational as well as career mobility (Tepperman and Tepperman, 1971). While in career mobility the limiting of high level competitors for a high level position is achieved by retirement and death, in intergenerational mobility the same limiting of high level competitors for a high level position is produced by differential family size, which varies inversely with social class (in industrial societies). This limit on the number of potential inheritors of high position, combined with a control rule that always gives first preference to children of higher class parents—analogous to the seniority rule in career mobility—both predicts that upper class children will continue to have the highest likelihood of entering an upper class position *and* maximizes the amount of upward mobility in society. While such a system does not permit long distance mobility, it ensures that the majority will move up at least one class each generation, and few if any will move down (*ibid.*: Table VII).

Summary

Organizations of unchanging size and hierarchy will vary in the amount of upward mobility people within them enjoy, according to the rules of promotion they utilize. The more controlled and predictable promotions are for all concerned, the more mobility there will be for everyone in the system. Therefore, the most controlled type of promotion, the age-graded or age-dependent system (and its subtype, the sponsored system), provides the greatest upward mobility for the greatest number. The more age-independent a promotion system is, regardless of whether it promotes by chance or by rewarding a talent unrelated to age, the less mobility there will be for all. While age-independent promotion offers the opportunity of more rapid ascent for a few, it offers most people unpredictability and insecurity: this may explain the prevalence of age-dependent ranking in contemporary and historical organizations.

Social mobility as a renewal process is much like two other renewal processes—aging and queuing—in important respects. This fact has allowed the utilization of techniques from demography and operations research in mobility analysis. Beyond this, we can look forward to research in which the structure of an informal hierarchy is revealed through the analysis of "normalized" mobility among specified states. This will allow more refined and more systematic studies of stratification and mobility than have been possible to date.

The next chapter will examine a variety of studies of career mobility that will both provide new insights into such mobility and put flesh on the theoretical skeleton inspected in this and the preceding chapter.

Chapter 3 Notes

[1] A ladder system of promotion allows anyone to challenge or compete against his immediate superior for that superior's position; the lottery system allows anyone to challenge any superior for his position. Under the ladder system, a vacancy is filled by a contest among holders of positions immediately below the vacancy; under the lottery system it is filled by a contest among holders of any position below the vacancy. In the "pure" ladder and lottery systems, all contests are won by chance.

4
CAREERS: INTRAGENERATIONAL MOBILITY

❧

Seven years, My Lord, have now past since I waited in your outward Rooms or was repulsed from your Door, during which time I have been pushing on my work through difficulties of which It is useless to complain, and have brought it at last to the verge of Publication without one Act of assistance, one word of encouragement, or one smile of favour. Such treatment I did not expect, for I never had a Patron before.

Is not a Patron, My Lord, one who looks with unconcern on a Man struggling for Life in the water and when he has reached ground encumbers him with help? The notice which you have been pleased to take of my Labours, had it been early, had been kind; but it has been delayed till I am indifferent and cannot enjoy it, till I am solitary and cannot impart it, till I am known, and do not want it.

From Samuel Johnson's *Letter to
Lord Chesterfield* (1755)

Careers: The Concept

This chapter will discuss careers of different kinds: careers that are normal and careers that are deviant (among these, artistic careers); careers that are formally organized in bureaucracies and careers that are entrepreneurial and informally organized. There will be a brief discussion of how a career relates to its historical-cultural context as well as to its immediate organizational context. This chapter will generalize from the existing literature on career mobility, while the following chapter will be given more to describing several kinds of careers in detail. This description may prove useful in helping the reader to understand the generalizations of this chapter, especially those relating to informal organization and historical context. But to begin we shall consider the distinction between careers as they are viewed structurally or objectively, by an outsider, and careers as they are viewed subjectively, by the person involved.

Viewed structurally, a career is a path of movement within some form of social organization. Following a career means going through a series of related and definable stages in a progressive fashion, in a specific direction, leading to a known goal or series of goals (Roth, 1963). The particular pattern of a given career will depend to a great extent upon its organizational context. In determining what a career pattern looks like, we look at the organizational structure and observe such things as: the positions at which the career begins and ends; how long it takes to reach the end of a career; the number of positions in the career hierarchy; the rate of advancement in the career; the determinants of this advancement; and the direction of mobility at different stages of the career.

An ideal model of a career is easily constructed. New recruits enter at the bottom levels; with experience, age and training they gradually move up in the hierarchy until they reach the top level, resign, or die. Yet few people in careers follow this route exactly. Many do not reach the top level by the end of their career; there is occasional downward mobility and horizontal movement (a change in job duties but not in the amount of responsibility or prestige); and not every entrant moves through all steps or through the same steps at the same rate. To be involved in a career, however, an individual must at least conform to the model to the extent that he occasionally moves from one position to another which is more responsible or prestigious and hence offers greater power. We can say, then, that not everyone has a career. People who remain at one status position, either because they lack the necessary training or motivation or because the activity in which they are involved does not offer an opportunity for more prestigious positions, do not have careers. Too frequent shifting of activities may prevent one from having a career, as involvement in a career may require both the investment of a good deal of time and commitment to one activity.

A career includes consecutive progressive achievements in a particular field of endeavour. These achievements are accompanied by different amounts of power; movement through a career, therefore, implies movement from at least one power position to at least one other. When we examine the change in position or resources an individual experiences in a lifetime (through involvement in one or more kinds of activity), we are looking at that individual's career mobility. The greater the change in power an individual achieves by this change in position, the greater his career mobility.

Viewed subjectively, however, a career is one way in which people engaged in a given activity can appraise their own competence and value in society according to the positions or resources they hold from the time they begin that activity until the time they leave it.

Career Rewards and Feelings of Success

A career is in one sense extremely personal: it is an important way people develop an identity. But a career is also worked out in some organized system without reference to which it cannot be described, much less understood (Hughes, 1958). The organizational contexts within which individual careers are worked out serve as a basis for understanding careers in general. In looking at the organizational structure, we can see career patterns, that is, typical ways in which individuals in the same activity are moved through different positions. They can tell us how all individuals—regardless of their personal definitions of success or failure—move through the organizational hierarchy and achieve success or failure according to the organization's definition of what constitutes achievement. When we look at the career associated with an occupation, we are usually trying to find out how all of those involved in the occupation have their careers worked out according to the way an occupation is organized to perform its characteristic activities.

Yet these patterns may not tell us anything about the personal feelings of any single individual in the career. Besides examining how individuals attain success or failure in the objective sense of attaining positions in the organization with more or less importance, we can also consider differences among people who share the same career but do not share the same personal evaluation of what the career means to them.

It is possible to succeed in a career by achieving a high rate of movement through an organizational hierarchy, and yet to have a sense of failure, feeling that nothing worthwhile has been achieved. For an individual in a given career there may be little or no self-perceived relationship between the amount of esteem he has objectively achieved and the amount of esteem he feels is due his position or effort. Alternatively, a man may feel uncommitted to the goals of the activity he is pursuing and may not even judge his own self-worth in terms of how much he succeeds in that activity, regardless of how much time he spends in it. A strict seniority system of promotion within an organization allows an individual to progress through the organization's hierarchy with complete indifference to the organization's goals; this is one of the disadvantages of gerontocratic organization. More often, however, we would expect that a positive commitment to the organization would aid an individual's mobility through the organizational hierarchy.

In looking at why individuals chose a career in the American military, one study revealed that the motivations behind the choice had changed over time. Those who had entered the military élite before World War II most often entered into a military career for one of four reasons: "tradition, or more precisely family and social inheritance; sheer desire for education and social advancement, with or without a career commitment to the military; experience in a military setting; and 'boyhood' ambition," (Janowitz, 1960). These individuals entered the military for different reasons but, from the data collected in this study, all who were successful were satisfying strong motivations and, for them, involvement in the military was more than just an occupation. There was, in fact, a missionary zeal associated with the performance of duties.

After the 1930s the recruitment pattern of the military changed as the size of the military forces increased. Formal and bureaucratic techniques of selection replaced the older system based on tradition and interpersonal connections. This change brought about a change in the career motives of entrants into the military élite. Careerist aspirations often replaced the old ideas of the military being a unique profession. Some of the older motivations still operated to recruit personnel but were more often replaced by a cold-blooded evaluation of the employment conditions offered in the military. The individuals who entered for careerist reasons were not interested in the goals of the organization as such, but had weighed the advantages of a career in the military against those they could receive in other professions. They chose the military as the most advantageous profession, and often continued in their military career simply because they had accumulated a good deal of seniority. Seniority was regarded as an investment that they did not want to lose.

Those who entered the military for strong personal reasons and achieved entrance into the élite with a feeling of enthusiasm and mission for the goals of the military were very successful in two senses. They achieved a personal feeling of success, as well as an objective success, defined by procedure through the hierarchy of positions in the organization. Those who had careerist motivations were successful in the career, objectively considered, in that they had moved through as many positions and were consequently given the same amount of prestige within the organization. They did not, however, achieve the same degree of subjective success in their careers, as they did not personally feel as important or as fulfilled by their movement through the organizational hierarchy as did those who felt strongly about the goals of the organization.

Organizational careers are limited in what they can offer to people. They provide a certain degree of prestige and authority at each level within the organizational hierarchy. This hierarchy, however, exists within a larger society which itself gives various amount of prestige to different careers. If one is working in a career which one feels is unsatisfying or unimportant, even a high degree of objective success in that career may not erase a feeling of failure.

An individual who chooses a career that is most compatible with both his own qualifications and his concept of value, personal worth, or success will experience the greatest degree of career satisfaction. Once the career is chosen, a person can determine how much success he is likely to achieve in his particular pursuit by comparing the qualifications he possesses with the necessary qualifications for mobility in that career. He can then decide how best to achieve maximum career mobility within the organization's structure and methods of promotion. What is more problematic is that people often change their goals and values during their lifetime and by the time a goal chosen at an early age is achieved, a person may no longer value its accomplishment. More is said of this problem in the final chapter. Also, as an individual progresses through different stages in his career, different demands and responsibilities, as well as increased power and authority, are available at each level in the organization. If too much time and/or effort is required to compete for the top positions, some potential competitors may deliberately drop out of competition, putting a higher priority on participation in activities that are unrelated to the career.

Commitment and Feelings of Success

An individual need not feel strongly committed to the organization in which he works, nor is it necessary that he feel that the activity of the career is especially worthwhile. The example of the military élite demonstrated how an individual could achieve a successful career, in the objective sense, without having a strong belief in the goals of his occupation. Others can pursue their careers without any great commitment to a particular organization if their skills are of a kind that allows them to move easily between organizations. For example, scientists who are employed in industry may feel little commitment to the goals of the industry, being devoted to pure research and a scientific professional career. Regardless of their official position in the organizational hierarchy, these individuals evaluate their own worth in terms of whatever scientific accomplishments they make. A move to a different organization would not constitute a disruption of their careers as long as their scientific endeavours were uninterrupted.

A study of the Pacific Electronics Company (P.E.C.) laboratory demonstrates how an industrial firm, aware of the lack of corporate commitment among the scientists it recruited, attempted to keep these workers within the firm by broadening their interests and developing a commitment to organizational goals (Marcson, 1960). In this company, each new recruit was placed in a group of people with whom he carried out all of his work. Work satisfaction became bound up with this group; the scientist eventually developed a loyalty to it and formed alliances and personal friendships within it. The new laboratory member evaluated and ranked those (including himself) in his network of relationships, and in so doing came to internalize the norms of this working group, and thus the norms of the P.E.C. laboratories. He thereby came to recognize the importance of applying his scientific research to the specific industrial situation. In this case, then, the lack of commitment among new recruits to the goals of the organization was overcome by a socialization process devised by the industry.

It should be stressed that the goals of the industry were accepted to varying degrees by the scientists it employed. Four career pathways were found through which the scientists became more or less devoted to the particular organization in which they were employed. First, the scientist might remain largely committed to research career goals and a scientific professional career. Second, he might become committed to administration, and steer his career up the administrative ladder. Third, he might remain interested in research but turn to administration for more financial security. Fourth, he might turn to a career in administration when he could no longer compete successfully in research with the younger scientists.

The first career pathway demonstrates that an individual can follow a career by committing himself to the goals of his activity rather than to the organization within which his career exists. In the second career pathway, a career is followed by acquiring a primary devotion to the goals of the organization. Those who followed the third career pathway forfeited their professional scientific career for an administrative one without—unlike those who followed the first two career pathways—having any real commitment to the goals of the activity they were pursuing. The fourth career pathway also demonstrates a lack of commitment to the activity of the career, but one differing from the preceding. Those who followed the fourth pathway no longer had the choice of achieving a very successful career in the activity in which they were primarily interested.

Varying degrees of commitment to the activity and organizational structure of careers probably exist in every career. To follow a career, however, one must devote a substantial amount of time and energy to achieving whichever goals one is pursuing. It is not necessary to feel that the goals are worthwhile ones, but it is necessary to be committed to the idea of achieving them, and to take the necessary time and effort in order to meet the requirements of doing so. These requirements will vary according to the type of career; that is, they will vary according to how the career is organized and how it measures success and failure.

We cannot assume that every entrant into a career seeks upward mobility to the top positions, for various reasons. First, an individual's background (age, training, education, etc.) restricts the range of mobility the individual can reasonably expect in a given career. Secondly, advancement usually depends, at least partly, on an understanding of how the prevailing mobility or promotional system works. Willingness to understand and master the methods of advancement may depend upon how committed an individual is to the goals and incentives of the organization within which the career exists. That is, if an individual's sense of self-worth differs from or conflicts with that which is attainable in his career, he may not seek or achieve advancement in the career hierarchy.

This last aspect may become especially important in cases where professionals are employed in industry. Those who followed the first career pathway in the P.E.C. laboratories (that is, those who remained committed to a professional scientific career) are an example of this kind of potential conflict between organizational and personal values. An industrial organization defines success according to the hierarchy of positions established in the industry: power increases with each higher level in the hierarchy. The professional may feel that organizational authority and prestige are unimportant, and that feeling successful depends on professional colleagues who recognize and reward accomplishments in the common field of activity. The organization then finds itself in a double bind. It may wish to offer promotion for success in a professional endeavour, but the professional worth so rewarding will not be interested in organizational rewards; he may even refuse them if he thinks higher rank will conflict with professional pursuits. Such an employee who does re-orient himself towards organizational goals is apt to be one whose professional worth is declining. To avoid this conflict between professional and organizational values an organization will try to socialize new recruits in a devotion to the goals of the organization and a willingness to work for the fulfillment of these goals.

Careers in Formal Organizations

Whatever kind of career we look at, different patterns emerge according to the shape of the career line and the amount of time in the career. By "shape" we mean first, its length—or where in the organizational hierarchy the career begins and ends. Education, friendships, training, sex and ethnicity, as well as organizational definition will determine where the career begins. The end of a career pattern will be determined by a person's capabilities, age and other factors accounting for promotion or demotion at any particular stage in the career, as well as by the ceiling imposed by the organization for any given career within the organizational hierarchy (Glaser, 1968).

The shape of a career pattern is also defined by the direction of the movement in the career; it can include promotions, demotions, and simotions (movement sideways). Career patterns may be prescribed and standardized or they may be fairly well molded by individuals for themselves. The type of work and the division of labour necessary to carry out the work are two influences upon the shape of prescribed career patterns.

The second important element of a career pattern is that of time:

for example, time spent throughout the career from entrance to exit or the rate of advancement between positions or the length of time in any given position. Again, an organization may or may not make changes in personnel routine scheduled and well-ordered. If these mobility processes are planned and known to all in the career, then a person can easily assess his career relative to others and judge his degree of success at any given time. Finally, organizational career patterns exist within a particular historical time (Warner and Abegglen, 1968). Thus, their shape and temporal aspects will vary with changing social conditions and changing determinants of recruitment, success, failure and exit from a career.

The structure of an organization can tell something about the possibilities for mobility in careers within that organization. For example, organizations with tall hierarchies usually produce careers with many stages and offer a steady climb with frequent promotions. Organizations with a high ratio of managers to managed—a short span of control—also offer much career opportunity because there is a greater likelihood of a high prestige job at the end (Wilensky, 1960). It must be remembered that these factors affecting career opportunities assume the constancy of other factors, some of which are internal to the organization (such as promotion procedures), and others which are external to it (such as economic pressures on the organization).

Structure and Planning in Organizational Careers

People in the same occupational career do not advance at the same rate even though they exist in the same organization at the same time. In order to understand career mobility, therefore, it is necessary to determine how much movement through different positions is due to individual merit, and how much is related to the form of the social organization within which the career exists. That career mobility can be best understood as the flow of people through various levels of an organized system does not imply that an individual within the system has no choice or control over where his career goes. Rather, it suggests that if an individual really wants to have some control over his own success or failure, he must understand the functioning of the system within which his career exists.

Every individual, when entering a career, has his own personality, values and desires placed in an organizational context. The organization—whether it is formal or informal—has goals of its own to fulfill and it achieves them by positioning people as the division of labour necessitates. The organization exists within a larger social context which affects the organization and ultimately the careers of individuals in various ways. Economic factors encourage or inhibit expansion and contraction in the structure of the organization. Expansion and contraction in turn create more or fewer positions to be filled and thereby help or hinder the movement up, down and sideways of individuals within the organization. The personal goals and assessments of self-worth of individuals are affected by this movement and will ultimately determine success or failure in the career. Similarly, the demographic characteristics of a society (and the particular demographic characteristics of an organization) will affect the number of competitors for a given number of positions, the amount of movement possible in a career and the individual's chances of fulfilling goals he has set for himself.

All of the factors mentioned above interact with one another, and it would be difficult to establish in every individual career which factor was most important in determining its shape. It is possible, however, to see one factor or another predominate at a given time. For example, in the description given in Chapter Three of the mobility of Canadian professors, it was asserted that the static structure of Canadian universities, accompanied by a seniority system of promotion, meant that the career opportunities for young professors were not very good in the early 70s. There were too many competitors (a result of a preceding period of rapid growth) for a fixed number of positions (a result of the current absence of growth). If the method of moving people to higher level positions were based on some criterion other than seniority, some of the newer recruits who met this criterion could achieve a much faster rate of advancement.

Most formal organizations would acknowledge merit, ability and/or seniority as valid criteria for promotion. Formal organizations usually try to plan the flow of people through some or all levels of the organization. Any vacancy must be filled by the organization if it seeks stability and continuity of operation, and all movement is intended to mesh with and support the organizational structure. The planning of succession reduces disruption within the organization by making rules for promotion known and formalized, and hence reducing excessively competitive behaviour in many cases. Everyone in the organization knows that the criteria for advancement are fixed and will not be much affected by extra efforts made by an individual. This does not mean that the organization fails to encourage employees to work hard and achieve organizational goals. The advantage of planning successions within the organization—and of making everyone aware of how successions are planned—lies in allowing the organization to choose individuals for positions in such a way that the organization will function smoothly, and in allowing individuals within it to be aware of what the channels of mobility are and how to enter them.

Careers in formal organizations are interdependent to the extent that one replacement may set off a chain reaction of succession down the line. Hierarchical succession develops if individuals are moved in sequence, and echelon succession will predominate if groups are moved (Glaser, 1968). The individual (or group) directly below someone who has just been promoted will likely become aware that his own chances for advancement have improved, as a replacement is needed for the position directly above him. If, however, his anticipation of promotion is left unfulfilled, it may cause disillusionment with the career. The planning of succession may be disadvantageous, therefore, in that by making the criteria for advancement known and routinized the organization generates an anticipation of mobility among those in the career: if this mobility is not achieved (or not achieved as quickly as is usual), an individual may feel that he has been cheated and stop working to achieve the goals of the organization.

An organization can plan only a limited amount of the career mobility of individuals. Not only is it limited in its ability to predict when individuals will choose to leave a career, and limited in its control over larger economic or demographic changes, but it must sometimes recognize that informal and unrecognized procedures intrude into rationally planned methods of moving individuals through positions. A power structure based on individual personalities may evolve and become superimposed upon the rationally planned organization (Martin and Strauss, 1956). The necessary qualifications for a successful career may include not only merit, ability and/or seniority, but also the right combination of circumstances, temperament, accident, patience and personality (Mills, 1951). Success may also be related to age, sex or ethnicity and to having the right clique affiliations or sponsor. Fixed lines of ascent are difficult to maintain; in an organization which is changing rapidly it may be relatively easy for personnel to evade them and use informal criteria to determine career lines. Personal sentiments intrude into the professional functioning of large organizations, and when individual or group interests conflict with each other the weight of formal techniques in making careers is further reduced (Dalton, 1951).

The amount of routinization which an organization imposes upon a career affects the individual in that career in various ways. Formal organizations stabilize career lines: categories for advancement are planned, known and routinized. For management, this stabilization provides a rational method of moving people through positions. It may also contribute to the efficiency of operations, because the hierarchy of responsibility and authority, being ordered and controlled, is therefore predictable. The individual in a career is provided with a stable set of expectations, rules of conduct at various positions and a number of channels through which to move (Martin and Strauss, 1956). The stabilization of career lines also allows a timetable of advancement to be established. An individual can judge, by his knowledge of the average rate of advancement, whether or not his career is progressing more quickly or slowly than is usual.

Status and Self-Esteem in Organizational Careers

The passage of time affects career lines differently according to the different processes an organization uses to move people through positions. A strict seniority system, for instance, means that as time passes and so long as the individual remains in his career, he comes progressively closer to high status positions. This was illustrated in Chapter Three with the example of the Coldstream Guard. If an individual does not improve his position over time, the amount of prestige he commands may actually decline. For example, it may be very prestigious for a new recruit into business to hold a job at the middle management rank, but if he is still there when he retires, his career will be labelled a failure. For any career, then, there is some kind of timetable of advancement (informal or formal average mobility reference points) which helps to define objective success or failure. A comparison of one's own timetable with the average will also affect subjective evaluations of success, and thereby influence feelings of self-esteem.

If a seniority system is used by the organization to move people through positions, and the individual with greatest seniority is bypassed for a promotion, then he has really experienced a form of demotion. Demotion can result from a change in occupation, a loss in rank within the organization (or within the same occupation), or a change in organizational affiliation within the same occupation [for example, a move from professorship in a high to one in a low prestige university (Caplow, 1954)]. Douglas M. More has, in fact, outlined eleven forms of demotion: (1) lowered job status with the same salary; (2) lowered job status with a lower salary; (3) retained status with lower salary; (4) being bypassed in seniority for a promotion; (5) a change of job to a less desirable function; (6) maintained status with a decreased span of control; (7) exclusion from a general salary raise; (8) an increase in the number of steps in the hierarchy above a given position; (9) movement from line to staff authority; (10) retention of the same job level, salary, authority, responsibility, but transfer out of a direct line of promotion; and (11) position elimination and reassignment (More, 1962). The (intended) subtlety of many of these forms of demotion may better serve to obscure the fact of demotion to outsiders, including sociologists, than to insiders familiar with organizational custom.

Any of the forms of demotion which More describes are likely to be recognized and resented by the person being demoted. In all cases he will be aware of some loss of status—some loss of authority, power and responsibility. In order to make a demotion socially acceptable and to lessen the destruction of motivation or the creation of alienation within the organization, mechanisms are created by the organization which make demotions ambiguous. For example, new positions may be added to the hierarchy and if no clear amount of prestige is associated with them, the person moved into such a position does not know where he stands relative to others. Another form of obscuring demotions is "zig-zag" mobility, which combines demotions and subsequent promotions so that the individual is not sure whether he is gaining or losing status at any time. One further method of allowing demoted individuals to save face is to promote an alternative goal system to substitute for the conventional goal of occupational success: for example, making competition so tough that an individual finds it easy to forego promotions in order to have more free time to spend on activities outside the career (Goldner, 1965). The organization's reluctance to use demotion blatantly is a clear demonstration of the degree to which organizational careers are competitions for prestige and self-esteem. Much effort is expended by individuals to "save face" during organizational conflicts; nowhere is this clearer than in the competition for prestige and self-esteem between staff and line personnel.

Careers of staff personnel, having an advisory or "back-up" nature within a bureaucratic organization, differ in several respects from the careers of line personnel, who are directly involved in movement through the hierarchy of positions and with whom we have been concerned to this point. "Staff personnel, especially when they occupy strictly advisory positions, must obtain cooperation and compliance mainly through the authority conferred by their superior knowledge—that is, through normative power," (Etzioni, 1961). Advisers called in from outside the organization must convince administrators that their ideas and suggestions are worthwhile. The expert who is called in to help with a problem in an organization becomes involved in the decision-making processes of the organization. In doing so he also becomes involved in the personal ambitions and competitions of line and other staff personnel who are trying to improve their positions in the hierarchy or their degree of prestige in the organization. Often an expert is called in because executives of the company could not solve a problem. The hiring of an outsider for expertise implies a slur on the competence of those already in the organization. If a situation develops in which the adviser and his advice become important in the power game within the organization, ambitious executives may or may not support the adviser, without a totally objective regard for his advice (Bryson, 1951).

If the expert enters into the power competitions within the organization he is jeopardizing his sense of objectivity and his reputation for disinterested knowledge. One author has used the following story to illustrate the touchy relationship between power and knowledge which may develop:

> There is a story that tells of the conversations which used to be held on the palace hill in Rome to entertain the Emperor Hadrian. He loved disputes about grammar and usage and work origins; professors were invited to dine with him and argue for his pleasure. Sometimes, he ventured an opinion of his own and on one occasion one of his experts rejected the emperor's theory summarily. The argument waxed hot and the emperor shouted. The deipnosophist shouted less and less as the exchanges went on, until at last the administrator, Hadrian, pronounced a final truth and his challenger was silent. "Aha," cried Hadrian, "my arguments have left you nothing to say." "Sire," replied the visiting expert, "who am I to disagree with the master of thirty legions?" (Bryson, 1951: 210).

An administrator's power in an organization relies on his ability to convince those with whom he works that he has a great deal of knowledge about how the organization does and should work and that he can put this knowledge to work in solving any problems which arise. When a problem is very specialized or technical, administrators may fail to solve it despite their efforts to do so, and an adviser who is considered an expert on such a problem may be called in.

Administrators and advisers may come into conflict, however, at the very outset, in defining exactly what the problem is that needs solving. The administrator may assume that because of his thorough knowledge of the organization he is the only one capable of defining what needs to be done, while the adviser may feel that his expert knowledge gives him more ability to understand where the problem lies. Nevertheless, the administrator's version of the problem will likely be the one with which the expert will work, because the expert is hired only if the administrator thinks it necessary. The administrator needs to protect his position in the organization, through the recognition of his knowledge; therefore he will often dismiss the opinions of an expert who disagrees with him on the nature of the problem to be solved. An expert who was too convinced of his own opinions and refused to work within the administrator's framework could be dismissed.

After agreement on what the problem is, the expert suggests alternative courses of action to solve it and predicts the consequences to be expected from each. Before accepting or rejecting any of the expert's ideas, those in the organization interpret these ideas according to their own knowledge of the organization. This interpretation may seem to the expert to distort his ideas and give them consequences he did not intend. "The expert can protest and argue; he may find himself silenced by the claim that his expertness goes only to the general idea and that translating it into action requires knowledge which he does not possess, that is, knowledge special to the time and occasion and occupational in character," (Bryson, 1951). Again, it is necessary for such staff personnel to assert their right to make decisions on the basis of their knowledge, for it is on this that their prestige within the organization rests.

Those who are employed outside the regular hierarchy of advancement in an organization probably have a much less certain sense of their positions in the organization: they have only their knowledge and the persuasiveness of their arguments based on this knowledge to guarantee their power. The expert who is called in from outside is not involved in this competition for power, but the basis of his career also is the knowledge he possesses. In transferring this knowledge into an organizational context, the expert becomes involved in the power relationships of those in the organization, and he must recognize the nature of these relationships if he wishes to continue to work in the organization.

Careers Outside Formal Organizations

In a career outside a formal organization, which we shall call an "entrepreneurial" career, one creates one's own career line and sets one's own timetable to evaluate success. Involvement in an entrepreneurial career means accepting less certainty of objective success or failure in the career. Advancement is not formalized or timed in any way, nor is there a specific number of discrete steps to pass through in a well ordered hierarchy in which different amounts of power are given at each step. This does not mean that those involved in careers outside formal organizations have their careers exempt from any kind of structure or organization. Strategies and patterns of advancement can be found in entrepreneurial careers as in all others; however, they are probably more varied and more difficult to trace because they are not formally established or explicitly stated.

Even if we look at what is now a non-existent form of successful independent entrepreneur, we can see patterns of behaviour which were thought to guarantee or at least help in achieving success in the entrepreneurial career. C. Wright Mills discussed the pattern of success in a society based on the liberal capitalism of small properties:

> The way up, according to the classic style of liberalism, was to establish a small enterprise and to expand it by competition with other enterprises. The worker became a foreman and then an industrialist; the clerk became a bookkeeper or a drummer and then a merchant on his own. The farmer's son took up land

in his own right and, long before his old age, came into profits
and independence (Mills, 1951).

Mills suggests that the old entrepreneur's ideology was based on sober
personal virtues like will power, thrift, habits of order and neatness,
among others.

Strategies of advancement exist in entrepreneurial careers today,
and they vary with the kind of activity involved in the career. Those
who work outside formal organizations must know how accomplishments in their careers are rewarded (that is, how they can judge their
objective status position) and how to go about attaining such rewards.
They must judge themselves relative to others in the same career
without the help of a formal structure in which differences of responsibility, authority, and prestige are easily evident. Informal criteria for
judging one's success in a career outside a formal organization sometimes arise.

For example, a clique of the most successful in a given profession
may exist, and acceptance into that group would provide one demonstration that a career has been a success. Members of the profession
must watch their colleagues in order to determine which accomplishments are rewarded by acceptance into the clique. By contrast, small
businessmen and self-employed people must generally set their own
standards to evaluate what success in their endeavour "looks like".
They must decide how successful they want to be and how to measure
their success (whether in terms of income, a particular life-style, or a
combination of a number of different objective criteria). People in
formal organizations may make a similar choice but they are provided
(through a recognized hierarchy of positions) with a great many more
reference points. Those in entrepreneurial careers must not only find
out which kinds of positions are available to them, but they must also
determine how the activity with which the career is involved is organized to achieve them.

Structure and Planning in Three Entrepreneurial Careers

A recent study traced the career patterns of real estate agents in
Montreal (House, 1974). The sample in this study was small, but
adequate for our purposes because it demonstrates the ways in which
career patterns can change along the dimensions just described. Five
career patterns were distinguished and those who conformed to each
pattern were named *abortives, marginals, regulars, upwardly mobiles,*
and *perenially high producers.* The differences among their careers
were explained according to variations in their sales success, mobility
opportunity, and individual decisions. Selling real estate is an entrepreneurial career, where the amount of success is dependent to a great

extent upon the individual's desire to devote a great deal of time and effort to it especially in the beginning stages. The patterns of success and mobility are typologized in Table 4.1.

Table 4.1

Residential real estate career patterns by sales success and mobility

Upward Mobility	Sales Success		
	High ($20,000 + /yr)	Medium ($10-20,000/yr)	Low (>$10,000/yr)
Yes	upwardly mobiles	—	abortives
No	perennials	regulars	marginals

Source: House (1974: Table 3)

Abortives and marginals did not invest enough time and effort in the beginning stages of their careers and hence did not achieve a great deal of success. Abortives left because they did not make enough money, while marginals made the decision to stay despite their lack of success. Regulars enjoyed a medium degree of success, having put forward enough time and effort initially to make a satisfactory living but choosing a less demanding life style after having established themselves. Both upwardly mobiles and perennially high producers continued to invest a lot of time and effort after establishing a good income, and accordingly their incomes rose further. The upwardly mobiles could transfer their success into a higher status selling or managerial position while the perennials could not—often for reasons of ethnicity, sex or age. The perennial eventually reached the point where his income could not be further improved because he simply lacked the time—in which case any surplus possibilities for making money could be transferred to less successful colleagues in return for esteem.

The shape of each of the five career patterns was different. All real estate agents began at the same point, the bottom of the status hierarchy. A career was organized in such a way that success depended on three determinants: entrepreneurial strategies (and devoting enough time and effort to learn them); decisions at crucial career phases; and the social characteristics of the agents. For the abortives and the marginals the career ended at the same level at which it began: no upward mobility was achieved. The careers of the regulars ended above those of the abortives and marginals in the status hierarchy, as this group had learned the methods of success in the beginning stages of their careers. This group did not choose, however, to continue to employ the methods of success as much as they had when they first entered the career, and their mobility was arrested in the middle of the status hierarchy. The perennials' careers ended at the top of the real estate status hierarchy, as this group had learned and continued to use fully the strategies of advancement learned upon entering the career. The upwardly mobiles also used the methods of advancement as much as they could throughout their selling career, but their careers ended within a different higher status sector of the organization than that in which they had begun.

Little advancement could be expected in the first few years of selling real estate. In this period much time and effort need to be spent building a strong base of listings and clients that could be drawn on later. Advancement was cumulative: the more clients one accumulated over time, the more new clients one could be expected to recruit. The timing of advancement was not externally ordered or planned in any way, due to the entrepreneurial character of the occupation.

All entrepreneurial careers exist in the framework of constraints imposed by other persons who are members of the same occupation. An extreme example of the weight of informal constraints is given in the following description of a sponsorship process in the medical profession (Hall, 1946). In this study an "inner group" of doctors was discovered. This group was spatially segregated, religiously and ethnically homogeneous, and involved in the lucrative specialized fields of medicine. It occupied dominant hospital posts, had preferred claims on the high paying clientele of the city, and controlled the local medical practice by sponsoring the entry of new members into the group. The sponsorship process by which the inner group protected its position involved six dimensions: the selection of recruits to the profession; the selection of interns; the appointment of externs; the appointments to staff positions; incorporations into office practices; and incorporation of clientele into the system. Unless an individual had a willing sponsor from this inner group he was not likely to achieve much career mobility.

In this case it was the sponsorship process which most determined success or failure in a career. A strict seniority system may limit the importance of sponsorship, as advancement in the career is relatively unaffected by any factor other than length of service. The sponsorship system is also inherently unstable, for promotion in this kind of system rests ultimately on the power and position of the sponsor. If the sponsor loses his position, those whom he sponsors will be similarly dragged down. A sponsored individual, therefore, must not only keep track of his own chances for career mobility, but he must also carefully watch that of his sponsor to be certain that he can disassociate himself from a sponsor who is losing his status position (Glaser, 1968).

A study of the career patterns of lawyers shows other informal promotion procedures at work, albeit within the context of a formally organized law office (Smigel, 1968). The study tried to determine how a lawyer would advance through the ranks to a partnership position in the law firm in which he was employed at the time. Very few lawyers ever do become partners and those who do generally take between nine and eleven years. The required length of time, however, varies from firm to firm. Smigel's study looked at the career patterns of ten imaginary apprentices hired from the class of 1951. The firm usually evaluates lawyers from any class alongside the ones that graduated the year before and after it. When the time comes to select partners for the firm, only one of the cohort of 1951 will probably be made a partner. The rest will have been weeded out by a variety of "tests" taking roughly ten years.

Little competition is evident among new recruits to the law firm. The recruits do work of a general nature and form close in-groups. After the third year, individuals begin to do more specialized work and are distributed among the various departments and partners. With specialization, some colleagues leave the firm and by the eighth year only two or three of the cohort will be left. It is at this point that competition is greatest; it focuses on the amount of work an associate is willing to do and how much time he is willing to spend on it. The effect of competition as a selective agent depends partly on the personality of the participants. A lawyer who finds the competition too severe or unpleasant will probably leave and, as the type of work done becomes narrower or more specialized, so does the process of weeding out. The few lawyers who have survived after eight years face another test. They are now given assignments by most of the main partners, who will observe and judge the associate's work for two or more years. At the end of this period, one from the cohort of 1951 graduates will likely have been made a partner.

Hard work has been named as an important criterion in becoming a partner but Table 4.2 illustrates that it is not the only one, according to the answers given by associates and partners when asked how to become a partner. Most answers suggested a combination of techniques for achieving partnership, although hard work and ability were assumed by a majority to be minimal requirements. One associate who claimed that he did not know how to become a partner but knew how *not* to be one had the following comment:

> You won't be a partner: (1) if you don't have awareness of interpersonal relationships on the partnership level—and poor relations with the clients doesn't help either; for example how you dress is a factor; (2) if you're married to a girl with no money or client contact; (3) if you're a man trusted to do a job by the top people in the office, think you can do a job, then don't do it well; (4) if you're not one of those fellows who are

reaching out and looking for work . . . . One thing I do know: if there is anything that typifies these downtown firms it is thoroughness. If you're sloppy in the clutch, you're in deep trouble . . . (Smigel, 1968).

Table 4.2

What can an associate do to help himself become a partner?

Techniques to partnership	Associates		Partners	
	(N)	(%)	(N)	(%)
Be a good lawyer, work hard	33	18.8	32	24.0
Bring in business	23	13.0	19	14.3
Maintain good relations with client	21	11.9	12	9.0
Have proper social background and contacts	20	11.5	7	5.3
Obtain sponsorship	18	10.2	6	4.5
Have proper personality	14	8.0	14	10.5
Have luck	13	7.4	12	9.0
Fulfill needs of the firm	6	3.3	7	5.3
Become indispensable to firm	5	2.8	4	3.0
Choose right department	3	1.7	0	0.0
Take responsibility	3	1.7	4	3.0
Go to right schools	3	1.7	0	0.0
Engage in outside activities	2	1.1	2	1.5
Don't know	2	1.1	1	0.8
Have leadership ability	0	0.0	3	2.3
Other	10	5.7	10	7.5
Total	176*	100.0	133*	100.0

*Totals more than lawyer sample since multiple answers were given.
Source: Smigel (1968: Table 1)

The career pattern of the successful lawyer according to this study shows not a series of discrete jumps in a hierarchy, but a gradual process whereby the competitors decrease in number over an extended period of time. All competitors reach crucial testing points in their careers. For instance, an associate who has survived the eight year period has survived many tests:

He has ignored the call of immediate riches ("I damn near left three times. One job was many times my salary"); judged correctly the managing partner's mention of a position with a corporation ("I was asked once if I wanted to take an invitation to leave"); stuck it out when it did not look as if an opening existed in his field ("When after I had worked for eight years in the tax department, they asked me to change to corporation law, I did not know what to make of it, but I changed. They had an opening in this other department and were trying me out") (Smigel, 1968).

The next two or so years also involves testing, this time by the main partners in the firm. Working hard was obviously important, but as the comment above by the associate who knew how not to become a partner indicates, other informal factors carry a great deal of weight.

Just as lawyers are tested at crucial points in their careers for promotions, so are those in the other professions. If an individual fails to perform adequately in the period of time between testing points he may be asked to leave or be pushed out of the organization. For example, those in academic professions are "tested" for promotions. Their testing is peculiar in that academics are hired to perform teaching services but are evaluated as candidates for appointments or promotions according to the research contributions they have made to their discipline. Such a criterion for judging advancement is likely to have the effect of making those involved in the academic professions less oriented towards the institution in which they are employed (in terms of teaching, administration, internal service to the university) and more oriented towards their discipline. A discipline-oriented attitude will have the effect of both furthering an academic's professional prestige and making for more mobility within the organization (Caplow and McGee, 1958).

The Historical Context Of Careers

Structural and Attitudinal Changes

Every career has structure and meaning only within a particular historical-cultural context. This kind of context has been examined in a comparison of business and legal élites in the nineteenth and twentieth centuries (Smith and Tepperman, 1974). According to this study, the major change that has taken place between 1870 and 1970 is that more organizational control is now exerted over the processes of entry and socialization into an élite. The development of Canada into a corporate society has affected careers in so far as those involved in the Canadian élite now fill corporate expectations; their power is no longer an inherited patrimony. A second change that has taken place is the separation of careers in business and law. Career patterns in either profession remain within their own professional sphere of activity more often now than in the nineteenth century, when the boundary between business and law (and between both and civic activity) was easily crossed.

The structure of the élite has changed most importantly in that the routes to, and the holding of, directorships in corporations have become increasingly determinant of membership in the élite (and of the accumulation of power resources). To understand any individual career pattern, one must be aware of how a society is organized at a particular moment. If today bureaucratization and corporate control (and a division of labour that promotes specialization and a pseudo-professional outlook) dominate, then careers will follow lines in keeping with this form of social organization because it is the corporation that controls recruitment, socialization, and success or failure in most careers.

Whether the nature of rewards offered in careers changes through historical time is more problematic. One can study élites of different historical periods and explain the requirements for success in a career as part of a larger social system, the nature of which creates specific career patterns. It is more difficult to judge, however, whether the individual who is successful in a career created by one kind of social system feels himself more or less satisfied and/or important than a successful individual whose career is conditioned by another set of social circumstances. Personal feelings about what gives meaning to life aside, one might expect that the form of organization within which a career exists exerts a subtle influence on how gratified one feels by the career mobility afforded. In order to feel successful in a corporate career as opposed to a nineteenth century entrepreneurial one, one must accept the corporate organization's status hierarchy as a valid way of earning status and self-esteem. Status is usually carefully marked out and limited at each stage in the career. It is the task of socialization processes in formal organizations to make new recruits feel a part of a career which offers future important status rewards. This task, however, becomes more difficult if other social values suggest that to succeed in a corporate career is not a particularly worthwhile goal; that no matter what one's position in a corporate entity one is not vitally important to its existence, nor does one have control or even understanding of its total functioning.

It is obvious that the positions of authority and power which corporations offer are widely valued and sought after. This is so because they are a common way in which people today achieve success in careers and hence accumulate status and self-esteem. Gratification is possible in a corporate career because such a career is what is possible in corporate societies. It is probably also true, however, that the self-esteem of those who wield the most power in our century (when status is often shared through an extremely long hierarchy in a formal organization) is quite different from that of the most powerful in past centuries. Then positions were often inherited and those who held the most power were unquestioned in their authority, indispensable in their sphere of influence, and protected in their position by an elaborate set of legal and religious sanctions. It hardly need be said that a sixteenth century lord wielded a different kind of power and achieved a different kind of status than that of a twentieth century corporation head, and this is noted here only to illustrate that the larger society and the specific form of the organization within which a career exists influences not only how a career proceeds but possibly what career achievement means to an individual and how he views himself in relation to others.

The achievement of successful careers by women certainly means something different today than it has in the past. Not only is it easier for women to be involved in careers now, but as the perception of women's role in society changes so does the perception (both her own and others') of what success in a career means for a woman. The Department of Labour (1960) conducted a study which traced the occupational histories of married women working for pay in eight Canadian cities in 1959. The work histories of these women demonstrated an interaction of the women's own circumstances with the changes which took place economically and socially during her time of employment.

Many of the married women (sixty per cent) had been in and out of the labour force and of those who had at some time withdrawn from it, eighty per cent gave reasons for the first withdrawal associated with marriage and family. Older women more often stopped working because they got married than did women under twenty-five, who quit usually because they had children. The study concluded that withdrawal on marriage was diminishing because many companies at the time of the study had ceased the practice of not employing married women.

Table 4.3

Percentage distribution of women who have been out of labour force by reason for first withdrawal, by age group: MWW*

Age group	Reason for first withdrawal					Weighted Total
	Marriage	1st child	Other child	Other reason and Unknown	Total	
	%	%	%	%	%	
14-19	33.3	44.4	–	22.2	99.9	(45)
20-24	38.3	45.1	–	16.6	100.0	(3080)
25-35	46.4	27.2	4.3	22.1	100.0	(1,123)
35-44	58.2	18.7	2.5	20.6	100.0	(1,135)
45-54	70.5	12.7	16.8	–	100.0	(684)
55-64	76.1	8.5	15.3	–	99.9	(176)
65 or over	100.0	–	–	–	100.0	(4)

*MWW refers to the weighted sample of married women working, i.e. the number corresponding to 100 per cent is 5,967.
Source: Department of Labour (1960: Table 12)

Forty per cent of the entire sample were continuous workers. This group was less likely to have children, were generally younger than those who had been in and out of the labour force, were more likely

Table 4.4

Percentage of continuous workers and others in each socio-economic class: MWW*

Socio-economic class of woman's occupation	Continuous workers		Others	
	%	weighted total	%	weighted total
Rank†				
1	82.6	(38)	17.4	(8)
2	46.2	(217)	53.8	(253)
3	46.1	(982)	53.9	(1,147)
4	25.7	(57)	74.3	(165)
5	42.6	(493)	57.4	(664)
6	38.0	(418)	62.0	(682)
7	22.7	(22)	77.3	(75)
8	47.7	(255)	52.3	(280)
Unknown	4.7	(10)	95.3	(201)
All socio-economic classes	41.8	(2,492)	58.2	(3,475)

*See footnote to Table 4.3.
†From high to low status scored 1 to 8 respectively.
Source: Department of Labour (1960: Table 24)

to have spent several years in their present job, but were less likely (presumably because they were younger) to have contributed many years to the labour force. The proportion of continuous workers was found to be greatest in occupations of the highest socio-economic classes. The greater amount of time required by occupations in the highest socio-economic classes can account for much of this difference between continuous and non-continuous workers.

The women varied widely in age and, therefore, entered the labour force during different time periods. Economic opportunities for women varied with the period during which they first began looking for a job. For example, those who entered the labour force during the war years when labour was scarce had much better opportunities than those who entered during the economic depression of the 1930s. In periods of surplus labour, employment prospects were very poor for women, especially since employers favoured hiring men over women. It was also determined from interviews with the women in the sample that many older women would have gone on working at the time they married if it had been acceptable to their employers. Others would have continued to work after they had children if the children could have been cared for properly in the mother's absence.

It is obvious from the reasons given in this study that women in 1959 were severely restricted in their career mobility. They were hired after men, sometimes had to stop working once they married, and most often had to stop working once they had children. In the sixteen years since the 1959 study greater opportunities for career mobility for

women have developed. Men and women do not yet have equal opportunity to establish successful careers, as we shall see in Chapter Six;
nor is a woman in a given career thought of in the same terms as a man
in the same career. A successful woman lawyer or business executive,
for example, is still viewed by many as an unusual individual—as
someone who is out of place and not as capable as men in such traditionally male occupations. Even if women do succeed in establishing
a career, they do not always receive the same recognition or income as
men, nor are they as likely to advance as quickly or as far, although they
may have the same qualifications (Royal Commission on the Status of
Women in Canada, 1970).

It is, however, now unlawful to discriminate in hiring on the basis
of sex, to refuse to keep a woman employed simply because she
marries, or to pay different amounts (on the basis of sex) to individuals
doing the same work. It is probably also less necessary now than in the
past for a woman to stop working when she has children, as the number
of facilities to care for children when both parents work have increased
in number. The inability to afford adequate child-care facilities probably still prevents many women from having a career. Still, the changes
which have taken place and the social movements which have
promoted them, urging the acceptance of women in careers on an equal
basis with men, have improved the ability of women to establish more
successful careers. Chapter Six examines the situation of Canadian
women more closely.

Equality of Opportunity as a Social Value

One point about careers which we have so far been assuming as always
true is that success in a career is viewed favourably, not only by those
who achieve success but also by those outside the career. That is, we
have assumed that the attempt to succeed is generally well looked upon.
We are probably safe in this assumption when referring to careers that
take place today in societies placing a strong value upon equality of
opportunity, if not equality of condition. This is not universally true
and it was certainly not true in the past: "In earlier times, and certainly
before the French Revolution, inequalitarian norms were supported by
an organic ideology of society, an ideology that justified not only the
fixity of the system itself but the appropriateness of the particular place
occupied by each individual and class in the system," (Barber and
Barber, 1965).

The success of the upwardly mobile servant in eighteenth-century
England is one example of a context in which success in a career is
viewed disapprovingly by society in general. When a domestic entered
into service his social status depended upon his nominal rank (a stable
boy, a footman, a valet or whatever) and the social status of his

employer (a domestic being employed by an upper class family having of course a higher social status than one employed by a middle class family). The domestic had opportunities to improve his position by receiving promotions in the family for which he worked or by changing his employer to one with greater social status (Hecht, 1965).

By staying with a family for a considerable length of time, the domestic had the opportunity to improve his position if he provided satisfactory service over an extended period. The following case is illustrative:

> Taken from the local poorhouse by the Hackmans of Lymington to be a weeder in their garden, Nancy Bere was later employed by them as a kitchen maid. She evidently discharged her duties in that capacity satisfactorily; for in time Mrs. Hackman preferred her to the post of lady's maid, having first had her carefully instructed in all elementary branches of education, (Hecht, 1965: 79).

The disapprobation in which such promotions were held by many is shown by the remarks, quoted by Hecht, of a newspaper correspondent in the *London Chronicle* in 1765, who signed himself "Clytus". "He assails the practice of 'setting some minion to the government of the house, brought from the most servile drudgery, and without the least education, more than barely writing his name.'

> How is it possible, he asks, to suppose such a person, assisted by a female ... who never studied anything beyond the use of the mop and duster (set aside airs and impertinence) should be able to dispose a family of thirty, forty or fifty servants, in that good order which should redound honour and give a grace to dignity.

The badness of upper servants, he contends, is due largely to the fact that they are frequently persons who have been promoted from the lower staff; and he comments with surprise 'that these promotions are rewards of a disposition which all gentlemen seem to hold in the utmost contempt,'" (*ibid.*: 81-82).

The improvement of a domestic's career by a change in places is illustrated by the following examples of two of a Rev. Woodforde's servants:

> In 1784 his maid Lizzy, having been recommended by him, left his service to join the household of the local squire. Again, in 1793 his footboy, whom he described as "being too big for his present place and deserving of a better," was taken on by the squire's brother. In both instances the servant gained prestige by passing from the employ of a lesser man to that of a greater. But the footboy's social status may also have been improved in another way. From Woodforde's remark about his having outgrown his place, it seems likely that his new position may

have been of a higher nominal rank than his old one; in changing places he may have received promotion, (*ibid.*: 85).

During a career of service, promotions of this sort might be combined
with a kind of demotion if a servant moved back and forth between
middle and upper class families. How often either kind of change of
place occurred is not known, but both were possibilities in a servant's
career in the eighteenth century.

A career of service often led to social mobility of another sort. The
successful domestic might eventually be able to secure other employment or establish some business through the use of the experience and
training he had gained while employed as a domestic. A career of
service provided the opportunity to accumulate enough capital to
establish a business, a beneficent patron with whose help he could gain
suitable employment or be launched into a suitable trade, and the
necessary skills to establish different kinds of businesses (particularly,
according to Hecht, the skills necessary to become keepers of public
houses).

Some domestics entered government service, and the majority did
so through the exertion of influence on the part of their masters. Again,
however, such a practice was often disapproved of, as is shown in the
following by a writer in 1750:

If any gentleman of a small estate applies to a lord or member
of parliament, to get some little place in the government's
service for a younger son, he may perhaps succeed, after his
lordship or his honour, has provided for all his favourite
servants, even down to his postilion; for the footman or valet
of a lord, or member, now stands a better chance of being thus
provided for, than the best qualified poor gentleman in the
kingdom, (*ibid.*: 90).

From such statements we can see that some disapproval of success (and
of social mobility in general) existed in eighteenth-century England.
Those who expressed their disapproval of the upwardly mobile servant
interpreted such mobility as the usurpation of positions by individuals
who had no right to the amount of responsibility, authority and prestige
they were given. It was not thought to be in the natural order of things
that a servant be given a position which a gentleman might fill. Nonetheless, the fact that some servants did improve their social status (and
usually did so with the help of their masters acting as patrons) is proof
that such sentiments were not universal or universally acted upon.

Perhaps part of the "justification" for improving the position of the
servant can be found in another eighteenth-century sentiment; that is,
that those so employed were both useless and enslaved. The following
statement by a newspaper correspondent in 1757 expresses this idea:
"I consider an Englishman in Livery, as a kind of Monster. He is a
Person born free, with the obvious Badge of Servility, and I should

think myself in better Company with the Farmer's Servant who buys his own Clothes ... " (*ibid.*: 78). The more idle a servant (and livery servants were considered to be among the most idle), the greater his social stigma. To elevate an individual out of such a position could not, then, be entirely wrong. The danger appears to be that in improving the servant's position one could go too far and give him a position to which he was not entitled, as in the case of servants given places in government while many gentlemen remained without employment.

From this examination of the career mobility of the eighteenth-century servant we can see how at a particular historical time, opportunity for success varies with the existing norms concerning who is entitled to the available positions of authority and responsibility, and what involvement in a given career says about individuals so involved. In our society today, we generally applaud the efforts of individuals to succeed in their careers and we do not accept the idea that one's position in society is fixed at birth. However, as in the case of women in the 1959 study, these general sentiments have exceptions. Women during the 1930s, for example, were often hired only if a man could not be found to fill the available positions, and today women who are employed in occupations traditionally thought of as male are still sometimes thought to be intruding into positions to which they are not entitled.

Summary

This chapter has reviewed many of the subjective and objective aspects of a career. Every career takes place within some form of social organization which influences, restricts and even defines the career. Although individuals may feel differently about the same career and may experience somewhat different events, the concept "career" has meaning only in respect to the general experiences of many individuals.

It is for this reason that we look to the organizational structure within which a career takes place for hints about the nature of the career. There is a reciprocal relationship between careers and social organizations: any organization is the sum and interaction of careers within it, and any career pattern is specific to a particular kind of organization. For these reasons, careers differ according to their organizational context: formally or informally organized; normal or deviant in character; bureaucratic or collegial in work relations; and entrepreneurial, sponsored or hierarchical in division of labour.

Every organization reflects the historical reality of which it is a part, and for this reason careers will be specific to a particular time and place. Changes in the pattern of a given career will reflect some kind of cultural or technological change in society, and the same change will cause some careers to disappear and others to develop. Other careers will continue but will recruit different kinds of people or will take on a different social meaning.

The next chapter will illustrate the workings of general principles discussed in this chapter with some case studies of "deviant" or statistically abnormal careers. Where we are able to gain information about such careers we find their very unusualness reveals more about the normal flow of events than normality itself.

5
FOUR DEVIANT CAREERS

～

Prisoner at the bar, you have been accused of the great crime of labouring under pulmonary consumption, and . . . you have been found guilty. . . . It pains me much to see one who is yet so young, and whose prospects in life were otherwise so excellent, brought to this distressing condition by a constitution which I can only regard as radically vicious; but yours is no case for compassion: this is not your first offense: you have led a career of crime. . . . You were convicted of aggravated bronchitis last year; and I find that though you are only twenty three years old, you have been imprisoned on no less than fourteen occasions for illnesses of a more or less hateful character.

Samuel Butler, *Erewhon*

People who are involved for all or part of their lives in an unusual or socially suspect activity may follow career patterns in the same way as those who are engaged in "normal" careers. A deviant career will be affected by the same kinds of factors which have been discussed in Chapter Four: subjective feelings about success and failure on the part of individuals; informal and formal constraints on mobility within a career; and other factors which vary with the historical or cultural context.

The way in which the deviant feels about his career will affect his amount of success in it and his general feeling of success or failure in his life. The way in which the deviant career is organized to achieve its goals will affect the way in which people are moved to different prestige positions within the career. The amount of formality in the organization of the career and the particular ways in which time can alter mobility possibilities can be as important in deviant careers as in normal careers. Professional thieves, for example, do not all share the same amount of prestige within their occupation, and in order to gain prestige they must learn the necessary techniques of advancement in the same way as the real estate agents we looked at earlier had to learn the methods of success particular to their careers if they wished to advance in prestige and authority within their occupation.

Because the activity of a deviant career is often thought to be unacceptable or undesirable by society in general, these careers will differ in several respects from other careers. In becoming involved in a deviant activity, an individual is stigmatized by society in general as being either "bad" or abnormal—often both. Success in the deviant activity is not usually thought of (unlike success in other careers) as a measure of skill in accomplishing the tasks of the activity, but more often as a measure of the degree of "badness" or abnormality of the individuals involved. Those involved in deviant careers must therefore receive their sense of success entirely from within their own careers, for they will receive little praise for their efforts and abilities to succeed from people outside the career. The very successful prostitute, for example, is not likely to receive more praise from society for having been successful in her career than is the less successful one. In fact, because prostitution is usually considered not only a deviant activity but also a criminal one, success in the activity derives partly from the ability to evade agents of social control whose purpose it is to seek out and put an end to deviant activities of a criminal nature. The prostitute (or any criminal) who is successful has more often and more success-fully been engaged in activities which are formally disapproved of by society in general. The greater the involvement in these activities, the more disapproval we would expect an individual to receive.

There are exceptions to this general observation that success in deviant careers goes unrewarded outside of the career itself. Particu-larly successful individuals who are involved in deviant careers are sometimes thought of as heroic or romantic individuals whose actions, while formally disapproved of, are adventurous, exciting, or contribut-ing to some worthy cause. Those involved in a career in radical political movements, for example, are sometimes thought of in this way by sympathetic outsiders.

The deviant careers we shall look at here are entrepreneurial in nature and do not take place within any kind of formal organization. An examination of these kinds of careers is useful because it demon-strates how individuals can make careers for themselves outside of formal organizations, and further, how they can do so despite the fact that formal agents of control in society often try to prevent the occurence of the activity in which they are involved. It also demon-strates some of the kinds of informal organization of careers and how such organization affects career patterns.[1]

The Professional Thief

The first deviant career we shall consider is that of a professional thief. The source for this description of a career in theft is a book written by one involved in such a career, *The Professional Thief* (annotated and interpreted by Edwin H. Sutherland). This particular professional thief's biography is briefly stated at the beginning of the book:

> He was born in Philadelphia about fifty years ago. His family was in comfortable circumstances. In adolescence he was ushering in a theater, formed an attachment for a chorus girl, married her, began to use narcotic drugs occasionally in association with her, left home, and became a pimp. In that occupation he became acquainted with thieves and through them learned to steal. He worked during subsequent years as a pickpocket, shoplifter, and confidence man. He stole in practically all of the American cities and many of the European cities. He lived in the underworld for twenty years and was thoroughly acquainted with it and with the techniques of many types of professional thieves (Sutherland, 1937: iv-v).

This thief also served several short terms in houses of correction and three terms in state and federal penitentiaries, totalling about five years. During the years between terms, he was stealing almost continuously. After the third term, he worked regularly at legitimate occupations (when he could find work) until his death in 1933.

As with any other career, we should not expect any two individuals who are involved in this particular career to have exactly the same career pattern. To be a professional thief, however, one must share with others in the profession certain technical skills, a definition of how status is achieved within the profession, and a complex of more of less common and shared feelings, sentiments, and overt acts. Too, there is differential association in which those received in the group and recognized as fellow professional thieves *are* professional thieves and all those who are not received and recognized as such are not, regardless of how they make their living. All of these shared characteristics make up the organized system in which a career as a professional thief is worked out. This organization is not formal or bureaucratized but it is none the less effective or real for its informality (*cf.* Becker, 1963; Bryan, 1968).

It requires time and effort to become a professional thief. In order to become a member of the profession it is necessary to be recruited and trained by those who are already in it. Some professional thieves started their occupational lives in other illegal occupations but, according to the account given by the thief in this book, most began in legitimate occupations. Whichever kind of employment the future professional thief is involved in, he must have some contact with professional thieves and will only be able to join the profession if he asked to do so, trained in the necessary skills, and successfully passes a testing on the job by those already in the profession. "He is first filled in for a day's work on a particular job of no great danger and calling for no particular ability .... If he does this unimportant part well, he may be called on later for more important parts, and gradually acquire the expert skill of the professional," (Sutherland, 1937: 23).

The abilities and skills of the professional thief are those necessary to perform his activity: "the planning and execution of crimes, the disposal of stolen goods, the fixing of cases in which arrests occur, and the control of other situations which may arise in the course of the occupation" (ibid: 197). The professional thief needs wits, "front" (dress or appearance), and talking ability in order to perform his work adequately. Besides these general abilities the professional thief must also have learned specific techniques which can be developed only by education secured in association with other professional thieves. Many of the techniques require cooperation among thieves if a job is to be performed adequately, and this further strengthens the bond among them.

Some specialization according to the type of theft in which the professional thief is involved does occur, owing to the specificity of some of the techniques and the time needed to perfect them. On the other hand, some of the techniques are of a more general nature and professional thieves can sometimes transfer their knowledge from one specialty (or racket) to another. The amount of specialization may be affected by economic factors, which can influence the possibility of success in any particular kind of theft. One author asserted during the 1930s that specialization had decreased, and he explained the decrease as a result of the war, prohibition, and the depression. "He asserts specifically that confidence men, who, a generation ago would have been ashamed to engage in any theft outside of their own specialty, are now engaging in banditry, kidnapping, and other crimes. ... " (ibid: 199).

Having learned the techniques of his profession and having been accepted by other members of it as a true professional, the professional thief may gain or lose status within his profession. Some thieves divide those in their profession into "big-time" and "small-time" according to the size of the stakes for which they play, their connections, and so on. Others, however, deny the existence of essential gradations of status within the profession, as the following statement by a professional thief demonstrates:

> I have never considered anyone a small-time thief. If he is a thief, he is a thief—small-time, middle-time, eastern standard, or Rocky Mountain, it is all the same. Neither have I considered anyone big-time. It all depends on the spot and how it is handled (ibid: 201).

Despite the commonness of this kind of sentiment among some thieves, professional thieves do receive more or less prestige from other professional thieves according to their professional skill, financial standing, connections, power, dress, manners, and wide knowledge acquired in the migratory life typical of the profession. As Sutherland notes, the difference of opinion concerning status in the profession is similar to that which would emerge if lawyers or doctors were discussing the gradations within their professions (*ibid*: 202).

Because the professional thief's career is a criminal one, he must look within his own profession for consensus and sympathy in regard to his professional activities. The profession of theft provides a system of values and an *esprit de corps* which allows the individual thief to follow his criminal career despite the condemnation of society in general. In some respects this consensus segregates the professional thief from those outside of his profession, and his need to keep his occupation secret intensifies this segregation. Nonetheless, the profession of theft is influenced by the social order in which it exists:

> The public patterns of behavior come to his attention as frequently as to the attention of others. . . . His interest in money and in the things that money will buy and his efforts to secure "easy money" fit nicely into the pattern of modern life. Though he has consensus within his own profession in regard to his professional activities, he also has consensus with the larger society in regard to many of the values of the larger society (*ibid.*: 209).

As in any career, then, a career in theft involves an interaction between the values and hierarchy of prestige particular to the career itself, and the values and ways of earning prestige generally acknowledged by the whole society.

To summarize the informal organization of a career in theft: the career begins with the continuous process of selection and tutelage; contact between thief and non-thief is the first requisite of selection, and it is a reciprocal selection, in which the non-thief must show the desire to become a professional thief and the professional thieves with whom he comes in contact must believe that he possesses the ability to become one. At the beginning stages of the career, an individual goes through a probationary period during which he is tutored in the techniques of the profession. He must continue to appreciate the values of the professional thief and he must continue to impress them as having the right character to continue in this career. Mental ability and honesty in dealing with other thieves appear to be among the characteristics most valued within the profession. Crisis points occur during the early stages of the career, and an individual must perform adequately in the task he has been given if his career is to continue. As he passes these testing points an individual gradually learns more of the techniques of the profession, until he is sufficiently skilled to be recognized by other professional thieves as a professional thief himself. When he is recognized as such, he is in fact a professional thief, for it is members of the profession themselves who define who is and who is not included in it.

Exit from the career may be voluntary or involuntary. An individual may be involuntarily excluded from the profession for a violation of its codes or for inefficiency. In either case, he will not be able to find companions to work with and will no longer be considered a professional thief. An individual may also leave the career voluntarily, in which case his status as a professional thief remains intact much in the same way as those who have been involved in legitimate professions maintain their status after retirement.

The Liquor Seller

We can examine the interaction between a particular historical time and the working out of a career both entrepreneurial and deviant in nature by tracing the career of Harry Bronfman who, we are told by James Gray in *Booze* (1972), made most of his money by taking advantage of the loopholes in Canadian prohibition laws and selling whisky to the United States during the early 1920s.

The Bronfman family came to Canada in 1889 as one of several hundred Jewish families escaping the pogroms in eastern Europe. In Brandon, Manitoba, the family prospered to a modest extent through the father's working at whatever was available. The two eldest sons, Abe and Harry, were also sent out to work as soon as they were able, and both spent several years working on railway construction and maintenance. When the family finances had sufficiently improved, Abe and Harry were sent to Winnipeg to learn a trade; both did so but neither spent much time pursuing the trade after having learned it. In 1904, Abe began a serious career in the hotel business by taking over the Balmoral Hotel in Yorkton, Saskatchewan with the money he had earned while working at his trade and the expertise he had acquired by running a small country hotel in Manitoba. The hotel business in the west survived mainly by the profits from whisky, and when Harry joined his brother in Yorkton he began his career in the field of activity in which he was to remain and succeed.

During the economic boom period between 1905 and 1910, Harry managed to clear off the mortgages on the Balmoral, buy out its main competitor, the Royal, and acquire hotels in two nearby towns. He next bought the entire city block on which the Balmoral stood. Harry Bronfman was now one of the most successful businessmen in Yorkton, but the nature of his business gave him a poor public image. "He was the hotel owner, which automatically classed him with the forces of evil for half the people of the community" (*ibid*: 109).

Both Harry and Abe Bronfman might have continued in the hotel business, but the First World War, prohibition, and an economic depression intervened and they transferred their interests to what were now more lucrative ventures. Many of the young single men who spent their time in the hotel bars were siphoned off by the war; the influx of immigrants ended abruptly, and a fairly serious depression gave new impetus to the prohibition crusade, as there was less income available to be spent in the bars. Prohibition shut down Abe's hotel in Port Arthur, but loopholes in the legislation gave him another way of surviving financially. He went to Kenora, and like many other former hotel owners, set up a mail-order house to supply the prohibition provinces of the west with beer and whisky. Mail-order liquor sales were not illegal, because the provinces were restrained from interfering with inter-provincial trade, this trade being a federal matter. In 1918, however, an order-in-council was passed under the War Measures Act which made illegal the shipment of liquor into any province where the purchase was forbidden by provincial law. The order-in-council expired in 1919 and a new Canada Prohibition Act was needed if the country were to remain dry. The Canada Temperance Act passed in November 1919 made it illegal to ship beverage alcohol into any province that had voted to forbid the importation or sale of liquor, but the act required each province to hold a referendum on the question before it came into full force. The prairie referendum was to take place October 25, 1920. During the interim, the mail-order whisky dealers once more began to capitalize on the demand in the neighbouring provinces.

Harry Bronfman used this period between the passing of the act and the holding of the plebiscite to stock up with supplies and to establish connections with American rum-runners. These markets would last long after the interprovincial flow had stopped. In 1919 Bronfman got a license to establish a wholesale drug company (the Canada Pure Drug Company) and then obtained a bonded warehouse license for it so that he could import alcohol from abroad for re-export. There was a pent-up demand for whisky before the holding of the 1920 plebiscite and Harry Bronfman (with the help of another brother, Sam) took advantage of this demand and made enormous profits. The Bronfman brothers were not satisfied, however, with merchandising other people's goods, and although they knew nothing about the manufacture of liquor, they did manage after an initial setback to succeed in this endeavour as well.

By 1922 Bronfman's wholesale drug warehouse and makeshift liquor-blending plant in Yorkton had expanded to the point where he dominated the whisky trade in the prairies and was a millionaire several times over. Taking advantage of American prohibition laws, he had established a string of export stores close to the border. American bootleggers were invited to bring their own vehicles and load them at one of his stores. To reduce the Americans' fear of being caught by the

R.C.M.P., Bronfman assured them that if their liquor was seized while they were still in Canada, he would replace it and would put up the double-duty bond for the release of their vehicles. There was little risk involved in this promise, however, as the Mounties were thinly scattered across the prairies and few seizures were made.

As the Americans became more confident of not being caught, they moved farther north for their supplies and in doing so they became aware of the inadequate policing of Canadian small towns. Several bank robberies took place in 1922, and on October 4, 1922, a murder was committed and connected, as many of the robberies had been, with the liquor traffic. Henry Matoff was murdered at Bienfait; not only had he been in charge of the Bronfman stores at Gainsborough, Carnduff, and Beinfait, but he was also married to Harry Bronfman's eldest sister. The robberies and this murder prompted the Saskatchewan government to apply to the federal government for permission to outlaw all exports of liquor from the province except from breweries and distilleries. Permission was granted and Bronfman was ordered to dispose of his stocks and get out of business by December 15, 1922. This is as far as we shall go in Bronfman's career, for he left Saskatchewan shortly after this to establish a more permanent distillery in Montreal.

Harry Bronfman's career seems to have been much his own making: it was carried on without the help of others in the same occupation and at any particular time took whichever form he felt was most advantageous to him. We have said, however, that careers take place within some organized system and Bronfman's is no exception. There was no formal organization to tell Bronfman which steps to take to succeed in his career or how to go about taking them, but there were opportunities and restrictions in his liquor career which existed because of the way in which the larger society was organized at the time Bronfman was involved in his career. We can go through this career again to examine some of these external influences.

Harry and Abe Bronfman began their careers in the hotel business during the economic boom period before the First World War. The Bronfmans took advantage of economic opportunities which might not have been available at another time. This was also a time when a large number of immigrants were coming to the Canadian west; many of these people did not settle immediately and provided the hotels (and hotel bars) with a substantial source of income. But these factors did not guarantee success in the hotel business, and part of Harry Bronfman's economic success was probably due to his own ability to do what was necessary to manage hotels successfully. The social context did provide, however, a set of circumstances which made success easier.

This social context also influenced Bronfman's success in another sense. However gratified hotel owners might feel about their economic success, a large number of people at this time saw them as contributing to the moral degeneracy of the population by their selling of alcohol. Because Bronfman's career took place during prohibition crusades, he was not given the same amount of prestige as equally successful businessmen who were involved in "respectable" activities. The stigma imposed on Bronfman's occupation meant that his own sense of success had to come from his economic success and/or his own conviction that what he was doing was not wrong, despite public opposition to it.

When the prohibitionists won the legal right to stop the selling of liquor, a career in the hotel business was no longer profitable and Bronfman accordingly changed direction. The hotel business had collapsed, not only because of the efforts of the Temperance people, but also because the economic situation had changed. The country was in an economic depression, the war had taken many of the young single men who patronized the hotel bars, and the influx of immigrants had ended. But there was still a demand for liquor and both Abe and Harry Bronfman made use of this demand, within the new economic and legal circumstances, to further their careers. Until the interprovincial flow of liquor became illegal, Abe supplied the west with his mail-order house in Kenora. The new prohibition laws, therefore, had provided opportunities for careers which had not previously existed.

The poor policing of the Canadian west aided Bronfman. Had the Royal Canadian Mounted Police been able and willing to make seizures of American vehicles which travelled back and forth between Bronfman's stores and the United States, Americans probably would have been much less likely to buy their liquor from Bronfman. Nonetheless, this inadequate policing eventually created a situation which made it impossible for Bronfman to continue selling. Whether or not the connection was entirely justified, the increase in crime during the early twenties came to be associated with the traffic in liquor. Bronfman's business became illegal in the drive to suppress the rise in crime; in 1922 the Saskatchewan government got federal permission to outlaw all exports of liquor from the province, except from breweries and distilleries. Nevertheless, by the time Bronfman was forced out of liquor-selling in Saskatchewan he was a millionaire several times over and had ensured his own and his family's future in more conventional areas of business.

Harry Bronfman's career cannot be understood outside of the economic and social context in which it took place. Liquor sales outside normal channels are more likely to succeed when the demand for alcohol is accompanied by prohibition legislation, and businesses succeed or fail at least partly through the opportunities and restrictions which the economy imposes on them. Careers within formal organizations will also vary with these kinds of factors, and may expand or contract (and hence offer greater or lesser chances for mobility) in response to them. Of course this does not mean that individuals who establish successful careers as Harry Bronfman did are in no way responsible for their own success. Career mobility is always at least partly a product of an individual's knowledge and use of the channels of mobility which are open to him at any particular time during his career. These channels are created by the organized system in which the career takes place, but movement through them depends on the individual's ability to deal with the informal and formal constraints on mobility particular to his career.

The Jazz Musician

We shall now consider a career which is not only entrepreneurial and deviant or abnormal in a statistical sense, but is one in which the factors influencing success and failure are very difficult to establish firmly. We shall look first at the career of jazz musician Ornette Coleman and try to discover how a career in such an occupation can be made, how success and failure can be measured, and how mobility can be achieved (Spellman, 1966).

Coleman was born in Forth Worth, Texas in 1930. He learned to play music in his high school band, and played outside of school at disreputable places in which the music was usually a cover for gambling. During this time Coleman met and played with other musicians who were passing through Fort Worth and one of them introduced him to, and got him interested in, serious jazz. Coleman wanted to leave Forth Worth because he could not find work playing the kind of music he liked. He had played with several of the bands that had stopped over in the city and was considered energetic, sincere and talented; but his style of playing was eccentric and none of the travelling band leaders were willing to take him on the road with them. "The most common means for young musicians anxious to leave their home towns and get into the mainstream of jazz had always been to hook up with a touring band ... " (Spellman, 1966: 96); but because of his strange style, Coleman could only find employment with a touring minstrel show. After being fired from this and a series of other groups, Coleman found himself unemployed in Los Angeles and living at the Morris Hotel, which attracted a large number of other jazz musicians who were not doing very well. This hotel was a good place for an obscure young musician to make connections with other jazz musicians who might help him in his future career. But Coleman's ignorance and naïveté were taken advantage of by the other musicians, who disliked both him personally and his unusual music. Disillusioned with Los Angeles, Coleman returned to Forth Worth for two uneventful years.

Coleman returned to Los Angeles in 1952 but jazz musicians were still almost unanimous in disliking his music. It was not, however, only his music which was considered unacceptable: "There were other factors that alienated Ornette from the Los Angeles jazz scene. He was physically conspicuous: he had let his face and head hair grow as long as it could, and he'd straightened and curled his hair. He had started to dress in clothes that were homemade in a fashion no one else wore." (*ibid*: 108) Most musicians would not even play with him and thought that his strange style was a result of his not knowing his music.

Coleman then began to work with a group of young musicians who basically agreed with his approach to playing. He was no more accepted by most musicians than before, but now at least he did not have to go alone when he went to sit in with the bands at various clubs. Because he could not get work in the clubs, Coleman decided to make a record. He went to a recording studio and introduced himself to the director as a friend of another jazz musician who had a good reputation. He made the recording, and it got generally favourable reviews but attracted little popular attention.

Coleman then managed to get together a group of his own and went to New York. This group attracted a lot of controversy and reactions were either very favourable or very unfavourable. The first year Coleman spent in New York was fairly successful. About a dozen articles had been written about him, he had gotten steady work in a club, and four of his records had been released. Some important jazz musicians came to hear him and admitted his influence on their music. He also acquired more important jobs, toured, and was considered an important figure at jazz festivals. After a few years in New York Coleman had moved up considerably in his career. We can judge the degree of his upward movement by the publicity he received, by admiration for his music from others in his career, and by his musical output.

Whether or not Coleman's career was a success at this stage is more difficult to judge. First, despite being widely known, he had made very little money. Secondly, Coleman himself felt that his career was not successful. He explained his lack of financial success as related to two things: the fact that he is black; and the fact that he does not own or control the music he produces. In his own words: "This has been my greatest problem—being short-changed because I'm a Negro, not because I can't produce. Here I am being used as a Negro who can play jazz and all the people I recorded for and worked for act as if they own me and my product" (*ibid*: 130). Coleman felt that his career in jazz was a failure for other reasons as well. For one thing he felt that his audience did not usually understand or appreciate his music, and he believed that such an understanding was an important part of what he was trying to achieve. He had also experienced problems of self-respect common to many jazz musicians who work in bars and are not treated respectfully by their employers: "They are employed by bartender types who treat them as disrespectfully as they treat waiters, cooks, and busboys, so that all the years of study and hard work that would give status to performing artists in other fields mean nothing in jazz" (*ibid*: 132).

In 1962 Coleman gave his last concert for three years. The concert broke even financially but Coleman felt that it was a failure, because he did not feel he had a group at that time which understood his music. He then removed himself from the public and refused to play unless his salary was what he considered high enough. He worked very little during this time as no one was willing to pay him what he demanded. In 1965 he went to Europe to continue his career.

If we consider Coleman's career in terms of his subjective feeling of success, he has not been very successful. He describes his position in the following way:

> If I was rich I wouldn't have to think that I'm fighting the system or that I was being exploited, because I could go out and do my best and be happy. If I was loved and felt that the people that gave me employment did so because they really wanted to see me do my best, I wouldn't have that problem either. But since I'm not loved and I'm not rich, I just feel fucked up, that's all. But being rich wouldn't make me play the saxophone any better, and I'm not loved because nobody is interested in what I'm doing; they're only interested in writing and talking about it, not the music itself (*ibid*: 149).

Yet Coleman has received attention and admiration from other people who are interested in jazz and if these are the criteria his career is more successful than the musician who is still unknown, poor and unadmired.

Trying to measure the success or failure of a career in jazz is very difficult. The amount of recognition and admiration a jazz musician receives from others both in and outside the career is one criterion of success. Having these, however, does not guarantee other things which the musician (and many other people in different kinds of careers) may feel are important—such as wealth, and prestige from society in general.

The achievement of upward mobility in a jazz career is also difficult to trace. A jazz musician must acquaint himself with others in his career, impress them with his talent, and be given help by them in finding employment. His mobility will be impeded, therefore, if other musicians do not like his music, or him personally. If an unknown jazz musician manages to impress someone who already has a good reputation in jazz then his career will be helped along a great deal. This is very much like the development of sponsorship in the medical profession we discussed earlier. If, on the other hand, his music is disliked by most others in his career, then he will not likely make the necessary personal connections. There is obviously no way to guarantee success in such a career because it is dependent to so large a degree on other people's opinion of an individual's talent. But the good opinion of colleagues is not enough. Coleman's career also illustrates that there does not seem to be any particular way in which the jazz musician can work towards a career successful in terms of financial rewards or large audiences. Perhaps Coleman is not typical in this regard, but if he is then it would seem to be an intrinsic part of this career that jazz musicians who are recognized by their peers as talented will not necessarily receive the same kinds of rewards that talented people in other careers often do.

The jazz musician's personal feeling of success and failure will depend upon how much importance he gives to these various criteria of success and failure. For example, if wealth is important to his sense of success or failure in a career, and yet he finds wealth unattainable—either because of the way his career is organized (in this case, around working for others who take most of the financial reward for what he produces) or because of other unalterable factors (in Coleman's view, his race)—then he will never be successful in a subjective sense. Like any career, therefore, a career as a jazz musician involves an interaction between the individual's personal definition of success and the definition of success as determined by the career itself.

The Painter

The careers of the professional thief, the liquor seller, and the jazz musician have been described in order to illustrate that however entrepreneurial a career may appear, there is always some organizational context to it and that without an examination of this context, a career cannot be fully understood. The organizational context may itself be subject to change, however, and careers which take place within a changing organizational structure will also be changing. We shall look at how artists' careers in France during the nineteenth century were affected by changes in the organizational framework within which their careers existed. Both the pressures for change in the existing organization and the factors which helped to determine the form of the new organization will be examined. This will demonstrate both how careers are affected by an organizational framework, and how such a framework itself responds to economic and demographic pressures from the larger society.

Harrison and Cynthia White (1965) have interpreted the changes which took place in French painting during the nineteenth century as a product of a change in the institutional system through which careers in painting were made. By institutional system they mean "a persistent network of beliefs, customs, and formal procedures which together form a more or less articulated social organization with an acknowledged central purpose—the creation and recognition of art" (White and White, 1965:2). The institutional system can be looked at in the same way we have looked at the organizational contexts of other careers: according to recruitment and training procedures, and determinants of career mobility. As the institutional system changes, these characteristics of careers change as well, and the nature of the changes is determined by the way in which the organizational context responds to pressures from the social environment.

During the late seventeenth and eighteenth centuries, the Royal Academy in Paris came to control painting careers in France. The Academy fostered a particular ideology concerning the artist and his work. The artist was given a higher social status than under the previous medieval guild system, for he was now treated as a learned man whose interests centred around the high principles of beauty and taste. In keeping with this new status of art and the artist, his subject matter was devised to teach him the "correct style" felt necessary in order to do justice to his subject matter. Because Paris was the centre of wealth and patronage in France, the Royal Academy's dominance over provincial academies increased in the eighteenth century. While the metropolis provided the artist with sponsorship and financial support, the Academy provided training according to its own definition of good painting and judged him as an artist according to his mastery of the skills which the Academy defined as significant.

The Academy had always been linked to the State, since part of its work had consisted in creating monuments to the king's glory. This work was of course interrupted during the French Revolution, but during the Napoleonic period the Academy returned (slightly changed in form) to the task of the legitimation of government. Napoleon, rather than the king, appeared as the romantic figure in the paintings of such members of the new Academy as Jacques Louis David. In return for legitimation, the State gave economic and structural support to the Academy. The Academy now had exclusive power over admissions and awards in salons as well as the real power of selection for state prizes, commissions, and teaching appointments to the new *Ecole des Beaux Arts*. The fourteen painters who were given membership in the Academy held their positions for life, and were more aristocratic in background than the previous membership, as the lower class of artist—the practical artist or journeyman-Academician—had been purposely excluded. High status and financial rewards were given to the members of the Academy, but the restricted membership meant that these rewards were available to only a small fraction of all aspirants.

The official route to success in a career in painting began with training at the *Ecole des Beaux Arts*. Entrance was competitive and the student engaged in a series of contests while he trained. Success in these contests allowed a painter to obtain admission to one of the painting *ateliers*, where he would paint and have his work judged by the master there. The main way for painters seeking official recognition to have their work reviewed and rewarded was to have it displayed in a Salon. In order to have a work hung in a Salon, however, an artist had to get approval from a jury, which judged the merit of his work. Jury members were either Academy members or other individuals who had a similarly conservative idea of what constituted good painting.

The major problem with the Academy system was that it could not accommodate large numbers of painters. The rewards were high if the painter was very successful, but they were also severely restricted in that only a very few could ever hope to achieve them. As the flow of students increased, the *Ecole* and the *ateliers* could not adequately cope with training them and official supervision became increasingly more cursory for the majority of students. As the number of paintings to be judged by the Salon juries increased, the juries found that their main task was to cope with and keep down the number of paintings to be exhibited, rather than, as was their official purpose, simply to judge which of the paintings submitted merited being hung. Table 5.1 illustrates the career characteristics of nineteenth-century painters. At the time this table deals with, it has been estimated that there were about three thousand French painters of some national reputation. From this table we can see that only a small minority of painters could hope to receive any official distinction or financial support. What is more, the different kinds of honours and support were often given to the same people, leaving an even larger majority unsupported and unrecognized than Table 5.1 indicates. The Academy focused on producing a particular kind of art, and this it did very successfully. What it failed to do, however, was to provide those who produced the art with a career: it failed to provide them with a secure income in keeping with the high social status the Academy itself had given to the artist.

A different framework for careers in painting was established later in the nineteenth century. This new system was a product of the increase in the number of painters, the Academy's inability to provide them with careers, and a change in the social context which expanded the market for paintings. The system was based on critics (who were not connected with the Royal Academy and who interpreted art for the public) and dealers (who sold art for profit and replaced the Royal Academy in its role as patron to young artists). The critics and dealers existed and survived because by the middle of the nineteenth century there was a large market for paintings, as well as a need to have them interpreted for potential buyers. French economic expansion had created a middle class with the money and the desire to buy paintings. The profits which could be made from selling to the middle class provided dealers with an income that was used in turn to support the aspiring artists whose work they would sell. Both the dealers and the

Table 5.1

Career characteristics of nineteenth-century French painters*

Characteristic	Sample 1: Males, birthdate known						Sample 2: males, birthdate unknown**	Males only Samples 1 and 2	Samples of women born 1785–1834 or first Salon from 1815–1865
	1785–1794	1795–1804	1805–1814	1815–1824	1825–1834	1835–1844			
1. Per cent attended Ecole des Beaux-Arts	12	26	33	38	26	36	4	18	0
2. Per cent born in Paris (excluding suburban towns)	60	48	36	54	39	29	30	41	43
3. Per cent received any official commission†	63	44	67	54	32		13	33	7
4. Per cent held any official job‡	37	11	25	8	3		1	8	7
5. Per cent received any Salon medal	56	52	50	38	32		6	26	7
6. Per cent received Legion of Honor, any grade	31	29	25	18	10	25	2		0
7. Average age at first Salon	29	29	24	27	26				
8. Average span of Salons°	31	26	27	23	17	25	11.9	18.4	7.9
9. Average age at first Salon medal for those who received them	34	29	30	30	32				
Sample size N =	16	27	24	39	31	14	113	264	59

*Where data not tabulated because not meaningful and/or not available, cells are left blank.

†Wide definition of official commission: includes works, whether easel or mural, hung in the Luxembourg Museum, Versailles Galleries, provincial museums subsidized by government, Paris churches, palaces, and ministry buildings, and works purchased by the State (including Emperor Napoleon III) without specific destination.

‡Wide definition of official job ever held: includes posts that are not entirely routine clerical ones in museums, ministry of fine arts, art schools in provinces or Paris subsidized by government, Sèvres porcelain works, Gobelins tapestry works.

°In years: the span for each individual was calculated by subtracting the year of his first Salon from the year of the last Salon for which the dictionary lists a hanging for him.

**First Salon from 1815 to 1865, implies birthdates between 1785 and 1834.

Source: White and White (1965, Table 5)

middle class needed the critics. By reviewing and interpreting art, the critics provided the middle class with a standard by which to judge what they should buy, and the dealers with a form of promotion for the paintings they wanted to sell.

The new system had the advantage of being much more adaptable than the old one. First, it could grow or shrink as the market demanded, and secondly, it could respond more effectively to the dominant tastes of the art market, even if these tastes fell outside the Academy's definition of good painting. In fact, as the institutional system of the French art world changed, so did the type of art it produced. The Academy had produced art for the State and for extremely wealthy individuals; the type of art it produced—history painting in classical style—well suited a palace or a millionaire's villa. It did not, however, suit the middle class parlour. Genre, landscape and still life were much more congruous in the bourgeois home, and it was with these types of painting that the dealer-critic system concerned itself.

The Impressionists were part of the movement which took advantage of the new market for decorative canvases. The evolution of the Impressionist school as a social as well as an aesthetic influence demonstrates both the decay of the Academic system and the strengths of the emerging dealer-critic system. All of the Impressionists (except Cézanne, who failed the entrance examination to the *Ecole des Beaux Arts*) went through some of the Academy's formal training procedures. They also, however, took advantage of the informal and unofficial opportunities for training, such as the "free" *ateliers* where they could work, untutored, for a small fee. During the 1860s the future Impressionists met each other, made friendships, worked together, and in the process influenced each other's style.

The critics played an important part in the Impressionists' careers. Most importantly, perhaps, the critics publicized them as a group and brought their work to the public's attention. The critics also interpreted the Impressionist paintings, not according to subject matter as the Academy did, but rather according to the technique and theoretical knowledge of the artist. The Impressionists were presented to the public as an innovative group which had made important discoveries in painting methods. More importantly, by interpreting the Impressionists in this way, the critics had undermined the Academy's criteria for interpreting art, and had given to these painters careers which were not dependent upon the Academy's judgment.

A dealer and patron for the Impressionists, Paul Durand-Ruel, also increased the painter's independence from the Academic system. In return for their pictures (which Durand would sell) the Impressionists could demand regular support, recognition, and praise. The dealer also had a ready-made clientele, and the painters could even make some direct sales, as they came into personal contact with patrons. The

Academic system could guarantee neither a steady income nor the praise and recognition which the Impressionists received through their contract with a dealer.

In sum then, the dealer-critic system was simply a more efficient method of providing painters with careers. It gave them more visibility and publicity: the dealer's exhibition assured them that their work would not get lost in the mass of Salon paintings, as his were one-man shows or independent group shows; and the critics' laudatory reviews substituted for Salon medals. It also gave them more financial rewards: a contract with a dealer assured the painter of a steady income and a chance to make direct sales himself. Finally, the dealer-critic system gave the painter more recognition, sympathy and encouragement than had the Academic system. Through his association with dealers, critics and buyers he was given social support totally absent for all but a tiny minority of painters under the old system. The institutional change which took place in French painting careers in the mid-nineteenth century resulted from a combination of factors: "growth of markets and dealers, increase in journals and critics, new variants in ideology, direct action by the growing mass of painters themselves as in organizing group shows, and so on," (ibid: 160). It is this combination of changes, and the Academic system's inability to adequately respond to them, which caused the organizational changes in painting careers. These organizational changes caused the careers of individual painters to change in terms of recruitment, training, and methods and determinants of mobility; without them Impressionism would almost certainly not have become the predominant art form of the late nineteenth century.

Summary

This chapter has examined four very particular cases of deviance; as with all attempts to generalize from the particular, we risk drawing the false conclusion that what is idiosyncratic is in fact characteristic. Yet what stands out most in these cases is the similarity of deviant to normal or usual career patterns as they were discussed in Chapter Four.

Deviant careers, it is true, may demand different kinds of skills and motivations than normal careers, and may therefore recruit different kinds of people, yet people within such careers are subject to social constraints like everyone else: both thieving and policing have a subculture, a socialization process, and a system of incentives, rewards and penalties regulating behaviour. The physician and the jazz musician must each cope with career uncertainty due to the entre-preneurial character of each occupation; each career will require patience, planning and "inner directedness", as well as skill and the proper contacts, for success.

The factors that influence deviant careers vary over time, as do the factors influencing normal careers; change of a career pattern—whether in farming or in painting—may come from within the occupational group itself or from outside it, as the pattern responds to the supply and demand for particular products, to technological change, and switches in public taste. Durkheim was the first sociologist to note the "normality" of crime, and his lesson has not been lost: deviant behaviour is a statistical and cultural phenomenon defined by the observer, as is conformity. The distinction between deviance and normality, conformity and nonconformity, is real only in a cultural context that defines norms. *Within* a deviant or nonconforming subsystem of society, what is deviant outside becomes normal.

Deviants do not, then, violate all of the rules of social conduct or escape all of the constraints placed upon behaviour by the significance of other people within career patterns. It is the *content* of a deviant career that is different from a normal one, not the degree of patterning, the number of constraints on an actor, or the importance of significant others'[2] expectations. The next chapter is about the careers of several types of people who likewise deviate from the mainstream of career activities. They do so less often by choice than by reasons of stereotyping and discrimination, which deter them from achieving "normality", in the sense of average-ness. Chapter Six will discuss the career patterns of Francophones in contrast to Anglophones, immigrants in contrast to native born Canadians, and women in contrast to men.

Chapter 5 Notes

[1] It is not quite true to say that these careers all existed outside the controls of formal organization. In particular, the change in nineteenth century painting careers illustrates how a career which had been formally organized, within the Royal Academy system, broke out of formal constraints to become a genuinely entrepreneurial career.

[2] The concept of "significant others", like that of "reference people" (Chapter Six, first section) refers to people to whom we compare ourselves, whose opinions we respect or whose characteristics we admire and wish to emulate. These people will tend to be like ourselves, and their similarity to ourselves provides a basis for expectation and self-evaluation. The importance of such people in career aspiration and achievement is dealt with further in Chapter Seven.

For discussions of the concept see George Herbert Mead's *Mind, Self and Society*, (1934) Part Three, and Merton, *Social Theory and Social Structure* (1965) Chapters Eight and Nine.

6
STEREOTYPES AND DISCRIMINATION

∾

Perhaps the most prominent feminine characteristic is the tendency to personalize. A man by nature follows an objective line of reasoning. A woman, by contrast, is inclined to look at each person, each product, each idea, each remark personally and emotionally. Her thinking is largely subjective....

What type of advertising approach is needed in French Canada? The French Canadian is a combination of Latin and Norman. As a Latin, he is noted for imagination, volubility, quickness of mind, warmth of feeling, and his artistic temperament. Being a Norman makes him practical, logical, thrifty, slightly cynical and sometimes suspicious.

Nariman K. Dhalla, *These Canadians:
A Sourcebook of Marketing and Socio-
economic Facts* (1966)

Some Thoughts on Method

In considering the mobility of units larger than individuals and families, we are thinking of abstract categories of people, and usually mean to imply one of several things. First, people of a specified age, sex, racial, educational, ethnic or other characteristic may be statistically over- or underrepresented in some types of jobs, and over the course of time their relative position *as a group* may change. This "group" is an abstraction in various senses. Most people categorized by age, sex, and so on are not true groups in the sense of carrying on intense and continuous interaction with one another. Not all nineteen year-olds or women or French Canadians interact with one another. Nor do they often or always have a group identity. Whether or not people interact exclusively with others of the same age, sex, or other characteristic, they may not perceive their interactions as being with others of the same "type"; they may not be aware of having such exclusive interactions; and they may not be conscious of any shared common interest or disadvantage.

Second, calculating the statistical overrepresentation or underrepresentation of "types of people" in "types of jobs" is at best a gross approximation of reality. No two positions are exactly identical, nor is the same position perceived identically by position-holders, or by reference people relevant to the position-holders. A professorship in one university is, in some respects, different from a professorship in another university, for example. Even if French Canadians were overrepresented in one set of university positions, it would be uncertain whether their representation were comparable to English Canadian representation in another set. Comparability must be judged in terms of the power each position gives its incumbent, not in terms of the name common to both positions.

These two points may seem trivial because we know intuitively that an excess or shortage of certain types of people in certain positions indicates some interesting social process. Where we often go wrong is in assuming that the social process is itself explained by categories. For example, a shortage of French Canadians in a particular position need not demonstrate discrimination in that position against French Canadians. There is no denying the existence of some discrimination which affects the way positions of status and power are filled. But we need more information in order to judge whether discrimination is actually the explanation, or whether other processes (such as self-selection or information about jobs) contribute most to the filling of positions in which French Canadians are underrepresented.

Although a social scientist may categorize people for ease of analysis, there is always some danger of "misplaced concreteness" (Parsons, 1964). Every human could be categorized in an infinite number of ways, yet a social survey may only classify a half-dozen aspects. Further, people are more than a sum of categories; as a result it is unlikely all relevant characteristics (and their interactions with one another) will ever be captured by a social scientist striving for generality and simplicity. Finally, the categories imposed upon actors by an observer may or may not be the categories actors take into account in their behaviour or interaction. For all that I am 5′10″ and have brown hair, play the piano and used to collect stamps, I never identify myself in these terms unless specifically asked to do so, for they play little part in my "self-concept" or present group allegiances. I do not seek out others who are 5′10″ and do not prefer to interact with people who used to collect stamps.

There is often a disjuncture between the ways we categorize ourselves and the ways others would categorize us. It is difficult to know which categorization, if either, will serve to explain our behaviour adequately in a given situation. As Nadel has stated the problem:

A great many actors can never "play their roles relative to one another", simply because the roles have no common locus, logically or empirically. The absence of a common logical locus precludes the assumption of a unitary coherent system.... Where the logical cleavages are absent ... one of the actors in his role would face a more or less broad public, of indetermin- ate role composition, so that the "ordered arrangement" of relationships contains so-to-speak zones of indeterminacy. Finally, the relational or correlative character of roles will tend to isolate the respective relationships from one another, in the manner of enclaves.... In a word, it seems impossible to speak of a social structure in the singular (Nadel, 1965:97).

Most of the effort expended in interaction with relative strangers is centred around finding a common basis for interaction. It may prove convenient to take as this common denominator a social category (e.g., a common age or sex), participation in a common situation (e.g., presence at a boring lecture), or experience of a common event (e.g., a fire, thunderstorm, or heat wave). People may impose categories on one another to expedite interaction, just as a sociologist does so to expedite his analysis. Yet these categorizations are often hasty and perhaps quite irrelevant; we categorize the world to bridge that "zone of indeterminacy" described by Nadel, but cannot be certain of all the consequences of this arbitrary act.

How one arrives at workable categorizations is too complicated to be discussed here at any length. One type of working categorization is the stereotype, a conventional and usually oversimplified charac- terization of a person or situation on the basis of some (often erroneous) belief about the group they belong to. A stereotype may or may not have good predictive power in practice, and it persists primarily because it serves to simplify interaction—that is, it makes interaction more determinate. If stereotypes are widely shared, they will become good predictors. Merton (1965: Chapter 6) has spoken of a "self-fulfill- ing prophecy", saying that when people strongly expect or believe that something is true, they will act so that it cannot help but become true. For example, if people believe (like Dhalla, in the quotation at the beginning of this chapter) that women are less logical than men, they will keep women out of situations where they could demonstrate their equal logical competence. This exclusion of women maintains the myth that they are incapable of logic; it is a "self-fulfilling prophecy" of women's illogicality, and serves to maintain stereotypes that are conve- nient for males.

Membership in a social category that is widely stereotyped, such as teenager, female, or French Canadian, will affect opportunities for mobility in a number of ways. First, membership may carry a stigma and lead to conscious discrimination. Second, membership may produce a self-fulfilling prophecy of failure or immobility, because category members are not given a fair chance to show their abilities. Unlike discrimination, this process may be largely unconscious and unorganized. Third, membership in a category that is negatively stereotyped may reduce a person's confidence in his or her ability to succeed, and thus lead to an avoidance of direct confrontation with the opportunity structure. Fourth, membership in a negatively stereotyped category may not so much lead people away from mainstream mobility channels as lead them towards more peripheral ones. People may be pushed or pulled into "enclaves", as Nadel has called them; or caught in a "mobility trap", in Wiley's terminology (1967).

Identifying Discrimination

Since we shall be directing considerable effort towards determining whether particular groups are discriminated against, it is desirable at the outset to define what is meant by "discrimination", and to specify how we shall identify its presence. One dictionary defines "discrimination" as "treatment or consideration of, or making a distinction in favor of or against, a person or thing based on the group, class or category to which that person or thing belongs rather than on individual merit." Discrimination, then, includes: 1) unidimensional classification; 2) evaluation on the basis of that classification; 3) action based on that evaluation. We rarely protest against discrimination in favour of talented people or against untalented people. Thus there is typically a fourth element in "discrimination" as we usually think of it: 4) the single dimension of classification is an *ascribed* status, one unrelated to merit or achievement, such as age, sex, race, religion, or ethnic background. Such discrimination seems unfair because it is based on a characteristic that is both involuntary (and unchangeable) and generally irrelevant to the classification, evaulation, and action that go into filling a job with a competent person.

We rarely have direct evidence of job discrimination, since most employers would deny that they discriminate against certain kinds of candidates for a position. For one thing, discrimination is often made illegal by a provincial human rights code. But employers may not be aware of the ways in which they discriminate, especially if asked point-blank whether they do so. Most commonly we are allowed to infer that discrimination explains a pattern of hiring *only after* we have exhausted other plausible explanations. In particular, we must first demonstrate that a certain inequality between groups is *not* explained by 1) differential aspirations; 2) differential skills; or 3) differential information.

If, for example, we find that in Canada persons of Serbian descent are disproportionately numerous in professional and managerial positions while persons of Bosnian descent are overrepresented in the ranks of unskilled labour, there are at least four possible explanations of Serbian success (and, similarly, of Bosnian failure). Serbians may want to achieve high status more than Bosnians; Serbians may, through the attainment of higher education, be more often than Bosnians qualified for high status positions; Serbians may, through networks of kin and friends, be more likely than Bosnians to hear of vacant high status jobs; or, finally, employers may discriminate in favour of Serbians and against Bosnians in filling high status positions.

To leave "discrimination" for last as a residual explanation reveals a bias in favour of not finding discrimination. This is so in practice, since we rarely have all of the data we need to estimate the significance of each of the factors besides discrimination, and therefore rarely feel secure in supposing that we have finally peeled away all else but discrimination as an explanation. To state this otherwise, the extent of discrimination must be very great in order for it to register as a mild influence, by this method. Thus, finding the extent of discrimination is methodologically very difficult at present, and our estimates will always minimize it. The question of inadequate or inappropriate education, for example, is especially delicate since it is both a real factor hampering French Canadian mobility and the classic English Canadian rationalization of French-English inequality. Yet this method of finding discrimination as a "residual explanation" is the one I have followed here, because it is the safest method and provides a baseline for more courageous estimates.

Yet even as I have defined discrimination, we cannot be certain whether our estimate is minimally adequate in practice; this is because aspirations, skills, access to information, and discrimination are inextricably tied together. A group (or person) that fears or suffers discrimination may adopt low aspirations, fail to acquire skills needed for higher positions, and not seek, or be deprived of, information about excellent opportunities. It may be best to leave a general discussion of this vicious circle and proceed to the specific cases, with the peculiar aspects each shows of the problem. The best we shall be able to do below is to review the relevant evidence in each case and, ever so delicately, try to assess the extent of discrimination as objectively as we can manage. The reader is forewarned that skepticism is in order and that the extent of discrimination is probably being systematically underestimated by this method.

Thinking usefully about the mobility of large units, or categories of people, requires an understanding that these are very abstract concepts. We must deal with processes that are complicated by the perceptions we have of ourselves, the perceptions others have of us, and the ways people act on their perceptions. At the very least, it is necessary to distinguish between conscious and unconscious discrimination in the opportunity structure. Some of these problems are illustrated below in an examination of differential mobility of Anglophones and Francophones, native born Canadians and immigrants, and men and women. In each case we shall consider how a group or collectivity perceives the opportunity available to it, how high it aspires, and how likely it is to succeed.

This chapter will be concerned with images of opportunity, aspirations for mobility, and the realities of the opportunity structure. It must be noted, before beginning, that this will be only a partial discussion of group mobility, for stereotypes and discrimination which affect the mobility of individuals are not the only impediments to group mobility. Other impediments may include forms of group subculture, social network, institutional organization, level of capitalization, or legal circumstances that are prejudicial to upward mobility; and some of these will be remarked on in due course. However the emphasis here will be placed upon showing how stereotypes and discrimination, by generally hindering individual members of a social category, work to reduce the mobility of that category as a group. The distinction between true group mobility and individual mobility is important, for the former will generally require group organization, protest, and legislated social change to overcome obstacles and build channels for mobility, while the latter will not.

Francophone Images of Opportunity

Johnstone (1969) sought to determine young peoples' perceptions of the Canadian opportunity structure. When respondents aged 13 to 20 years were asked which factors were very important in helping a young person get ahead in Canadian life, answers differed according to the ethnicity of the respondent and the part of Canada he or she lived in. Most notably, Francophones and Anglophones differed in the importance they attached to getting good grades in school and being able to speak both French and English. Over 90% of all Anglophone respondents, regardless of place of residence, thought good grades were very important in getting ahead, while only 66% of Quebec Francophones and 80% of non-Quebec Francophones thought good grades were very important. By contrast, 87% of all non-Quebec Francophones and 72% of Quebec Francophones felt that bilingualism was very important in getting ahead, while only 40% or less of all Anglophones living west of Quebec thought the same.[1]

Other differences in perception were found as well. Anglophones were much more likely than Francophones to think a university education was very important in getting ahead. Francophones were much more likely than Anglophones to think that "coming from the right religious group" or being born in Canada were important factors in success. The young Francophones appeared to believe that certain ethnic, linguistic, or religious groups had more opportunity for

Table 6.1

Images of Canadian opportunity structure, by language spoken at home and region

Factor*	French		English				
	Quebec (N = 337)	Non-Quebec (N = 192)	Atlantic (N = 122)	Quebec (N = 107)	Ontario (N = 291)	Prairies (N = 175)	B.C. (N = 98)
(1) Get good grades in school	66	80	99	95	93	95	94
(2) Work hard	42	73	91	97	95	94	92
(3) Have a nice personality	70	64	86	81	87	85	81
(4) Get a university education	44	67	82	82	75	82	87
(5) Know the right people	49	56	50	52	47	51	57
(6) Be able to speak both French and English	72	87	52	72	37	40	18
(7) Come from the right family	26	33	24	27	25	21	19
(8) Come from the right religious group	30	40	15	6	10	11	9
(9) Be born in Canada	22	26	10	5	10	11	10
(10) Have parents with a lot of money	10	12	2	8	5	7	6

*Per cent who said each factor was very important in helping a young person get ahead in Canadian life. All percentages computed from weighted bases. Table shows unweighted number of cases in parentheses.
Source: Johnstone (1969: Table 1-7)

advancement than others. Academic achievement was thought unlikely to overcome this disadvantage, while bilingualism (a form of assimilation) would help to do so. (It should be recalled at this point that until the Quiet Revolution of the early 1960s, Quebec students did not have the same educational options as the great majority of Anglophones. If educational opportunities are lacking or inappropriate, education may not be perceived as a realistic means of success.)

Respondents were sensitive to the problem of minority group status in achieving success. Quebec Francophones were about as confident of finding jobs in their own province as Ontario Anglophones; but Quebec Anglophones and non-Quebec Francophones were less confident than Quebec Francophones. Each of the latter two groups seemed to think that membership in an ethnic and linguistic minority would prove disadvantageous. Assessments of opportunities "elsewhere" in Canada gave the same indication. Quebec Francophones, who would be a minority group outside their own province, saw less opportunity available elsewhere than in Quebec. Ontario Anglophones, by contrast, were less pessimistic about opportunities outside their own province, for they would not be in an ethnic minority elsewhere in Canada, except in Quebec. Quebec Anglophones tended to imagine more opportunity outside Quebec, where Anglophones would not be in the ethnic or linguistic minority.

Johnstone found a high correlation, rho = .86, between a regional-linguistic group's perception of opportunities elsewhere (as compared with those in the home province) and the proportion of that group expecting to move to a different province. Quebec Francophones were most unlikely to move (2%) while non-Quebec Francophones and Quebec Anglophones were much more likely to change their province of residence (16% and 11% respectively), according to their own statements.

Bilingualism is viewed by young French Canadians as important for success, as we have seen. Francophones perceived bilingualism as useful in virtually all areas of social and economic life, including going on dates, talking to friends, and travelling around the country (Johnstone, 1969). Yet Francophones and Anglophones differed most in the importance they attached to bilingualism for "getting ahead in the line of work I hope to enter." Francophones were 34% more likely than Anglophones to see bilingual ability as necessary for mobility. Stated otherwise, 92% of Francophones said bilingual ability would affect getting a job, and 83% thought it would help them advance in their preferred line of work, as compared with only 67% and 49% of Anglophones respectively.

The same images of unequal opportunity are found in data collected by Roseborough and Breton (1971) for the Royal Commission on Bilingualism and Biculturalism. Their results were derived from questionnaires administered to a national sample of over 4000 Canadians 19 years of age and over. Respondents were asked whether they believed English Canadians had more chances than other Canadians of getting the best jobs in industry. Answers were grouped according to the ethnic group (English, French or Other) of the respondent.

Overall, French Canadians were 27% more likely than English Canadians to believe that English Canadians had more chances for the best jobs. However, some subgroupings of the respondents produced even larger English-French differences in perception of opportunity. A greater French Canadian perception of English Canadian advantage was noted among respondents to whom ethnicity was particularly salient: namely, for those who lived in predominantly French Canadian electoral districts, worked in organizations whose management was predominantly French Canadian, or were unilingual rather than bilingual. Wherever French Canadians lived and worked in primarily French cultural or linguistic surroundings, they were most often conscious of a disadvantaged status. This is not necessarily because French Canadians were actually more disadvantaged in such settings, although they may indeed have been stuck in firms offering less chance for mobility. They also had greater opportunity in these settings to discuss their disadvantage with others having the same perception.

Type of residence, whether rural or urban, and educational attainment appeared to make less difference to the perception of inequality by French and English Canadians. However, while large proportions of both French and English Canadians perceived inequalities in opportunity favouring the English, few believed these inequalities were just. Only 20% of English Canadians and 8% of French Canadians thought the English *should* have the most chances for the best jobs. Although wide inequalities were noted by many, few thought they were legitimate; the French Canadians, not suprisingly, were least likely to think them legitimate.

A similar set of ethnic differences was found when respondents were asked whether all ethnic groups had an *equal* chance of getting the best jobs in industry. Here the "Other" Canadians were most likely to imagine an equality of opportunity, followed by the English Canadians, and then at a distance, by the French Canadians. As before, the differences between English and French Canadian in perception of equality was greatest where the respondent's electoral district was predominantly French and the respondent was unilingual. When the investigators controlled for[2] the respondent's educational level and the ethnicity of management at his workplace, the differences in perceptions of French and English Canadians widened: English Canadians became more likely to perceive equality of opportunity. As before, type of residence (rural versus urban) made little difference to the respondents' perception of equal opportunity.

To summarize, French and English young people and adults appear to believe that people of different cultural and linguistic backgrounds have different opportunities for success. French Canadians have dealt with this in part by becoming fluently bilingual; English Canadians have felt little need to achieve similar bilingual fluency. Although fluently bilingual French Canadians continued to perceive inequalities of opportunity which favoured the English Canadians, there is little doubt that such bilingualism enhanced their chances for mobility.

Because they consider bilingual ability especially important for success, French Canadians feel obliged to send their children to English schools if they live outside Quebec. Yet Havel (1972) has shown some decline in this tendency with the government decision following publi-cation of the Royal Commission on Bilingualism and Biculturalism, to ensure that the French language enjoy equal status with English throughout Canada. Havel found in 1970 that French-speaking parents in Sudbury, Ontario were more likely to send grade 4 children than grade 9 children to French schools (94% and 54% respectively). Families in which only one parent was French-speaking were also more likely to have grade 4 than grade 9 children in French schools (46% and 13% respectively). Havel concluded that French Canadian children outside Quebec are being sent to French language schools more often now because parents are less fearful today than five years ago that this training will limit their children's future success.

Similarly, Francophone parents were more likely to speak French in the home if their children were in grade 4 than if they were in grade 9. This greater willingness to speak French at home was found even in "mixed marriages" between a Francophone and Anglophone or a Francophone and a person of a third language. This general increase in the use of French at home may have resulted from the *formal* elevation of French to an equal (and no longer a second) language in Canada or, alternately, from the establishment of French language secondary schools in recent years. Moreover, the increased willingness to use French is found even outside of purely Francophone households. Ethnic intermarriage does not eliminate the willingness of parents to speak and educate children in French. Havel's study supports the hypothesis that facility in French was no advantage and possibly a disadvantage before this present decade, but that this is changing.

Francophone Aspirations for Mobility

A study by Breton (1972) that is examined more closely in the next chapter investigated the educational and occupational aspirations of Canadian high school students. Breton found that fluently bilingual English Canadians were more likely than fluently bilingual French

Canadians to aspire to white collar occupations; but unilingual French Canadians were more likely than unilingual English Canadians to aspire to white collar occupations. This set of differences is maintained with no exception, even when we control for the occupational status of students' fathers. Therefore the socio-economic status of the student is not the explanation of these French–English differences in aspiration.

Ignoring bilingual fluency, and controlling instead for the socio-economic status (SES) and mental ability (IQ) of each student, Breton found little systematic difference in the aspirations of English and French students having high or medium SES and IQ. French students of low SES were more likely than English students of the same status to aspire to white collar occupations, regardless of their mental ability. That is, low IQ and/or low SES are more likely to sustain high aspirations among French than among English Canadian students. This is worrisome because both low IQ and low SES tend to restrict the attainment of high occupational status, as we shall note in the next chapter. Thus, French Canadian students of certain types hold aspirations that will not be realized for reasons of IQ and SES as much or more than for reasons of ethnicity.

Table 6.2

Percentage preferring a white collar occupation by language, controlling for mental ability rank and occupational status of father (boys only)

| | Language | |
	English	French
High occupational status		
Mental ability rank		
High	87.4	84.2
Medium	76.3	80.1
Low	62.2	60.8
Middle occupational status		
Mental ability rank		
High	80.9	76.1
Medium	65.4	69.3
Low	50.9	54.1
Low occupational status		
Mental ability rank		
High	66.6	76.1
Medium	52.7	63.8
Low	43.1	47.6

Source: Breton (1972: Table A-91)

It is clear that the aspirations of French and English Canadian students are somewhat different, and that these differences are magnified by degree of bilingualism, SES and IQ. Because it is conceivable that the well known difference in status achievement between French and English Canadians is a result of differences in aspiration as well as in opportunity, it is worthwhile considering whether the French and English cultures orient people differently to the Canadian occupational and status system.

Norman Taylor (1964) has argued that the Quebec economy in its "French Canadian aspect" has retained an eighteenth-century capitalist outlook. French Canadian businessmen have kept a traditional approach to entrepreneurship in refusing to take big risks, which might either bring big profits or, alternatively, threaten family security. Self-made men who have prospered through risk-taking are both admired and distrusted, but they are rarely emulated. Since family life and business life are little separated by French Canadians, according to Taylor, there is less separation of corporate ownership and management than has occurred elsewhere under the "managerial revolution" (Burnham, 1962). Thus the potential for corporate expansion is limited by the ability of a French Canadian family to administer an expanded enterprise. While Taylor recognizes that all business activities in North America have a personal or particularistic element, he asserts that this element is much stronger in French-Canadian business where "non-rational policies may even be implemented" on the basis of personal considerations.

Taylor concludes that "comparisons between (the French Canadian industrial entrepreneur's) attitudes and those of his English-speaking counterpart have emphasized the fact that by tradition, temperament and training (the former) clings to a different world of business from that which predominates in North American society." This leads one to hypothesize that French Canadians aspire to statuses or accomplishments different from those of English Canadians. For example, they might prefer family well-being to economic achievement. If French Canadians perceive the status hierarchy differently than English Canadians do, they may aspire less often to statuses English Canadians would consider "high" and more often to statuses English Canadians would consider "medium or low". If so, this would account for observed differences in French and English status attainment. On the other hand, Taylor's analyses may be muddied by either stereotyped notions of French Canadian attitudes and temperament, or an unrepresentative sample of French Canadian industrialists.

Nosanchuk (1972) analyzed the prestige rankings of selected occupations and found that across the broad spectrum of occupations, the agreement between French and English Canadians on the prestige or desirability of different occupations was extremely high (rho = .97). He noted, however, that this agreement is largely misleading. Within given situses, such as government, construction or manufacturing, the average agreement between French and English Canadians was very much lower, on the order of rho = .5 to .6. From this, Nosanchuk concluded there may very well be cultural differences in occupational ranking by French and English Canadians, although it is generally the case that correlations decrease in size within situses because of finer prediction. Yet these data could be interpreted to mean that different aspirations constitute one reason for the difference in French and English achievement.

Breton and Roseborough (1971) examined the importance of such cultural differences for status and mobility through a survey of about 700 white collar and 400 blue collar workers. Respondents were asked about their values and aspirations and were classified, according to ethnic group, as English, French or Other. The first set of questions in Table 6.3 deals with issues of the kind raised by Taylor: whether French and English Canadians differ in the value they attach to work, success, and the family. Breton and Roseborough found no significantly greater tendency among French Canadians than among English Canadians to value family over success. If anything, the French Canadians stated more willingness than English Canadians to work overtime and make themselves available for duty at any time, activities that would reduce the time workers could spend with their families.

English Canadian blue collar workers were more often willing to move to another province to increase their chances for promotion than were French Canadians. However, this finding can be explained through reference to perceived opportunities. Johnstone's study of young people showed that Quebec French Canadians do not believe there is more opportunity in other provinces than in Quebec. Perhaps Breton and Roseborough's respondents were answering this hypothetical question about moving to another province in terms of their fears that a better job would not really be available elsewhere.

French Canadians clearly differed from English Canadians in what the investigators called "mobility oriented behaviour". They were less likely than English Canadians to have applied for a promotion (white collar workers only), and less likely to have taken courses while working for the company. Their reluctance to apply for a promotion may be based on the supposition that they are less likely to be promoted than English Canadian employees. Similarly, their reluctance to take courses may follow the belief of French Canadian young people, recorded by Johnstone, that getting a university education or good grades in school—in short, educational attainment—is not very important for the success of Francophones in Canada.[3]

French Canadians did not differ from English Canadians in their responses to promotion. Indeed, French Canadian white collar workers turned down transfers to another place or job less often than English Canadians. While they may be reluctant to move to another province on speculation, French Canadians are not occupationally or geographically immobile if a genuine opportunity presents itself.

Table 6.3

Attitudes and behaviours relevant to mobility, by occupational status and ethnicity of respondent (percentages)*

	Occupational status					
	White collar			Blue collar		
	English	French	Other	English	French	Other
A. Value attached to work, the family and the community						
Would accept a job requiring heavy overtime and availability for duty at any time	65^{F,O}	75	54^F	44^F	57	53
Working long hours is not too high a price to pay for success	41°	44	32^F	33	32	33
Would move to another province in order to increase chances for promotion	48	41	40	43^F	30	31
Value education as a criterion of promotion	53	50	60	57	56	56
B. Mobility-oriented behaviour						
Applied or bid for a promotion	55^F	35	51^F	24	21	27
Have taken or are taking courses given by company	42°	34	29	27	20	16
Have taken or are taking courses in a school, university, or by correspondence, since working for the company	50^F	28	47^F	29^F	17	41^F
C. Responses to opportunities						
Turned down a promotion	18	14	15	8	13	10
Turned down a transfer to another job or place	21^F	12	19	8	9	14
Would take a 12-week evening course to increase chances for promotion	81	74	81	62	53	56
Would accept heavier responsibility to increase chances for promotion	85	81	83	63	67	61

* An "F" or "O" superscript indicates the percentage is (statistically) significantly different (p ≤ .05) from the percentage of French (F) or Other (O) responses on the same question.

Source: Breton and Roseborough (1971: Tables 2, 3 and 5), data rearranged

The results of the Breton and Roseborough study uncover few important cultural differences relevant to mobility. Perhaps because they fear discrimination, French Canadians are less likely than English Canadians to apply for promotions or take courses that might enhance their likelihood of promotion. French Canadian blue collar workers are also more reluctant than English Canadians to accept a move to another province in order to improve their *chances* for promotion. In these respects, Taylor may have been right in asserting that the French Canadians are reluctant risk-takers; yet these data give little overall support to Taylor's thesis.[4]

Johnstone (1969) provided data on the readiness of young people to advise (or undertake) a move that would improve their economic position. He found, as did Breton and Roseborough, that French Canadians would be more reluctant than English Canadians to move to another province in order to take a job which offered better pay than a job available in their home province. However, French and English Canadians would be equally reluctant to move to the United States in order to secure a better paying job. Indeed, the French young people would be slightly more willing to move to the United States than to another province in order to take a job which offered better pay than the French Canadians are not opposed to moving as such, but rather opposed to moving within Canada to a province where they may experience anti-French discrimination worse than what might arise in the United States.[5]

Johnstone found that Quebec Francophones would be more willing to move to the United States than to another province under economic (job) incentive. Non-Quebec Francophones would be more willing to move to another Canadian province, and they showed generally greater willingness to change location than Quebec Francophones. Anglophones varied in their willingness to move for economic betterment, but they always preferred moving to another province over moving to the United States. It is interesting to note that the Quebec Anglophones are, of all Anglophones, least hesitant about moving to the United States. This and the response of Quebec Francophones suggest that residence in Quebec Province, regardless of ethnicity, creates a sense that little opportunity is to be found in Canada and much is to be found in the United States.

To summarize, there is some evidence that French and English Canadians differ culturally in their aspirations for status and mobility. This difference may play some part in explaining actual status differences and the perception of unequal opportunity. However, empirical study has not produced sufficiently strong evidence of cultural differences to explain the differential power of French and English Canadians. One might suppose on the basis of the foregoing section that French Canadian aspirations are molded by a realization, or a belief, that French Canadians will be at a disadvantage regardless of merit, educational attainment, or willingness to change location or jobs. The "reference group hypothesis" presented by Breton and Roseborough suggests that French Canadian workers in low status positions may compare themselves with other French Canadians in equally low positions, and as a result develop "more limited goals (in absolute terms) and . . . be satisfied with a lower level of achievement." However, as even Breton and Roseborough note, the same data can lend themselves to a different interpretation, in which the selection of a low status reference group is a response to real or expected discrimination at higher levels. To reach a conclusion on the direction of causality we need studies on past and present stereotyping of French Canadians by Anglophone Canadians; these studies do not yet exist.

It is now useful to examine the realities of French-English stratification in Canada, and consider whether they can be explained away by differences in educational attainment, merit, willingness to move, and other similar factors.

The Realities of Francophone Opportunity

After examining the ethnic composition of the top three socioeconomic (job) classes, Blishen (1970) argued that native Canadians are statistically overrepresented in these top classes in Ontario and underrepresented in these same top classes in Quebec. Since most native Canadians in Ontario are Anglophone and most native Canadians in Quebec are Francophone, this suggested that Anglophones are overrepresented in Ontario élites and Francophones are underrepresented in Quebec élites. Add to this the observation that persons born in the U.S. and U.K. are overrepresented in the élite classes of both provinces, and we are forced to conclude that Anglophones dominate the élite classes in both provinces.

A study by Lanphier and Morris (1974) noted that French Canadians in both 1961 and 1968 income surveys had lower incomes than English Canadians. However, these income differences decreased significantly when the authors controlled for average educational attainment, occupation, and age. That is, most ratios of French-English incomes come closer to 1.0 (meaning income equality) when only people with the same education, occupation, or age, and different ethnic origins, were compared. To take the most clearcut case, in 1968 the income difference between French and English Canadians of the same educational attainment was virtually zero. French and English Canadians had different income levels because they had different (average) educational levels; French Canadian educational attainment was lower. The statistical reduction in income inequality achieved by controlling for education was less marked in 1961 than in 1968, suggesting that educational attainment became more important in determining income in the seven-year period between surveys.

Controlling for occupational status and age also shrank the size of (apparent) French-English income inequalities. The French Canadians had a lower average income, at least in part because they held lower average occupational statuses (due presumably to lower educational attainment) and tended to be younger (due presumably to the high fertility levels) than the English Canadians. Although French-English inequalities decreased between 1961 and 1968, they did not disappear. Indeed French-Canadian unskilled workers were worse off in 1968, in comparison with English Canadian unskilled workers, than in 1961; and clerical and skilled workers were not much better off than in 1961. French Canadian managers, professional, and sales people had higher incomes than their English counterparts in 1968, showing a great improvement over the 1961 conditions.

French-English income differences were visibly least among the youngest (age 15 to 24) and oldest (age 65 and over) members of the work force. This may have resulted from greater educational homogeneity among French and English Canadians in these age groups: the youngest group has relatively high educational attainment and the oldest group relatively low educational attainment. Young people and old people are typically at a disadvantage in the labour market, regardless of ethnicity; this too may account for the similarity of French and English incomes in these age groups.

Breton and Roseborough (1971) tried to determine whether differences in status and mobility in respondents' workplaces resulted from differences in ethnicity. Table 6.4 shows few significant variations between French and English respondents in their absolute and relative satisfaction with status and promotions. Where any significant difference appeared, as in one instance, French Canadian blue collar workers were more satisfied than English Canadian blue collar workers. In most cases ethnicity had made little difference in obtaining promotions, although French Canadian white collar workers were significantly less likely than English Canadians (86% as opposed to 95%) to have been promoted after having applied for promotion.

There were no significant differences between the two ethnic groups in access to senior management. However, college and high school educated French Canadians in the white collar sample were significantly less likely than English Canadians of similar education to be in middle management, perhaps as a result of this difference in promotions; and significantly more likely than English Canadians to be in non-management (other white collar) positions. This suggests discrimination against French Canadians at the middle management level, a point that is questioned in the light of data provided below by

Table 6.4

Mobility experiences, by occupational status and ethnicity of respondent (percentages)*

A. Having applied for a promotion and having been promoted	White collar sample			Blue collar sample		
	English	French	Other	English	French	Other
Have applied for a promotion	95F	86	95	65	61	69
Have not applied for a promotion	73	67	76	41O	39	21F
B. Respondent's job compared to that of other people and to his own previous job						
Job is better than that of closest friends	20	18	24	7	11	11
Job is better than that of father	56	59	65	49	52	56
Job is better than that of close relatives	26	23	31	16	17	16
Present job is better than that held before working for this company	74	72	83	54F	71O	55
C. Job Satisfaction						
Satisfied with job in general	89	91	85	89	93	90
Satisfied with promotions received	85	90	79F	81	90	80
Dissatisfied with not having had a promotion	40	29	35	38	28	38
Satisfied with salary	74	76	70	73	76	59F
Satisfied with responsibility	84	86	79	83F	91	85

*Statistical significance is indicated as in Table 6.3.
Source: Breton and Roseborough (1971: Tables 4, 6, 7), data rearranged

Armstrong. English Canadians were significantly more likely than French Canadians to be skilled workers and less likely to be semi-skilled workers, given the same educational attainment. This fact also suggests discrimination against French Canadians, if we assume French Canadians desired promotion as much as English Canadians. However, these results, and the inference of discrimination in middle management and skilled jobs, are not unambiguous.

Differences in Mobility Within One Occupation

The data have thus far shown only small differences in French and English occupational and income attainment and promotions, especially when we allow for differences in average educational attainment. Yet some inequalities persist, despite similar educational attainment. Can this be explained by the attainment of different *types* of education and jobs by French and English Canadians? Would we find inequalities persisting if we narrowed our investigation to very particular occupational and educational levels?

Armstrong (1970) attempted to answer this question by confining his attention to university educated engineers of French and English origin. He asked first whether engineering graduates of French language universities had higher or lower salaries than the average Quebec engineer. Data from a 1964 survey showed that French-speaking Bachelor's and Master's graduates, and especially those graduated since 1945, had a higher than average income. These 1964 data represented a marked improvement in French Canadian incomes over the findings of a 1962 survey. French-speaking Bachelor's and Master's graduates earned a slightly lower than average salary in the 1962 survey: only 97 to 99% of the average for postwar Bachelor's graduates and 88 to 96% of the average for postwar Master's graduates. Armstrong had found that where education and occupation level are identical, there is little if any income discrimination against French Canadians in Quebec today. However, such discrimination must have existed in the past and has tended to decrease during the 1960s.

Data from the same 1964 survey compared the "management achievement" of French speakers and of others of the same educational attainment. They show that the French Canadian engineers, far from being underrepresented in management, are overrepresented, at least in Quebec. In Ontario, French speaking engineers are overrepresented in management only if they are relatively recent graduates. It appears, then, that French Canadians in Quebec are not kept out of management if they have appropriate education. If they have been kept out of management somewhat more in Ontario, this kind of exclusion seems to have declined during the last decade.

But French Canadian managers of engineering background in both Quebec and Ontario typically earn lower average salaries than English managers of the same background. The reason for this was suggested by data discussed earlier: French and English Canadian managers typically occupy different management levels, and as a result, they are paid different amounts of money. Armstrong asserts that French-speaking managers are utilized as a "bilingual belt" to provide an interface between the French-speaking work force and English-speaking upper management. Francophones are not kept down in lower management because they are incapable but rather because it is necessary to have bilingual management at the middle and lower levels, and most English Canadians are unilingual. It is for this reason that unilingual English managers have moved ahead while bilingual French Canadian managers were kept behind to deal with the Francophone work force.

Despite this, Armstrong feels there is little evidence of general discrimination against French-speaking candidates for management positions. He shows that top Francophone executives have lower average educational attainment than their Anglophone counterparts in the same organization, and this suggests to Armstrong that French Canadians are actually given preference in promotion, *despite* low educational attainment. The French-speaking managers are much less likely to have been trained in engineering, business management or science than English-speaking executives. The reason why so few French Canadians are found in management is not discrimination but inadequate or inappropriate education for business.[6] This would accord with the assertions by Taylor that French entrepreneurship is culturally different from English entrepreneurship, being founded on little education or on a classical education rather than on specialized training and expertise.

It seems that the finer grained our analysis becomes and the more variables (such as educational attainment) we take into account, as in the Lanphier and Morris, and Armstrong studies, the less plausible becomes a theory of discrimination against French Canadians.[7] Yet there is no denying that some discrimination exists. As Armstrong has shown, Francophone managers are at a disadvantage in terms of promotion as long as only they are capable of manning the middle level "bilingual belt". This "discrimination" is sufficient reason for requiring bilingual fluency in all companies in which workers of both major language groups are employed; this, of course, is a major requirement of Quebec's recently enacted Bill 22 on provincial language use.

Returning to the question posed at the beginning of this section, we find that all differences in French-English stratification cannot be explained away as differences in education, merit, and willingness to move. French Canadians do pay less attention to formal education than their English Canadian counterparts, whatever the historical reasons for this attitude, and are less willing to move geographically on the chance of securing better employment. These two factors must work against their opportunities for mobility, since education actually does play a critical part in upward mobility, as may willingness to gamble with the future. (Although what is at stake for the French Canadian, community and cultural identity, may not be at risk for the Anglophone contemplating a comparable move.) Outright discrimination remains a factor that must be taken into account, although most evidence is ambiguous or contradictory. Certainly there is a vicious circle of distorted perceptions (or old realities) shaping present aspirations and behaviours, which in turn limit the future mobility of French Canadians. Action must be taken to eliminate both discrimination against French Canadians and French Canadian misperceptions of the opportunity structure. Both work to reduce French Canadians' income and status achievements.

Current Changes

The relative position of Francophones and Anglophones in respect to status and mobility has been changing, especially in Quebec. Dofny and Garon-Audy have given the following reasons for the "decrease of the gap between English Canadians and French Canadians" in that province:

a) *an expansion of the structure* at the top due to industrial growth so that the English Canadians no longer suffice to fill available positions; b) *the proportional shrinkage* of English Canadians in the upper categories which may result when: 1) some jobs disappear when certain English-Canadian enterprises are replaced by American and French-Canadian enterprises more willingly employing French-Canadian staff; 2) emigration of English-Canadian personnel occurs and French Canadians succeed them, as in the case of the nationalization of Hydro-Quebec; and c) *the promotion of French Canadians* to the detriment of English Canadians. Let us note, in conclusion, that the decrease of the gap should not obscure the fact that English Canadians have kept a clear overrepresentation in the upper categories (Dofny and Garon-Audy, 1969; translated by Turrittin, 1974: 27-28).

The first of these three factors accounts for Francophone status improvement in terms of pure structural mobility, and the second, in terms of pure demographic mobility—the emigration or forcing out of Anglophone competitors for power resources. The third of these describes exchange mobility and the improved ability of French Canadians to compete against English Canadians for a given set of positions. It is here that the reduction in stereotyping and discrimination against French Canadians would be noted. However there is great difficulty in assessing how much of French Canadian status improvement is due to this third factor as compared with the first two.

Reitz (1974) has provided further evidence that the inequality between French Canadians and English Canadians (i.e., Canadians of British stock) declined (by about 14%) between 1950 and 1961, "reversing a trend for the decades immediately preceding 1951" (*op.cit.*: 20). However, this finding may be somewhat less intriguing than the finding from the same data that the British, French, Italians, Indians and Eskimos all fell further behind the Jews in this same period, even while overall inequalities between the Jews and all other groups decreased slightly. This observation provides a good point of entry into the discussion of immigrants and "non-charter group" members of Canadian society.

Immigrants' Progress

Skill as an Import

Somewhat less is known about the mobility of immigrants (as compared with native-born Canadians) than about the differences between French and English Canadians. There is, for example, little systematic information about immigrant perceptions of opportunity in Canada, or immigrant aspirations. For this reason immigrants cannot be discussed in quite the same detail as we have discussed Francophones to this point. Immigrants have played an important part in Canadian history and have experienced mobility that is somewhat different from that of native-born Canadians. Likewise, they have both as immigrants and as members of particular ethnic groups been stereotyped, and in some cases victimized, by discrimination. Yet here too our data is less complete than one would wish.

The section that follows will discuss the mobility of immigrants in Canada with special reference to John Porter's work, *The Vertical Mosaic* (1965). Porter emphasized that immigrants and immigration have played a special role in the development of Canadian society. In some senses, this role has been unhealthy from the standpoint of both Canada and the immigrants themselves (Porter, 1965: Chapters 2 and 3, *et passim*). Immigration has allowed Canada to continue filling important positions without reducing inequality of opportunity and may have locked particular ethnic groups into statuses held on entering the country. In both ways, immigration has promoted immobility. It is worthwhile examining Porter's thesis and the data which address this thesis, for such an investigation will improve our understanding of Canadian industrial development as well as of social mobility. Porter's theory has been widely discussed; some of this discussion has recently been collected and summarized (Heap, 1974), and a review of *The Vertical Mosaic* by Irving Horowitz (1974) in this collection points up the relevant issues nicely.

Porter has suggested that the Canadian educational system does little to promote social mobility (Porter, 1965: Chapter 6). It fails to train all of the skilled and professional people Canadian society requires, and as a result fails to promote movement of large numbers of talented people into the élite. Thus the Canadian governmental, business and intellectual élites stagnate, through inadequate renewal mechanisms in Canadian society itself (*ibid*: Chapter 9).

Skilled workpower must be imported from abroad through immigration. This manages to answer the workforce needs of Canada but at the same time keeps the upward mobility of native Canadians at a low level (*ibid*: Chapter 2). The Canadian system of mobility may be somewhat more closed than the American one, although one may reasonably doubt that this is so. Baltzell (1964) has shown that Anglo-Saxon Protestants have excluded all others from the American establishment, just as Porter suggests ethnic minorities are excluded in Canada. Blau and Duncan (1967) have shown that educational attainment is the great determinant of occupational status (and hence mobility) in the United States; it serves to reduce or eliminate disadvantages of birth in most instances. A replication of this large-scale study in Canada will be needed before we can finally conclude that educational attainment has less importance, and ethnic origin greater importance, in Canada than in the United States; however, some tentative conclusions are drawn in Chapter Seven. But the available data do not support Porter on this point.

Just as immigration serves to provide the workers Canada needs but does not train herself (or whom she excludes from higher occupations), so emigration to the United States in particular serves as a safety valve to reduce the discontent of socially immobile workers. This discontent might promote change in Canadian society if there were no emigration. But because emigration has occurred on a large scale throughout Canadian history, our rates of unemployment have remained relatively low and the educational élite systems largely unchallenged. High rates of emigration probably always indicate a rigid system of stratification, low mobility and little receptivity to social innovation. Because of the high rates of emigration, the Canadian population has grown little through migration, despite very high immigration rates (Keyfitz, 1950; Jones, 1971).

Because immigration policy is shaped by particular racial and ethnic stereotyping and skill qualifications are imposed through quotas (Kalbach, 1970), if there is little mobility after arrival particular ethnic groups tend to preserve their "entrance status" for decades and perhaps generations after entering Canada. Thus, Horowitz notes, "Canada displays a reciprocal relationship between ethnicity and social class absent in the United States developmental process," (Horowitz, 1974). This point is subject to some debate, for it is unclear that immigrant and minority group mobility is quite as limited as Porter (*ibid*: Chapter 3) has postulated. One should likewise question whether ethnic groups "tend to accept their inferior economic position" (Horowitz, 1974) even if they do retain it. That ethnic groups develop and maintain their own subcultural enclaves in Canadian society may be as good an illustration that Canada makes no American pretense of being a single-culture melting pot as it is that ethnic groups fail to assimilate for reasons of restricted opportunity. Data collected in the United States (Glazer and Moynihan, 1963) have raised doubt that the United States is itself a melting pot of ethnic cultures despite the American ideological commitment to such assimilation. Beyond this, there is reason to doubt that cultural separateness and economic assimilation are incompatible. Ethnic subcultural distinctiveness simply cannot be taken to demonstrate restricted social mobility; what Porter calls "behavioural assimilation" and "structural assimilation" are indeed distinct and perhaps independent (Porter, *op. cit.*: 72).

Immigrant Economic Assimilation

The relationship between education and mobility is treated at some greater length in the next chapter. This section will discuss the evidence that immigrants are disadvantaged with respect to status and mobility. We shall also consider whether immigrants have tended to preserve their entrance status in Canadian society or have, instead, managed to assimilate economically through upward mobility. After reviewing material that shows immigrant groups typically do not maintain their entrance status, we shall consider whether there is any evidence of mobility among immigrants lower than among native-born Canadians.

In an article mentioned earlier, Blishen (1970) showed that native-born Francophones are found less often than native-born Anglophones in the top three (élite) occupational classes. Chart 6.1 displays data from this article showing that some immigrant ethnic groups are overrepresented and others underrepresented in the élite classes of Ontario and Quebec. Postwar immigrants from the United Kingdom and the United States are overrepresented in the top three (élite) classes in both Quebec and Ontario; immigrants from north, central, and eastern Europe and from Asia are overrepresented in these same élite classes in Quebec but not in Ontario. The latter immigrant groups are less often overrepresented in Ontario because native-born (Anglophone) Ontarians dominate the élite; while the relative exclusion of Francophones from the Quebec élite leaves room for immigrants to enter that élite in numbers disproportionate to their group size. It would seem that provinces differ in the amount of opportunity made available to immigrants, with more opportunity in Quebec (at the expense of native Francophones) and less opportunity in Ontario.

A paradoxical feature of our society is that Canada imports talent, in the form of immigrants, at various levels of the occupational hierarchy. "Especially since 1946, immigration has not only met a demand for unskilled workers but has helped to overcome the shortage of highly skilled workers resulting from the demands of organization and technological change which could not be met by the native labour force due to the low birth rates of the 1930s and the early 1940s, and the emigra-

Chart 6.1

*Rank distribution of Canadian-born and postwar (1946–1961)
immigrant groups in Quebec and Ontario in terms of their degree of
over- and underrepresentation in the top three socioeconomic classes,
I, II and III**

| | Class | | | | | |
| | I | | II | | III | |
Rank	Quebec	Ontario	Quebec	Ontario	Quebec	Ontario
1	UK	US	US	US	US	US
2	US	Asian	UK	UK	UK	UK
3	Scandinavian	UK	Scandinavian	*Canadian*	Scandinavian	*Canadian*
4	Asian	*Canadian*	Asian	Scandinavian	Hungarian	Scandinavian
5	Hungarian	Hungarian	Other European	Asian	Asian	Asian
6	USSR	Scandinavian	Hungarian	German	German	German
7	Polish	USSR	German	Other European	Polish	Hungarian
8	Other European	Polish	USSR	USSR	Other European	USSR
9	German	Other European	Polish	Hungarian	USSR	Other European
10	*Canadian*	German	*Canadian*	Polish	*Canadian*	Polish
11	Italian	Italian	Italian	Italian	Italian	Italian

*In each column, groups above the italicized group are overrepresented and those
below are underrepresented in classes I to III.
Source: Blishen (1970: Table VI)
Note that Blishen includes the Ukraine in this chart under USSR.

tion of native Canadians," (Jones, 1971: 429-430).)
prewar immigrants conformed in occupational sk.
postwar immigrants than either group conformed in
to native Canadians. It seems clear that the Canadi
needed skills is a practice of long standing.

Yet it is evident that immigrants assimilate ecoi
sense that their occupational distribution converges w.   .- ui native
Canadians in the course of time. This convergence indicates that
immigrants are socially mobile. For example, data provided by Kalbach
(1970) suggest that immigrants who arrived in Canada in the early
postwar period (1946–1950) are very much more like native-born Canadians in their relation to the means of production than are immigrants
who arrived later. Indeed, early postwar immigrants are even more
likely than native-born Canadians to be the employers of others. While
they are slightly more likely than native-born Canadians to be wage-
earners, they are less likely to be so than later immigrants. Similarly,
they are more likely than later immigrants to be self-employed. These
data imply that immigrants move over the course of time from their
entrance status (generally as wage earners) to the status of employer or
self-employed person, and suggest, however inconclusively, that
immigrants are upwardly mobile.[8]

Ethnic groups vary in the frequency with which they entered
Canada as wage-earners and then left wage-earning to enter an
employer or self-employed status. Immigrants from the United
Kingdom, Germany and the Ukraine offer particularly striking
examples of how recent immigrants (1956–1960) were very much more
often wage earners and less often employers or self-employed than
earlier immigrants (1946–1950) or native born persons of the same
ethnic origins. Blishen showed (Chart 6.1) that these are three ethnic
groups that entered the Canadian élite in disproportionate numbers,
especially in Quebec, and the data in Table 6.5 suggest that this
entrance into the élite was gradual. These immigrants probably did not
for the most part enter élite positions immediately on their arrival in
Canada.

A similar kind of conclusion can be drawn from the data in Table
6.6, comparing the numbers of immigrants who intended to enter a
particular occupation and the numbers who were in that occupation
one to five years after immigration. These data are not fully trustworthy
since there is an occasional discrepancy between the numbers of people
who immigrated between 1956 and 1960 intending to enter the labour
force, and the numbers in the labour force in 1961 who claimed to have
entered Canada between 1956 and 1960.

Many more immigrants became managers and many fewer became
unskilled labourers than had intended or expected to; but some ethnic
groups did very much better in this regard than others. For example,

Table 6.5

centage distribution, by selected ethnic origins and class of worker, for native-born and postwar immigrants in current experienced labour force, by period of immigration for the foreign born, Canada, 1961

Ethnic origin and class of worker	Native-born*	Postwar immigrants		
		1946–50	1951–55	1956–61
British Isles				
Wage-earner	84.3	92.3	94.7	96.6
Unpaid family worker	1.9	1.1	0.3	0.2
Employer	6.0	3.3	2.6	1.4
Own account	7.8	3.3	2.4	1.8
German				
Wage-earner	75.5	82.1	87.1	93.9
Unpaid family worker	5.0	3.9	1.7	0.7
Employer	6.8	6.2	5.3	2.0
Own account	12.7	7.8	5.9	3.4
Ukrainian				
Wage-earner	72.3	86.9	90.5	91.7
Unpaid family worker	8.4	1.6	1.0	1.8
Employer	6.1	4.4	2.5	1.2
Own account	13.2	7.1	6.0	5.3
All Origins				
Wage-earner	82.9	84.7	88.1	94.3
Unpaid family worker	2.8	2.2	1.3	0.7
Employer	5.8	6.4	5.1	1.8
Own account	8.5	6.7	5.5	3.2
Totals, per cent	100.0	100.0	100.0	100.0
Totals, number (All ethnic groups)	5,089,512	167,990	317,361	318,560

*All columns total to 100% for each ethnic group.
Source: Kalbach (1970: Table 5.5.), data rearranged

many more French and German immigrants became professional and technical workers than had intended to; more German, Polish, Ukrainian and Italian workers entered clerical jobs; and more Polish and Italian workers became skilled blue collar workers (craftsmen) than had intended to. This shows that even recent immigrants experienced upward mobility in the short time (five or less years) they had lived in Canada. Overall, more immigrants became managers and fewer became unskilled workers than had intended or expected to at the time of immigration. Entrance status was not preserved, even for so short a time as five years.

Kalbach shows that later immigrants were, compared with native-born Canadians, underrepresented in most white collar jobs. While the latest group of immigrants in Kalbach's study—those entering Canada in 1956–1960—were more overrepresented in the professions and in the skilled blue collar jobs than were the native-born or earlier immigrants,

Table 6.6

Ratio of actual to intended occupational attainments by immigrants who arrived in Canada 1956–1960 and who were resident in Canada on June 1, 1961, by ethnic origin

Occupation Attained	All	British Isles	French	German	Polish	Ukrainian	Italian
				Ethnic origin of immigrant			
Managerial	2.36	5.04	4.83	12.66	21.00	17.00	8.21
Professional and technical	0.71	0.67	1.20	1.38	0.96	0.84	1.01
Clerical	0.81	0.73	0.90	1.18	1.17	2.61	3.66
Sales, service and recreation	0.83	0.80	0.89	0.70	1.31	1.98	0.78
Transportation and communication	0.66	0.50	0.46	1.06	0.65	0.46	1.33
Farmers and farm workers	0.34	0.31	0.34	0.52	0.55	0.42	0.25
Fishermen, trappers, hunters and loggers	0.93	0.33	0.98	0.76	1.00	0.40	4.56
Miners, quarrymen and related workers	0.90	0.35	1.50	1.23	0.81	0.64	2.05
Craftsmen, production process and related workers	0.83	0.49	0.70	0.70	1.02	0.83	1.89
Laborers, n.e.s.	0.44	0.37	0.43	0.44	0.60	0.45	0.44
Not stated	4.29	1.87	2.63	2.50	1.00	9.92	15.50
All	0.75	0.66	0.85	0.77	1.00*	1.00*	0.91

*In these instances there were more immigrants reporting arrival in 1956-60 and in the labour force in 1961 than had arrived in 1956-60 and had intended to enter the labour force. The ratios were calculated on the basis of identical numbers of intended and actual work force entries.

Source: Kalbach (1970: Table 5.7), data recomputed

they were likewise overrepresented in the unskilled labour jobs. As Jones has suggested above, recent immigrants were a heterogeneous collection of people who filled various jobs created by industrialization throughout the occupation hierarchy. They were more clustered, or less dispersed, in the occupational structure than native-born Canadians and earlier immigrants, although immigrants belonging to different ethnic groups varied in their degree of occupational clustering. Later immigrants were generally more clustered than earlier immigrants, and immigrants were generally more clustered than native-born Canadians. These findings support Kalbach's thesis that immigrants to Canada assimilate economically over the course of time; dispersion throughout the occupation structure is perhaps the best indicator of economic assimilation.

Native-born Canadians of British stock are least clustered, and people of Italian, Ukrainian, Jewish and Asiatic origins are most clustered, whether they are native-born or not. Ethnic groups fall into three levels of clustering: low clustering (the British and French); intermediate clustering (the Germans and Poles); and high clustering (the Ukrainians and Italians, for example). The stability of these clusterings suggests discrimination in favour of the English and French charter groups and against certain other groups—such as southern and eastern Europeans. Stable clustering may also be taken to indicate that ethnic groups select different occupations more or less voluntarily. If immigrants of particular ethnic backgrounds migrate to and remain in particular parts of Canada where they can obtain jobs through previously established relatives and friends of the same background, their range of occupational choices may be relatively limited.

Thus for example, the Portuguese may tend to immigrate to central Canadian cities, where their education and social contacts make available only certain types of skilled and proprietary work (Anderson, 1974). Ukrainians heading for the Canadian prairies will find another set of job opportunities that is relatively limited in variety. It is likely that "chain migration", the strength of kinship ties, occupational experience in the homeland, and educational preparation will all affect the degree to which immigrants assimilate economically or, conversely, cluster disproportionately in certain kinds of jobs.[9]

Variations in Earning Power

Recency of immigration and immigrant status *per se* affect not only occupational attainment; they also affect earnings within a given occupation. For all but the most recent immigrants (1956–1960), immigrants in every occupation but farming earn more than native-born Canadians. In many instances, prewar immigrants earn the most of all immigrants. There is no smooth progression from high earnings to low according to period of immigration, but the most recent immigrants earn least in almost all occupational categories. The greater earning power of immigrants compared to native-born Canadians may be in part attributable to higher education. Controlling for age, prewar immigrant family heads have the highest average education of all Canadian family heads aged 25 to 44, followed by postwar immigrants and then by native-born Canadians. This order is slightly reversed for family heads 45 to 54 years of age; in this age group postwar immigrants have attained the highest average education and prewar immigrants and native-born Canadians are tied for second place (Kalbach, 1970). This difference in education would help explain the differential earnings of immigrants and native-born Canadians within occupational categories. Such education differentials exist ultimately because immigration quotas select people with particular skills (which often imply relatively high educational attainment), while native-born Canadians can "enter" and remain in Canada without any particular skills whatever.

The earnings of immigrant groups vary with their place of origin (or ethnicity). Generally, all immigrants but the most recent earn more than their native-born ethnic counterparts; Jews and Asiatics are the notable exception to this rule. In these ethnic or racial groups, native-born people earn more than immigrants, and median income is highly correlated (inversely) with recency of immigration. With immigrants of other ethnic origins, there is a much weaker correlation between recency of immigration and earnings, and in many instances it is the immigrants who arrived in 1951–1955 who earn the most money of those in a given ethnic group.

Controlling simultaneously for occupation and ethnic origin, Table 6.7 shows that the median earnings for workers of British and French origins are higher for immigrants, especially postwar immigrants, than for native-born Canadians, while the converse characterizes workers of Jewish and Asiatic origins. Workers of other ethnic origins typically earn most if they are prewar immigrants. This finding first sustains the hypothesis that native-born Canadians—at least those of the charter groups, English and French—are less mobile and less "successful" than their native birth would predict. Native birth ought to be an advantage in the job market; if it is not, this may mean that native-born Canadians receive too little education to benefit from the mobility created by industrialization; or that employers prefer immigrants from the United Kingdom, United States, and France over native-born workers of the same ethnic origins.

But if there is a general prejudice against immigrants in Canada, there is some difficulty in explaining how the Jews and Asiatics have done so well; why they are apparently more mobile than people of French and English stock; and why their occupational level and earnings are highly correlated with the length of time they have been in Canada. The achievements of these two groups suggest that even if the educational system is, as a whole, inadequate to the needs of Canadian society, certain ethnic groups will acquire the education needed to prosper if the motivation for upward mobility is sufficiently great.[10]

The European immigrant groups—excluding the English, French and Jews—behave like the Canadian charter groups in several respects. Unlike the Jews and Asiatics, they assimilate readily both economically and culturally, as shown by rates of ethnic exogamy, for example, in which Jews and Asiatics are lowest of all ethnic or racial groups. Because they assimilate more readily, they do worse (i.e., earn less) as native-born than as immigrants. To state this another way, as they become socially "acceptable" the Europeans lose the social and economic marginality which has so often served as a strong economic motivation for minority groups. It is the permanency of marginality that has made the Jews and Asiatics ambitious and successful wherever they have been in a minority. Where this outsider status is absent, the drive to overcome obstacles imposed by rigid stratification, discrimination, and limited educational opportunity may disappear.

Summarizing to this point, immigrants come to Canada through a combination of self-selection and immigration laws which select in favour of particular groups and particular skills. In this way, the Canadian labour force receives skilled and talented people under-supplied by the Canadian educational system. Immigrants are not often brought in "at the top" even though immigrants are found overrepresented in élite positions, particularly in Quebec. Immigrants enter Canada in low occupational positions as well as high ones; it is upward mobility that allows them to enter the occupational élite.

Typically, immigrants enter Canada as wage-earners but move up to employer and self-employed roles if they remain in Canada, becoming in this respect more like native-born Canadians. The economic assimilation of immigrants is, at least at first, a matter of becoming more like native-born Canadians—moving from positions of occupational and economic inferiority to positions of equality. Some immigrant groups move faster than others, and after a certain period of time some, such as the Jews and Asians, enjoy success that surpasses that of the average native-born Canadians. Immigrants experience both occupational and income mobility, although some groups do so more than others. Part of this mobility can be attributed to relatively high educational attainment, and another part to the willingness of immigrants to enter new sectors of the economy, such as sales, service and recreation, that native-born Canadians may be reluctant to enter. Immigrants enter the work force in relatively few occupational levels; they are overrepresented in some occupations and underrepresented in others.

Some ethnic groups remain more occupationally segregated than

Table 6.7

*Median total earnings for native-born, prewar and postwar
immigrants in the labour force with incomes, by occupational groups
and ethnic origins, Canada, 1961*

Occupation and ethnic origin	Native-born	Foreign born	
		Prewar immigrants	Postwar immigrants
	$	$	$
Managerial			
British Isles	5,778	6,076	6,387
French	4,786	5,054	6,452
Northwestern European	5,168	5,038	5,118
Central, eastern and southern European	5,234	4,876	4,494
Jewish	7,392	6,084	5,438
Asiatic	3,286	3,084	2,836
All origins	5,438	5,612	5,352
Professional			
British Isles	4,714	5,330	5,230
French	3,747	4,992	4,640
Northwestern European	4,226	5,072	4,332
Central, eastern and southern European	4,376	5,664	4,434
Jewish	6,256	7,396	4,476
Asiatic	4,650	5,700	4,094
All origins	4,404	5,364	4,774
Clerical			
British Isles	2,876	3,323	2,867
French	2,746	3,095	2,766
Northwestern European	2,673	3,138	2,710
Central, eastern and southern European	2,763	3,230	2,771
Jewish	2,520	3,329	2,668
Asiatic	2,885	2,694	2,638
All origins	2,814	3,286	2,799
Sales			
British Isles	2,813	2,865	3,261
French	2,649	2,954	3,332
Northwestern European	2,496	2,588	2,865
Central, eastern and southern European	2,797	2,975	2,667
Jewish	4,182	3,315	3,089
Asiatic	2,453	2,477	2,220
All origins	2,734	2,873	2,970
Craftsmen			
British Isles	3,817	4,240	4,250
French	3,202	3,516	3,584
Northwestern European	3,654	3,783	3,620
Central, eastern and southern European	3,806	3,690	2,959
Jewish	3,832	3,119	3,210
Asiatic	3,582	3,246	2,618
All origins	3,531	3,992	3,355

Source: Kalbach (1970: Table 5.26), data rearranged

other groups, despite the passage of time; this gives some support to the contention that Canadian society is a "vertical mosaic" of ethnic groups. However, it supports neither the contention that immigrant groups accept inferior status nor that they remain in a low status. One can more readily assert that the two Canadian charter groups, the majority of native-born English and French Canadians, have accepted and remained in inferior socio-economic positions, than assert this of immigrants not belonging to these charter groups.[11]

Direct Measures of Immigrant Mobility

There are some data available that allow direct measurement of the mobility of immigrants rather than inference from cross-sections of the immigrant population as with Kalbach's data. Table 6.8 compares the intergenerational mobility of native-born Canadians with immigrants; however, as the sample sizes are so small, these data can be taken as no more than suggestive. They will nonetheless help to judge whether immigrant mobility is substantially less than the mobility of native-born Canadians.

Table 6.8 shows that immigrants from the United Kingdom are more *upwardly* mobile from manual to non-manual occupations than are native-born Canadians, and European immigrants are more upwardly mobile from farming into non-manual occupations than are native-born Canadians. Immigrants from the United Kingdom are likewise less *downwardly* mobile from non-manual into manual occupations than are native-born Canadians. However, of all groups native-born Canadians are the least downwardly mobile from non-manual into farming occupations. These data generally support the contention that immigrants experience a great deal of upward mobility, and that they are greater beneficiaries of Canadian industrialization than native-born Canadians.

The top half of Table 6.8 includes estimates of Canadian mobility derived from the computer simulation described in Chapter Two. These estimates are reasonably close to the observed mobility rates of native-born Canadians, although they predict less movement out of farming than has actually occurred in Turrittin's sample. The fit between predicted and observed mobility rates is little changed if we calculate the mobility of all respondents together, regardless of birthplace, except that the fit between predicted and actual mobility out of farming into non-manual occupations is then worsened.

If we standardize these same data by iteration in order to equalize the marginals (or occupational distributions) of the various subsamples, the results yield a slightly different interpretation. Standardization prepares the data as they would have appeared had Canadian-born and

Table 6.8

Intergenerational occupational mobility in Ontario, 1968, by birthplace of respondent (per cent)

A.

Father's occupation	Respondent's occupation	Birthplace			
		All*	Canada	United Kingdom	Europe
Nonmanual	Nonmanual	66	71	75	59
	Manual	32	29	20	41
	Farmer	2	0	5	0
	Total	100	100	100	100
Manual	Nonmanual	27	33	37	21
	Manual	70	67	60	72
	Farmer	3	0	3	7
	Total	100	100	100	100
Farmer	Nonmanual	24	35	60	2
	Manual	49	47	40	94
	Farmer	27	19	0	4
	Total	100	101	100	100

B. Data standardized by iteration:

Father's occupation	Respondent's occupation				
Nonmanual	Nonmanual	64	68	30	78
	Manual	26	32	10	22
	Farmer	10	0	60	0
	Total	100	100	100	100
Manual	Nonmanual	26	27	18	19
	Manual	57	61	42	27
	Farmer	17	12	40	54
	Total	100	100	100	100
Farmer	Nonmanual	10	5	52	3
	Manual	17	7	48	51
	Farmer	73	88	0	46
	Total	100	100	100	100

*These are estimates based on a computer simulation discussed in Chapter 2. The first set of estimates (Part A) is based on Stages 12 and 15 industrialization; estimates in Part B are the "basic nucleus of association" derived from 29 mobility tables.

Source: Computed from data provided by Turittin (1970: Table 2-11), and Tepperman (1975b: Table 2), and unpublished data

immigrant workers had fathers with the same occupational distribution and had entered an identical distribution of jobs. Under these hypothetical conditions, the odds that an immigrant would move out of farming into a non-manual occupation would be very much greater than for a native-born person, but the odds of moving from a manual into a non-manual occupation would be somewhat worse. This implies that the greater upward mobility and lesser downward mobility of immigrants over native-born Canadians, noted earlier, is primarily structural mobility. When we eliminate differences in structure, as we do through the standardization of marginals, we thereby eliminate structural mobility and find that exchange mobility tends to favour native-born Canadians over immigrants.

Comparative Mobility of United Kingdom Immigrants

Richmond (1971) has investigated whether immigrants from the United Kingdom are more mobile than immigrants to Canada from other places of origin, a question of interest for several reasons. Immigrants from the United Kingdom are overrepresented in the élite occupations of both Ontario and Quebec, and perhaps in all Canadian provinces. We want to determine whether this occurs because they are more mobile than other immigrants, or because they are imported directly into the élite. If the élite classes are filled directly from outside, thus restricting the upward mobility of both other immigrants and native-born Canadians, this may be taken to indicate the seriousness of British-American *economic* domination of Canada. Second, we want to determine whether being an immigrant with an ethnic origin in one of the two charter groups bestows advantages unavailable to people not belonging to these charter groups. This may serve to indicate the extent and seriousness of British-American *cultural* domination of Canada. The data provided by Richmond will address more directly the issues raised and tentatively answered with Kalbach's data.

United Kingdom immigrants moved upward more often and downward less often by immigrating from a job in their place of origin to a job in Canada than did "other" (i.e., non-United Kingdom) immigrants. In this sense, the careers of United Kingdom immigrants were greatly enhanced by a move from the United Kingdom to Canada. However, this conclusion should be modified by a separate examination of two aspects of career mobility: the mobility attributable to immigration, and the mobility that took place after arrival in Canada. Richmond has compared the amounts of career mobility experienced by United Kingdom and other immigrants after arrival in Canada, and these show that "other" immigrants moved upward after arrival much more than did United Kingdom immigrants. The "others" moved out of unskilled into skilled occupations, and moved (presumably) out of skilled into white collar or non-manual occupations much more than United Kingdom immigrants. They were also more likely than United Kingdom immigrants to enter the labour force after arrival, an additional indication that they were experiencing greater opportunity in Canada than the United Kingdom immigrants.

However, United Kingdom immigrants were much more likely than other immigrants to enter Canada as non-manual or skilled manual workers; for this reason, they could not move upwards proportionally as much as the "other" immigrants who originated in much lower occupations. Likewise, a smaller proportion of United Kingdom immigrants were outside the labour force on arrival in Canada than were other immigrants; they were proportionally more likely for this reason to be able to move outside of it. The following conclusion may be drawn from these data about career mobility. Immigrants originating in the United Kingdom entered Canada at much higher occupational statuses than did other immigrants. Such entries represented great upward mobility for United Kingdom immigrants in a comparison of last job held at home and the first job held in Canada. However, after immigration the "other" immigrants were proportionally more upwardly mobile; they never overtook the lead established by the United Kingdom immigrants but they were especially successful in moving out of unskilled into skilled blue collar jobs.

Movement from place of origin to Canada represented, for the majority of "other" immigrants, a net loss in occupational status. Almost half of the "other" immigrants took a first job in Canada that was of lower status than the job they had held in their country of origin. By contrast most immigrants from the United Kingdom either maintained their original occupational status or improved it by immigrating. This suggests an ambiguous answer to the question of whether immigrants of the British charter group are advantaged or disadvantaged in Canada. On the one hand, they benefit most immediately from immigration to Canada; but on the other hand, they tend to lose their advantage to "other" immigrants over the course of time. This is similar to what we had concluded from the Kalbach data.

"Other" immigrants were more often downwardly mobile and less often upwardly mobile *before* coming to Canada than were the United Kingdom immigrants. This suggests that many immigrants came to Canada from countries other than the United Kingdom in order to achieve upward (or escape downward) intergenerational mobility. Immigrants from the United Kingdom experienced more upward intergenerational mobility by immigrating to Canada than by staying in the United Kingdom, because, as we have already noted, they tended to enter higher occupational statuses in Canada than they had held in their last job in the United Kingdom. This suggest a motivation for immigration to Canada from the United Kingdom.

The differences between immigrants from the United Kingdom and "other" countries are summarized in Table 6.9, which simply shows differences in the frequency of upward or downward movement. Part E of Table 6.9 indicates that "other" immigrants have more upward mobility and less downward mobility than United Kingdom immigrants after arriving in Canada; while Parts B and C show that United Kingdom immigrants experience more upward mobility and/or less downward mobility than "other" immigrants as a result of moving to Canada.

Richmond prepared two matched samples of United Kingdom and "other" immigrants, confining himself to males aged 24 to 55 years who had been in Canada five years or more and had intended to stay in Canada. These groups were matched for marital and socio-economic status in the country of origin. That the matched United Kingdom immigrants experienced very much higher rates of upward mobility and lower rates of downward mobility (Part D, Table 6.9) indicates that a systematic preference is shown in Canada to immigrants from the United Kingdom. This may be ascribable to ethnic favouritism and discrimination; it is not easily explainable by differences in skill, education or other achieved characteristics of the immigrants.

To conclude, immigrants typically enter the occupational structure in positions below those held by persons already in Canada—whether native-born or earlier immigrants. Some immigrants do enter toward the top of the occupational hierarchy; however, the majority of immigrants who reach the top of the class structure have done so gradually through upward mobility within Canada, in competition with one another and with native-born Canadians. At the beginning of the "competition" immigrants may be at a disadvantage vis-à-vis native-born Canadians, but this disadvantage probably disappears quickly. Immigrants can validly perceive Canada as a country of great opportunity, for even if they do not benefit from great exchange mobility in competition with native-born Canadians, they benefit greatly from structural mobility—from the mere fact that Canada is highly industrialized and has many unsatisfied needs for skilled and non-manual workers. While the data are presently inadequate for full measurement of the frequency and extent of immigrant mobility, they are sufficient to challenge Porter's contention that immigrant mobility is insubstantial.

Being a member of one of the charter groups—being a British immigrant in particular—gives advantages not available to other immigrants. It provides an opportunity for instant upward mobility on arrival in Canada. Yet as Richmond points out, "This initial advantage diminished over time as immigrants from other countries became more acculturated." Immigrants from non-English speaking countries learn to speak English, to act and dress in a "Canadian" manner, and most important, to acquire whichever skills are currently most saleable, while lower class Anglo-Canadians do not. These immigrants become economically assimilated, but not "acculturated" in the sense of culturally assimilated. It is patently false that ethnicity and social class are interchangeable in Canada, that low status groups (especially immigrants) accept their inferior economic position, and "groups ranging from the Italian to the Irish tend to preserve their entrance status, rather than seek to trade it in for something higher (or at least different," (Horowitz, 1974). Whatever our desire to find characteristic

Table 6.9

Direction of mobility, by type of mobility and birthplace of immigrant (per cent)

Type of mobility	Birthplace		Difference
	Non-United Kingdom	United Kingdom	
A. Between father's occupation and immigrant's last occupation in Canada:			
Up	39.0	43.5	4.5
No change	15.6	13.9	-1.7
Down	45.4	38.6	-6.8
N =	295	101	
B. Between occupation abroad and first occupation in Canada:			
Up	14.8	14.5	-0.3
No change	36.5	52.7	16.2
Down	48.7	32.8	-15.9
N =	285	110	
C. Between occupation abroad and occupation in Canada, February, 1961:			
Up	28.5	37.1	8.6
No change	42.2	43.8	1.6
Down	29.2	19.1	-10.1
N =	287	105	
D. Matched sample. Between occupation abroad and occupation in Canada, February 1961:			
Up	12.5	37.1	24.6
No change	50.0	42.9	-7.1
Down	37.5	20.0	-17.5
N =	32	35	
E. Between first occupation in Canada and occupation in Canada, February 1961:			
Up	46.6	42.7	-3.9
No change	47.8	46.4	-1.4
Down	5.6	10.8	5.2
N =	318	110	

Source: Richmond (1971: Tables 3-7), data rearranged

differences between Canadian and American social structure or personality, we should avoid assuming of Canada and Canadians a conservatism, docility and torpor for which little evidence seems to exist.

The Position of Women in Canada

We have thus far considered the social mobility of Francophones and immigrants as compared with that of Anglophones and native-born

Canadians respectively. In each instance, an attempt has been made to describe and explain the contemporary Canadian situation in terms of explicit discrimination, stereotyping, and the presence or absence of aspirations for upward mobility. This last section will attempt a similar type of analysis, comparing the mobility of men and women. As in the preceding sections, the extent of this analysis will be largely defined by the limits of available data on the subject. Most available data are recent and a product of the Royal Commission on the Status of Women in Canada (1970).

One of the more frequently discussed aspects of female disadvantage is that of unequal salary for the same job as that performed by a man. Data published in the Report of the Royal Commission on the Status of Women in Canada (1970) have shown that women do not enjoy wage parity with men in most jobs. For example, in the making of underwear and outerwear there are at least three defined jobs—circular knitter, hand operator, and cutter. In Quebec, men earn on the average of 44¢, 20¢ and 69¢ per hour more than women doing these three respective jobs; in percentage terms, they earn an average of 32%, 16% and 49% more than women for these jobs, respectively. Quebec is not unique; Ontario and Nova Scotia, indeed all of Canada, show similar differentials between men and women performing these three jobs. What is even more remarkable is that the upper limit of women's hourly rates for these jobs is often only slightly above the lower limit paid men for the same job. That is to say, a highly proficient woman with seniority can work up to earning what an inexperienced or incompetent man is earning for the same job.

Bossen (1971a) found women in all full-time positions in Canadian department stores, save the position of cashier, earned an average of 80% of what men in the same position were earning. Data collected by Bossen (1971b) from employees of Canada's eight major chartered banks likewise show that men may earn a median salary anywhere from 3% to 67% greater than that of a woman in the same position. Similarly, in every position (save one) where salaries can go above $8000 per year, a much higher proportion of men than women in those positions earn these high salaries.

Robson and Lapointe (1971) analyzed differences between male and female salaries in universities, using multiple regression to estimate the financial impact of being a *female* academic, all other things being equal. They concluded that of the roughly $2250 average difference between male and female academic salaries, $1200 (or 53%) could be considered a "pure sex difference" after the effects of different rank, age, highest degree, field and various university characteristics were removed. Of the seven variables that affected salary most, rank came after sex, not surprisingly; and we shall note shortly that women achieve a given rank at an average age greater than that of men with the same highest degree. Being in a lower rank for a longer time means that women are losing a large amount of money each year; and even at the same rank, women are earning less than men. This, most strongly of all the data examined to this point, suggests the likelihood and significance of sex discrimination in formal organizations. Since so many factors besides sex have been held constant, we are largely convinced that sex discrimination alone can explain Robson and Lapointe's pure sex difference in salaries.

However, even these data are ambiguous. What Robson and Lapointe have not considered in their analysis are precisely those factors which ought, in an approximately meritocratic university, to affect pay and promotion most: scholarly competence, quality of teaching and research, amount of research productivity, and contribution to university or departmental administration. Neither have these authors measured seniority or years of service. Since the authors did not have these data, they did not use them to determine whether they reduced the pure sex difference in salaries. It remains premature to assume sex discrimination is the explanation until we have shown that these latter factors do not vary with sex. While there is little *a priori* reason to believe they do, it may be well to examine the pertinent data before deciding the matter is closed. In the next section we shall review some evidence pertinent to the question of discrimination. This includes studies of male attitudes and the position and mobility of women in departmental stores, banks and universities.

Evidence of Preference, Bias, and Discrimination

Geoffroy and Sainte-Marie (1971) interviewed over five hundred male French Canadian manual workers to ascertain their attitudes about women's place in the work world. It is worth noting at the outset that the majority of these men had wives who held jobs and this, we would suppose, would predispose them to viewing women's participation in the labour force somewhat more favourably than otherwise.

The picture we get of worker attitudes, as portrayed in Table 6.10, is along the following lines. Women should stay at home, if this is financially feasible; otherwise they displace men from jobs that men need to support their families. Wage parity between men and women does not and perhaps should not obtain in Quebec industry. Yet these workers would typically prefer that higher salaries be negotiated for men so that their wives could stay at home. Women are not as useful workers as men: they should not work at night—they should presumably be home taking care of husband and children—and this reduces their utility as workers in manufacturing firms. Women do not achieve positions of authority in either industry or the unions because, these men claim, they lack ambition, interest or competence. Yet they also admit that the majority of working men do not like working under the supervision of a woman; this comes in opposition to the expressed personal willingness of a bare majority to work under a female boss. As regards the issue that has proved especially thorny in reducing *de facto* disabilities of women workers—paid maternity leave—under one-third indicated they were willing to go on strike to support such a demand by their female co-workers if it arose.

Table 6.10

Percentages of male unionized workers agreeing with each statement

Statement	% agreeing
Women displace men on the labour market ("yes", "sometimes")	67.5
For me, working under the direction of a woman would be pleasant, not unpleasant	51.7
The majority of working men do not like having women as their bosses	67.7
Women should not be allowed to work the night shift in manufacturing firms	67.5
I prefer that my wife stayed at home, didn't work	56.8
Few women achieve executive or managerial positions, because women lack ambition, interest, competence or authority	63.7
Few women are in positions of responsibility in the unions, because women lack interest, information	62.5
The principle of wage parity between men and women is not accepted everywhere in Quebec	78.6
The principle of wage parity is not applied in my field of employment	45.7
Prefer that higher salaries were negotiated for male workers, so wives could stay at home	61.1
Would go on strike in order to secure for female workers maternity leave without income loss	32.1

Source: Rearranged from data provided by Geoffroy and Sainte-Marie (1971: Appendix I *et passim*)

This leads us to infer that women workers in Quebec industry suffer from income and other disabilities; it remains for us to determine the extent and generality of such sex-determined disability. Marianne Bossen (1971a) sent questionnaires to the management of 38 large department stores in all major Canadian cities. These stores employed 23,000 full-time and 25,000 part-time workers, of whom 56% of the full-time workers and the great majority of part-time workers were women. She asked for information on the positions and income attained by male and female employees, and on their career mobility within these organizations.

Bossen found that female employees were much more likely than males to be employed in sales or office work in those stores, and only one-sixth as likely to be in management or executive positions. Analyzing 24 selling departments, Bossen observed that females were rarely department managers, and a majority of female managers (77%) were located in one of 5 departments: women's outerwear, women's underclothing, apparel accessories, boys' and girls' wear, and economy apparel. On average, these 5 departments employed women as 95% of their salespeople; it should be unremarkable that they had females to manage them. Yet a high proportion of female salespeople gave no guarantee that a female would be hired to manage. Another 5 departments—piece goods, drugs and cosmetics, jewellery and china, books, and toys and games—employed women as 91% of their salespeople and yet relatively few female managers were employed in these departments. Although the latter 5 departments employed 26.9% of all saleswomen working full-time in these sampled stores, only 11.2% of all female managers were hired to work here; there was a distinct underrepresentation of female managers in these latter departments.

Management was asked to indicate whether male or female salespeople were preferred as employees in each of these 24 departments, and why; the answers are presented in Table 6.11. We note first that there were few departments of the 24 in which management indicated that salespeople should be of *both* sexes. Thus in most cases, there was a preference for one or the other sex, but not for a mixture of both sexes: men and women would be "separate but equal" as salespeople. Men were preferred as salespeople for mens' clothing, household furniture, appliances, hardware, cameras, sporting goods, and auto accessories, while women were preferred for those departments we have already noted as employing very high proportions of women, the 10 departments named earlier.

Asked whether these preferences were based on "objective" or "subjective" considerations, management indicated that in most cases the preference was based on such "subjective" considerations as customer, employee, or employer preference or on tradition, rather than on "objective" considerations such as physical job requirements or technical knowledge. However, reference to "subjective preferences" was most frequent in respect to jobs that were primarily held by women. An average of 95% of all preferences were subjective in those 5 departments that employed the majority of female managers; and 91% of all preferences were subjective in regard to those 5 departments that employed primarily female staff but fewer female managers. Job requirements such as physical strength or technical knowledge were more often invoked to explain preferences for male employees, wherever such preferences occurred.

About 18% of all management and executive (M & E) staff in these stores was female, yet a strong difference between western and eastern Canada can be seen in this regard. Women in eastern Canada were over three times as likely as women in western Canada to be on the M & E staff. The same differential holds for promotions to M & E staff in the

Table 6.11

Percentage preferences expressed for male or female sales staff in 24 selling departments

	Preference				N =	% preferences based on subjective* considerations
	male	female	mixed	no pref.		
Men's clothing, furnishings	72.1	1.6	13.1	13.1	61	60.7
Women's outerwear	0.0	100.0	0.0	0.0	49	100.0
Women's underclothing	0.0	100.0	0.0	0.0	55	100.0
Apparel accessories	0.0	91.5	0.0	8.5	47	91.5
Boys' and girls' wear	0.0	79.6	4.1	16.3	49	79.6
Footwear, all kinds	23.7	7.9	13.2	55.3	38	26.3
Household furniture	80.4	0.0	1.8	17.9	56	51.8
Household appliances	53.7	4.9	0.0	41.5	41	43.9
Radios, etc.	88.9	0.0	0.0	11.1	54	61.1
House furnishings	20.0	25.0	0.0	55.0	40	42.5
Hardware, housewares	60.0	0.0	6.7	33.3	45	33.3
Piece goods, etc.	0.0	80.5	0.0	19.5	41	80.5
Drugs, cosmetics	0.0	85.7	0.0	14.3	49	85.7
Jewellery, china	0.0	68.4	0.0	31.6	38	68.4
Books, etc.	0.0	72.1	0.0	27.9	43	72.1
Cameras, etc.	64.1	0.0	0.0	35.9	39	48.7
Sporting goods	83.9	0.0	0.0	16.1	56	64.3
Toys and games	0.0	46.3	2.4	51.2	41	46.3
Food products	8.7	34.8	21.7	34.8	23	43.5
Tobacco products	0.0	60.9	0.0	39.1	23	60.9
Auto accessories	85.4	0.0	0.0	14.6	48	56.3
Economy apparel	0.0	63.3	3.3	33.3	30	63.3
Economy house furnishings	38.1	0.0	0.0	61.9	21	28.6
Economy other	0.0	56.0	0.0	44.0	25	56.0

*"Subjective statements are all those statements of preference related to 'people' requirements (customer, employee, employer) and tradition, while objective statements. . . (are) related to 'job' requirements (physical job requirements and technical knowledge)" (Bossen, 1971a).
Source: Bossen (1971a: Table 10), data recomputed

five years preceding the study. Two-thirds of the present staff had been promoted to M & E in the preceding five years, indicating a tremendous amount of managerial turnover and/or structural expansion. This rate of mobility was higher for men than for women, and among women, much higher in eastern than in western Canada.

It is sometimes argued that women do not advance to positions of authority and responsibility as often as men because they drop out of a job in early or mid-career. However, Bossen found that neither in western nor eastern Canada were women more likely to drop out of M & E than were men. Further, women in western Canada were less likely than men to drop out of their training program, and in eastern Canada women were only slightly more likely than men to drop out of training. There was a much higher rate of dropping out and separation in eastern than in western Canada, which suggests that much of the mobility through M & E in the last five years was exchange mobility, not structural mobility. The ratio of promotions to separations from M & E in the last five years can be calculated, for women only, separately for eastern and western Canada. A comparison of western and eastern ratios should reveal the excess of western over eastern female structural mobility.[12] This allows us to infer that western women are experiencing more structural mobility than eastern women and this inference is sustained by the evidence that western women are being promoted to M & E at an average age of 34, three years younger than the average female promotee in eastern stores. Likewise, women in the western stores are being promoted to M & E at an earlier average age than the average male promotee, while the opposite holds true in eastern Canada.

That women are underrepresented in positions of authority is hardly a unique finding. Robson and Lapointe (1971) have found a similar underrepresentation of women in the higher ranks of Canadian university faculties, even while controlling for age and highest degree attained. For example, in the age group 45 to 59, 48.5% of all female academics with Ph.D.'s are still assistant professors or below, while only 8.1% of all male academics of the same age and highest degree are at the same rank or below. No female deans appear in a Canadian university before age 55 to 59, while male deans are to be found in all age groups, including those under 35. (These figures refer to Ph.D. degree holders only). Male Ph.D. holders are 3 to 4 times as likely as female Ph.D. holders to have attained the rank of professor by the ages 40 to 55; below these ages, the female-to-male differential is wider, and above these ages the differential is narrower.

These data are supplemented and reorganized in Table 6.12 in order to examine more directly the ages at which males and females attain various ranks, given the same highest academic degree. We will recall from Chapter Three that in any organization, such as a university, in which promotion is age-dependent or based largely on seniority, the difference in ages at which two groups attain a given rank is precisely the measure of differential mobility of these two groups. Depending on how we interpret the data collected by Robson and Lapointe, slightly different conclusions are drawn about male and female mobility in Canadian universities. However, the differences in conclusion are ones of degree, not kind; all analyses point in the same direction. Female Ph.D. holders are about 7 years older than male Ph.D. holders on attaining the rank of professor, 4 to 8 years older on attaining the rank of associate professor, and 1 to 5 years older on attaining the rank of assistant professor. These differences are of roughly the same magnitude for holders of M.A. degrees, although Robson and Lapointe's measure of present age difference in rank would suggest that the sex differential in mobility is more marked for M.A.s than for Ph.D.s while calculation using another method [devised by Hajnal (1953) to estimate the mean age of marriage from a similar kind of data] suggests the opposite.

Whatever the means of calculation, the message is clear: women attain higher ranks at later ages than men. One cannot tell whether or not this reflects different amounts of time spent in full-time service in the university, however. If women academics typically take five or more years off to raise a family before giving full attention to their career, it should come as no surprise to find them reaching higher ranks five or more years after their male counterparts. This can remain no more than a speculation at this point, for we have no data on this issue.

In her study of department store employees, Bossen (1971a) collected data on the average ages at which male and female employees attained different positions in the 24 selling departments of 36 major department stores. As already noted, jobs in these stores were highly sex differentiated; the data in Table 6.13 give an even finer-grained analysis of this sex differentiation. While women were very numerous in the lowest ranks of salesperson (classes A and B) they were few in the highest rank of salesperson (class C). Almost all cashiers were female, but females outnumbered males at the levels of head or senior salesclerk and first-line supervisor by much less. Finally, females were badly underrepresented in the positions of department manager and departmental buyer.

In all of these positions but one, that of buyer, females were older on the average than were males in the same position. These age differences ranged from a high of 12 years (in the position of head or senior salesclerk) to a low of 1 year (salesperson class C). Yet when we examine years of service rather than chronological age, the picture changes considerably. The buyer position continues to employ fewer experienced females than males and so does the position of salesperson class C. In those positions that men are attaining with fewer years of seniority than women, the male-female difference is only about 3 years

Table 6.12

The comparative mobility of male and female academics, by highest earned degree

A. Average age of males and females, with same highest earned degree, in each academic rank

	ACADEMIC RANK																
	Deans			Heads			Other full profs.			Assoc. profs.			Asst. profs.			Other		
							AGE IN YEARS											
Highest Earned Degree	M	F	Diff	M	F	Diff	M	F	Diff	M	F	Diff	M	F	Diff	M	F	Diff
Ph.D	49.3	60.7	11.4	48.1	54.2	6.1	47.1	54.6	7.5	40.1	44.3	4.2	33.0	37.5	4.5	35.7	36.7	1.0
M.A.	49.8	52.0	2.2	51.2	56.6	5.4	48.2	54.4	6.2	42.8	51.3	8.5	34.8	42.8	8.0	32.2	35.6	3.4

B. Estimated mean age at which rank was attained*

| | Other full profs. | | | Assoc. profs. | | | Asst. profs. | | |
	M	F	Diff	M	F	Diff	M	F	Diff
Ph.D.	43	50	7	36	45	9	30	32	2
M.A.	47	53	6	41	48	7	33	38	5

*Using the method devised by Hajnal (1953) for calculating singulate mean age of marriage.

Source: Robson and Lapointe (1971: Table VI); part B calculated from data in Robson and Lapointe (op.cit.: Table V)

in most cases. (There were 6 to 10 year differences favouring men when we considered chronological age). Females do experience slower mobility than men in most positions, but the difference is slight if we confine our attention to years of service. This gives some greater persuasiveness to the suggestion above that sex differences in mobility of university teachers may be largely explainable by differences in length of actual service (or seniority, rather than age).

Table 6.13

The comparative mobility and salary of male and female full time employees in 24 selling departments, 36 stores: Canada, 1966

	N =	Sex ratio (female/ male)	Average age female	Average age male	Average years service female	Average years service male	Ratio of female to male salary
Sales person class A or B	4521	3.91	42	34	7	6	0.83
Sales person class C	1025	0.38	42	41	9	12	0.77
Cashier	165	81.50	39	27	6	2	1.05
Head or senior sales clerk	332	1.50	45	33	11	8	0.82
Supervisor first line	940	1.55	47	38	13	12	0.79
Dept. management	1103	0.29	44	38	16	13	0.81
Buyer (specialist)	142	0.28	36	42	8	18	0.78

Source: Bossen (1971a: Table 8), data recomputed

Because the data on discrimination are suggestive but not conclusive at this point, it will be worthwhile to determine whether female aspirations are lower than male aspirations, or simply different. Such differences in aspiration might help account for the differences in status attainment and mobility.

Female Aspirations

Aspirations are generated very early in life, as the next chapter argues. Certainly they develop in the parental home and become channelled and specified, encouraged or discouraged, in secondary school if not before. These aspirations may be very general, or may change a number of times within a relatively limited variety of choices. Even more general than this is a sex-typing of "proper" behaviours and aspirations, which guides the development of more specific aspirations. It is appropriate then to begin by examining sex-typing or sex stereotyping of adult roles as this is carried out by children of primary and secondary school age.

Such a study was carried out by Lambert (1969) under the auspices of the Royal Commission on the Status of Women in Canada. Lambert asked 7,500 male and female children of various ages and places of residence to answer a long questionnaire on attitudes towards a wide variety of childhood and adult behaviours. His purpose was to discover whether children saw these behaviours as differentially characteristic of, and appropriate to, the two sexes. The questions asked dealt with four main areas: general behaviour, jobs, the feminine role, and authority.

In respect to "behaviour", respondents were asked to indicate which things boys and girls the respondent's age should or should not do: these included such behaviours as crying when hurt, doing dishes, playing softball, swearing, and making their own bed. As regards jobs, respondents were to indicate how suitable boys and girls would be for specified jobs when they grew up: the jobs included medical doctor, bus driver, librarian, clerk in store, and Prime Minister of Canada. Respondents were then asked how much they agreed with a set of statements about the rights and duties of males and females. These included such statements as, "It is more important for a boy to go to university than a girl," "A woman's place is in the home," and "Women should not have authority over men."

Finally, the questions on "authority relations" asked how boys and girls the age of the respondent behaved towards other people in their environment: whether such children had the right to wear what they wanted to school, decide for themselves what they wanted to be when they grew up, and pick their own friends, for example. Lambert also asked about the responsibilities of boys and girls of that age: whether they should do what their parents said, help parents with household chores, and try hard to please the teacher, among other things.

A respondent answered each question twice: once in terms of a male's rights and responsibilities, and once in terms of a female's. If the respondent answered very differently for males and females, he was characterized as showing high "sex role differentiation" (SRD). It was found that in all cases but that of authority relations, more male than female respondents displayed a high degree of sex role differentiation. This difference between respondents was greatest in respect to "feminine role": boys and girls clearly differed in how much they thought women ought to be segregated from men, e.g., in household as opposed to work situations; and how much difference there ought to be in the power of males and females in a family. By contrast, the male and female respondents differed least in their perceptions of appropriate male and female work, although as before male respondents saw a greater difference between the sexes than did females.

It is interesting to note that there was no systematic variation in male-female response differences according to the age of respondents. We cannot conclude that the inclination to segregate male and female behaviours increases or decreases with age. Put another way, it appears that sex role differentiation is well and stably established by the age of nine, the earliest age in Lambert's sample. However, there were noticeable differences in the response patterns of Anglophones and Francophones. The differences in SRD between male and female respondents were more marked for Francophones in most cases, chiefly because a smaller proportion of Francophone females than Anglophone females were given to a high degree of sex role differentiation. Lambert gives no explanation of the Francophone female's unwillingness to sex-type roles; and the observation runs contrary to our expectations. One typically assumes the French Canadian culture to be "traditional" in many of its values, and "traditional" as opposed to "modern" values generally support high SRD and sex-typing.

Lambert found that respondents answered each of these sets of questions differently from the way they answered each other set; there was little intercorrelation in responses to the four sets of SRD questions described above. He concluded that sex role differentiation is a multi-dimensional phenomenon. Since this is so, we shall confine ourselves to examining data relevant to the sex-typing of jobs, which is most germane to a study of social mobility. Lambert found that respondents sex-typed jobs quite a lot, and that males did so more than females. This finding would lend some support to a theory that males impose SRD upon females by discrimination and other means.

Lambert carried out little systematic analysis of the characteristics of respondents who did and did not sex-type jobs, but two interesting relationships did emerge. First, children who had a lot of interaction with the opposite sex were more likely than those with little interaction to sex-type jobs highly. It is certainly not clear which caused the other, or through what process; the finding is noted because it is strong, interesting, and there. This finding suggests that female children may internalize sex role norms through interaction with male children. Second, respondents who perceived a great difference in the power held by their mother and father were more likely to sex-type jobs than were respondents who viewed their parents as equals. This finding makes more intuitive sense than the preceding one, for it suggests that a child's family represents a microcosm of the (imagined) work world. The more a child perceived differentiation of power within the family, the more he imagined it exists and is proper in the work world.

Career Indecision

We have learned thus far only that male children are more likely to believe job differences are appropriate than are female children, and that some patterns of family and peer interaction influence general levels of sex role differentiation with respect to jobs. Breton's data on educational aspirations (1972) shed a somewhat different light on male and female differences. Breton asked high school students to identify their career plans, and then analysed the characteristics of respondents who had no career plans or goals. Not surprisingly in view of differential opportunities discussed earlier in this chapter and in the next, he found that children of lower intelligence (IQ), lower socio-economic status (SES), and of French ancestry were more likely than other students to have no career goals at the time of the interview.

More interesting for our present discussion, at each level of IQ and SES, and for each type of ancestry, girls were more likely than boys to be without a career goal. (Career indecision among boys was inferred from a failure to specify *which kind of job* would be sought in adulthood; among girls, it was inferred from a failure to state *whether* a job would be sought outside the home in adulthood.) When Breton examined the effect of each of these three variables while controlling for the other two, he found that ancestry made much more difference, and father's occupation much less difference, to girls' than to boys' career indecision. That is, other things being equal, a French Canadian girl was by reason of her ancestry less decided on a career than was a French Canadian boy, compared in each case with English Canadian children. Second, a lower class boy was much less decided on a career than was a lower class girl, other things being equal, and compared in each case with higher class children. It appears that linguistic (or ethnic) staus weighs more heavily on a girl than on a boy, while social class does the opposite. This we would suppose is because parents in different ethnic and social class groupings provide different amounts of support for sons' and daughters' career aspirations.

Yet if different parental aspirations were the explanation of the effect of such sex differences as were observed above, sex differences in career indecision would disappear when we controlled for parental aspirations, or compared children with similar parental support; but the results are ambiguous here. Controlling for parental aspirations does weaken some of the male–female differences in career indecision observed above. Specifically, boys and girls having the same IQ level and parents with high aspirations differ little in their amount of career indecision. However, high parental aspirations do not erase the male–female difference in career indecision for children of the same SES or language. Moreover, the career indecision of females whose parents have low aspiration is much more affected by SES and language than is the career indecision of boys with the same level of parental aspiration.

Thus it would be unreasonable to infer that male–female differences in career indecision among children of the same social class or language group are a simple product of different parental aspirations for sons and daughters. Indeed, the data show that boys and girls respond differently to similar parental aspirations. An increase in parental aspiration reduces career indecision more for high IQ girls than high IQ boys; more for French girls than for French boys (and more for English boys than for English girls); and more for high SES boys than for high SES girls. Parental aspirations interact with sex and social situation in a way that is difficult to interpret at this point.

A more easily interpreted finding of Breton is that the gainful employment of a mother reduces the career indecision of girls. This effect is almost uniformly great across various socio-economic statuses and both linguistic groups. And although mother's employment has little effect on the career indecision of girls whose IQ's are high, girls of medium and low IQ show a uniformly high level of response. These data suggest that girls with a role model of "working women"—namely a gainfully employed mother—can more readily make career decisions than girls without such a role model.

In Table 6.14, we examine the effects on career indecision of some attitudinal variables that are seen in the next chapter to predict (male) aspirations for a high status job. Typically, male students who aspire to high status prefer interesting work to a high income, see their school activities as relevant to their future status, consider their marks in school satisfactory, intend to continue their education beyond high school, and have a great ambition to suceed. Yet females who hold the same attitudes are, in every case, more undecided about their career goals than are males. Different factors seem to enter into male and female aspirations and decisions on career goals; such attitudinal factors as those just mentioned are much less significant for females than for males. Yet neither are they insignificant; each has a greater impact on girls' career decision making than does mother's gainful employment, for example.

To summarize to this point, sex role differentiation in general and sex-typing of jobs in particular develop early in life, and boys quickly come to differentiate jobs by sex more than girls do. When we consider the situational and attitudinal factors that most affect boys' career planning, we find girls with the same situational or attitudinal characteristic to be less decided on a career goal. What girls see in their homes—for example, a working mother or a mother with power equal to that of a father—influence both the sex-typing and role modelling of career-related aspirations and behaviours. It may or may not be accidental that the same proportion of girls in Lambert's study (roughly one-third) show high SRD in respect to jobs as show career indecision in Breton's study. One is led to wonder whether these are the "same" girls, and whether high SRD of jobs produces career indecision among girls.

At this point we know only that female high school students are more uncertain than their male counterparts with similar social and

Table 6.14

Percentage without a career goal, by attitudes toward work and achievement

	Boys	Girls
A. Evaluation of interesting work vs high income in a job		
Interesting work	28.9	33.7
About the same	35.2	38.2
High income	40.7	41.3
B. Relevance of school activities to future status		
High	25.5	30.1
Medium	33.9	34.5
Low	42.5	50.6
C. Marks considered satisfactory by student		
Above average	26.4	32.6
Average	33.1	34.1
Below average	41.4	42.8
D. Educational plans		
Continue beyond high school	28.2	32.8
Finish high school only	34.9	34.4
Leave before finishing high school	45.5	42.2
D. Ambition to succeed		
High	35.0	41.0
Medium	32.0	35.0
Low	31.0	32.0

Source: Breton (1972: Table I-2.8)

psychological characteristics.[13] This uncertainty, especially if it persists during a career in the work world, may contribute to an explanation of women's lower status and mobility in the work world; low status and immobility in turn feed this sense of uncertainty. However, alternative and equally (or more) plausible explanations exist and we shall examine them below.

The Mobility of Women, Concluded

Women, like any traditionally oppressed group, show career indecision. Their social environment has been historically hostile to female career-making, and futures are planned on true or false perceptions of the past. We know that high school girls are indecisive about their career goals; we do not have data to tell us whether this indecisiveness persists into adulthood. Yet some uncertainty must remain because there exist stereotyping, bias against allowing women into many positions, slow mobility in some careers, and poor and inequitable pay in others. If women sense they can little predict how prospective employers (or husbands) will respond to their career plans, they may well become indecisive, harming their own careers in a way similar to the French Canadians who do not value formal education or good grades. High motivation and proper training are always necessary for career mobility, especially where stereotyping and discrimination must be overcome.

Yet the current position of women in Canada cannot be blamed on the failings of Canadian females alone, for their fears and perceptions of opportunity reflect a social reality. Asked about obstacles to the career development of women in eight chartered banks, management cited three main problems (Bossen:1971b). One obstacle was said to reside in the women themselves: a lack of career mindedness, and an unwillingness to assume responsibilities outside the family, for example. Another was attributed to the banking community: women are assumed to be opposed to geographic transfers, for family reasons, and this aside, there is some opposition to female bankers among bank employees. Third, customer prejudice and tradition in the community create an obstacle to be contended with, as do domestic responsibilities restricting the active involvement of female bankers in community affairs, and mobility of the spouse, which may uproot the female banker at undesirable moments.

What bankers called "obstacles" were called "tradition" and "customer preference" by the department store managers referred to in an earlier section. Other issues raised by bankers remind us of the French Canadian workers' frank statement that men do not like to work under women: this may be part of the opposition to female managers in the "banking community" as in industrial labour. Most explanations, however, return to the theme that women should stay at home, if possible; and that women will, if forced to choose between work and family responsibilities (e.g., the career of a spouse), choose family. This belief receives some support from the data in Table 6.15 showing the differential labour force participation of women with and without children, controlling for the woman's education and spouse's income. Participation declines with the birth and upbringing of young children and with the increase in spouse's income (or his career mobility), regardless of a wife's level of education.

There is every evidence in our society that large organizations follow their own logic and sell the public what they want to, convincing us of the desirability of their product or service after they have committed themselves to providing it (Galbraith, 1967). One must therefore view with chagrined disbelief the assertion that tradition or customer preference limits organizational ability to promote women.

The idea that women favour a high degree of sex role differentiation with respect to jobs or careers is also largely fallacious. Where jobs are concerned, little girls display less sex role differentiation than little boys; further, while high school girls are less decided on careers than

Table 6.15

Labour force participation rates of married women*, by schooling and family type, by income of husband

Education of wife and family type	Income of husband					Total
	Under $3,000	3,000-4,999	5,000-6,999	7,000-9,999	10,000 & over	
Total	26.0	24.9	20.2	14.2	9.4	22.4
One or more children under 6						
elementary or less	12.0	9.7	6.2	5.2	6.2	9.7
high school	19.0	15.3	10.0	5.2	4.5	12.8
university	36.2	24.5	15.7	8.8	6.6	15.3
Some children, none under 6						
elementary or less	23.5	21.8	17.1	12.4	10.6	20.8
high school	38.6	36.4	28.7	18.1	9.7	29.8
university	56.1	53.7	44.2	29.0	11.4	33.3
No children						
elementary or less	28.1	27.0	21.3	14.2	15.6	26.1
high school	46.9	49.9	42.4	27.9	14.1	44.0
university	60.2	63.0	57.3	40.6	20.5	51.4

*In husband-wife families, living in urban and rural non-farm areas, husband in labour force
Source: Women's Bureau, Department of Labour (1966: Table 8)

boys of the same age, only a minority of girls (one-third) are actually undecided. It is female exposure to the biases of the real world, including their husbands', that creates female indecision and hinders careers despite decisiveness. Of the three "groups" we have examined in this chapter—Francophones, immigrants, and women—surely women are the most occupationally disadvantaged and probably the least mobile.

Summary

There is good evidence that French Canadians and women are stereotyped in Canadian society, and this stereotyping may contribute to the limiting of mobility in various ways. In all cases, these "larger units" of mobility suffer from discrimination in the occupational world and experience mobility that is slower than the mobility enjoyed by Anglophones, native-born people, and males respectively. Yet the prospects for immigrants and French Canadians are not as bad today as one or two decades ago, and they seem to be steadily improving; it remains to be seen whether the position of women will likewise improve.

Where evidence has been available, we have been forced to acknowledge that Francophones and women contribute to the restriction of their own mobility. Francophones, in believing that they are discriminated against, have been reluctant to attain the educational credentials that are necessary for mobility in our society. Females are more indecisive about their careers than males, and such a lack of planning and self-confidence may strengthen the traditional stereotypes, allowing men to deny women equal opportunity. There is least evidence that immigrants are immobile for reasons other than discrimination, or that they are content to accept low status in Canadian society.

Wherever stereotyping and discrimination occur, they are rationalized by those who enjoy the advantage: this is clearest in the case of women's mobility, for sex role differentiation pervades all sectors of Canadian society and is rationalized in a great variety of polite ways. More often than not, tradition is invoked to justify continuing injustice, as though tradition were necessarily to be valued. It is precisely where Francophones, immigrants and women are concerned that traditional norms and expectations most need a radical reformulation. The Royal Commissions on Bilingualism and Biculturalism and the Status of Women in Canada have provided a start in that direction.

The next chapter will continue the discussion of education, and its importance for mobility, hinted at in this chapter. We shall close with a consideration of successfulness and the ways people in contemporary society handle success as well as failure.

Chapter 6 Notes

[1] This amounted to an acknowledgement that in Canada as a whole the ability to speak English is more valuable than the ability to speak French.

[2] To "control for" variable A in considering the relationship between variables B and C, the investigators split variable A (e.g., education level) into n categories, and looked at how variables B and C (e.g., income and ethnicity) were associated within each of the n categories of variable A.

[3] It may also indicate a similarity of French Canadians to lower class Americans studied by Mizruchi (1964). Those studied were aware of the instrumental value of education for social mobility but so undervalued education as an end in itself that they did not acquire it, and so lessened their chances for advancement.

[4] Taylor may have examined entrepreneurs primarily active in declining industries; if so, the entrepreneurial conservatism he describes would have had an economic rather than cultural basis. As Taylor does not describe his sample at any length, we cannot judge whether this is the source of our problem with Taylor's findings. Yet we do fail to find confirmation of his cultural explanation in other research of a systematic kind.

[5] They may also have relatives or friends in such parts of the United States as New England, as a result of earlier migrations. These "connections" might assist the newcomers to the United States in finding a job, a place to live, and so on.

[6] Of course, the practice of discrimination against French Canadians may explain why so few French Canadians troubled to prepare themselves for careers in business.

[7] The studies suggesting an absence of discrimination are primarily recent ones, and it may be the case that discrimination has only recently diminished or disappeared, perhaps as a result of wider public interest in the matter, and separatist threats in Quebec.

[8] The conclusions are uncertain because they infer a longitudinal process (i.e. mobility) from cross-sectional data. However, immigrants entering Canada at different times after the Second World War may not have been identical to one another in all respects but their date of immigration; for example, their average entrance status may have varied significantly. Data displayed shortly will provide more direct evidence of upward mobility, supporting what is at present inconclusive for methodological reasons.

[9] The clustering of members of particular ethnic minorities in certain occupational situses has been said by Wiley to result from the ethnic "mobility trap". The retention of ethnic identity and contacts may prove useful in achieving mobility *within* these situses, but may also restrict the number and diversity of situses open to an individual and divert efforts from success-seeking in the dominant social structures. For a review of the Canadian literature analyzing ethnic mobility from the so-called "network perspective" akin to Wiley's, see Howard and Wayne (1975).

[10] These groups suggest the great importance of cultural predisposition to higher education and success, and of communal organization for group advancement.

[11] There is an alternative explanation for the relatively poor showing of native Canadians: many of the best educated and most talented of these have migrated to the United States. This substantial emigration has made the upward mobility of native Canadians *within* Canada appear slight, and has left vacancies into which the most capable immigrants may move. Immigrants to Canada are, therefore, the final beneficiaries of a booming U.S. job market.

[12] Calculating this excess of western over eastern female structural mobility as

(49.1/28.8)/(66.9/54.0), we conclude that western females employed in department store management are experiencing 38% more structural mobility than eastern females.

13 This is to some degree produced by the schools themselves. Richer and Breton (1968) showed that a large sample of secondary school principals, teachers and counsellors across Canada believed schooling ought to be differentiated by sex. While most felt that, "It is as important for girls to have a high school education as it is for boys," only one-half thought, "Boys and girls should follow the same high school curriculum."

7
ASPIRATIONS REALIZED AND UNREALIZED

∽

So here I am, in the middle way, having had twenty years -
Twenty years largely wasted, the years of l'entre deux guerres -
Trying to learn to use words, and every attempt
Is a wholly new start, and a different kind of failure
Because one has learnt to get the better of words
For the thing one no longer has to say, or the way in which
One is no longer disposed to say it.

T.S. Eliot, *East Coker*

Feeling successful results from a particular combination of aspirations and performance. When our aspirations for power resources are high, we must achieve great power to feel satisfied and subjectively success-ful. But the attainment of such power requires aspiration (or motiva-tion) to succeed as well as opportunity. The preceding chapters have discussed the opportunities or "structure of mobility" under the assumption that people in modern industrial societies have similar aspirations. The present chapter will examine how aspirations vary in Canadian society, the origin of these aspirations, and the problem of fitting aspiration to opportunity.

Aspirations of High School Boys

A study of Canadian high school students was initiated by Breton (1972) in the mid-1960s and the discussion of aspirations in this section will be based largely on that work. Clearly, some part of occupational aspi-ration develops long before entry into the job market, although Harvey (1972:304) has indicated that a majority of university students decide on a *particular* job field during undergraduate or graduate university education, not before. The decision to pursue a white collar or blue collar occupation is made long before this, for students are forced to choose a particular stream of post-elementary education that will lead them to either a white collar or blue collar job, and this choice is made around age 13 or 14. While there is some switching of educational streams in high school and even after high school, switching is relati-vely rare.

Of high school boys asked to name their occupational preference in 1965, two-thirds preferred a managerial or professional (white collar) occupation,[1] one-fifth preferred a skilled (or upper blue collar) job, and about one-eighth wanted an unskilled (lower blue collar) or farming occupation. The preference for "high occupational status" (i.e., a white collar occupation) was more often voiced by fourth year than by first year high school boys, roughly 61% and 75% respectively preferring this occupational status. High school boys apparently become more wedded to the idea of high status occupations the longer they stay in secondary school; and those boys who intend to enter a lower status (skilled or unskilled) blue collar occupation usually drop out of high school after a few years.

Determinants of Occupational Choice

The role of the school in establishing an occupational preference has been widely discussed in the last decade, for it has been shown that occupational status and intergenerational mobility in North America are largely dependent on educational attainment (Blau and Duncan, 1967). Father's social class or ethnic origin has little influence on occupational attainment for males who have attained the same level of education. Stated otherwise, mobility is more dependent upon achieved than ascribed status in North America, and educational attainment is a decisive influence on the extent of intergenerational mobility. Since education is crucial, whatever influences student aspirations will be of major importance in explaining the total amount of mobility in a society. Chart 7.1 sketches out some of the student attitudes and behaviours in a school context that appear to influence occupational aspiration. These relationships are ultimately derived from the analysis provided by Breton (1972), although a particular causal sequence has been superimposed that is partly hypothetical. This sequence is largely untested at this time but it is plausible, and I have used it to simplify the discussion.

The likelihood that a high school boy will prefer a white collar occupation is influenced by all of the variables in Chart 7.1. Let us suppose that a high school boy brings three kinds of beliefs to secondary school. These are based on home (family) experience and are modified by experiences in school. The first belief is that a boy has control over his own future: this belief is indicated by a strongly negative response to the assertions, "Making plans only makes a person unhappy because plans hardly ever work out anyway," "When a man is born, the success he's going to have is already in the cards, so he might as well accept it and not fight against it," and "Good luck is more important than hard work for success." Students who believe they control their own future tend to prefer white collar occupations, as

Chart 7.1

Aspiration to a white collar occupation, by high school boys in a school context: Canada, 1965

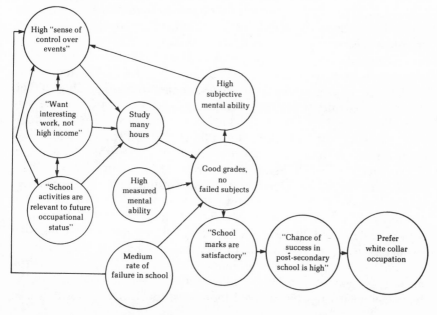

Source: Breton (1972: Chapter III-2), data rearranged

contrasted with students who feel they are dependent upon luck. Second, students vary in the type of work they want to do: some prefer "interesting work" while others prefer a job with a high income. Those who prefer interesting work indicate a preference for a white collar occupation.

Finally, students vary in the future importance they attach to their present school work, in responses to the questions, "What do you think the chances are that the things you are learning now will be useful in one way or another in your future career?" and "How important do you think your grades or marks will be in getting the kind of job you want?" Those who believe their school work will influence their future status tend to prefer white collar jobs, while students who think their present work is irrelevant prefer white collar jobs less often.

Students bring from home such beliefs about their own competence (or control over events), the desirability of "interesting work", and the relevance of school performance to success after the completion of schooling. Those who subscribe to these beliefs will probably work harder, i.e., study more hours per night, than students who do not hold these beliefs. Since success in secondary school depends on hard work, "brains" and the level of competition for high marks in the school, students who study many hours, have a high IQ and attend a school where few students *also* work very hard (and are very bright) will get better grades than students with the opposite characteristics. It follows logically that students who believe in their own competence will have the most success in secondary school.

The level of failure in a school also acts to encourage or discourage students, whatever their own level of performance. In a school where the level of failures is high, even those students who are passing all their courses will aspire to white collar occupations less often, because they feel less secure in an academic setting than those students in schools with a lower failure rate. Yet students who attend schools with a low failure rate are less encouraged to go on to P.S.S. than students in schools with a slightly higher failure rate. Students in a school where almost no one fails receive too little sense of their own ability relative to other students. Indeed, wherever there is too little variation in the likelihood of failing, i.e., where the failure rate is very high or very low, a student develops little knowledge of his relative merit and likelihood of success in future competition for grades or jobs. If the likelihood of failure varies little from one student to another, a student receives little encouragement to continue; and where the failure rate is high, he becomes positively discouraged by the prospect of prolonged risk of failure.

Achieving good grades will lead a student both to perceive his mental abilities (IQ) to be high and to judge that his school grades are satisfactory. These will in turn increase the student's sense of control over events relevant to his future, thus encouraging further hard work; and will lead him to judge that his chances of success in a post-secondary school are high. If he believed his school performance was important in determining future occupational status and if he valued "interesting work" over income, this student would have his preference for a white collar occupation reinforced (if not formed) by the achievement of satisfactory grades.

School experience only helps to specify and reinforce general attitudes about oneself and the future which have been learned at home. We should therefore examine the kinds of variables measured by Breton that refer to pre-school or extra-school influences on the preference for a white collar occupation. These variables and their (partly) hypothetical interrelationships are displayed in Chart 7.2.

The main family influences upon occupational aspirations, which are linked to the eventual influence of school experience, include the development of a sense of competence, generally high aspirations, and a belief that many opportunities for advancement are available. The focal variable in developing childhood aspirations is the social class—

Chart 7.2

Aspiration to a white collar occupation, by high school boys in a home context: Canada, 1965

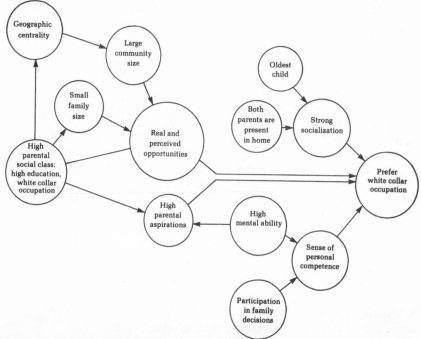

Source: Breton (1972: Chapter III-2), data rearranged

the occupational status and educational attainment—of a child's parents. Parents with white collar occupations and high (e.g., post-secondary) educational training will more often than other parents hold high aspirations for their children. They will also be more likely to believe in the existence of many opportunities for advancement, as is reasonable for people with high educational attainment. But these parents will not only believe in such opportunities and transmit this belief to their children: they will also *make* opportunities for their children.

Higher class parents "make opportunities" for their children in various ways, although only a few of these are measured in the Breton study. By having smaller families, higher class families increase the likelihood of "social capillarity", which we discussed in Chapter One. By settling in the urban centres of Canada, and especially urban centres in central Canada—Ontario and Quebec—parents increase the number and variety of jobs available to themselves and their children, and the number and variety of schools that will train their children for desirable jobs.

High parental aspirations and the perception of many opportunities are intensified by "strong" socialization. First-born or only children are known to have greater psychological needs for achievement and are different in other respects from later-born children (Schachter, 1959). Since higher class families are generally smaller than lower class families, a larger proportion of higher class children will have strong desires for achievement. Second, the presence of both parents in the home will intensify the inculcation of parental values and beliefs, whatever they may be. Thus the strength with which values about the future and occupational aspirations are learned will depend to some degree on birth order and parental presence. In the Breton study both of these variables predict a preference for white collar occupations.

A child's sense of personal competence is no doubt dependent on both his innate (mental) abilities and the dynamics of his family life. Where a child is encouraged to participate in family decision-making, he will develop a stronger sense of personal competence, (and a greater ability to make sensible decisions about his own future), than a child who is denied such experience.

The child's actual mental ability is likely to have some influence on a parent's aspirations for the child: the higher his IQ, the more likely it is that a parent will encourage the child to high educational and occupational attainment. Moreover high IQ greatly increases a child's preference for a white collar occupation, probably by increasing the child's perception of personal competence. Yet it is interesting to note that of students with a low IQ, a much higher proportion born into white collar families aspire to a white collar occupation than do those born into an unskilled blue collar family (63.3% to 45.7%, respectively). Measured mental ability has an impact upon a student's aspirations, but the absence of high ability does not remove the impact of parental class (and aspiration) upon a student's aspiration.

There has been much discussion of whether the IQ test is a valid measure of "high mental ability", especially in view of evidence that the test appears to favour particular racial, ethnic and socio-economic groups. Whatever the IQ test really measures, it appears to predict occupational preference very strongly. If the IQ test is "culturally biased" and reflects little more than parental social class, this only adds to the present evidence that social class is the major direct and indirect determinant of occupational aspiration among high school boys.

Schooling tends to reinforce and specify the aspirations a child brings from home. Some additional school influences are identified in Chart 7.3 which shows how general propensities to a high status occupation may get specified in a secondary school.

The selection of a particular occupation begins with exposure to, encouragement of, and role modelling upon significant others. A

Chart 7.3

Aspiration to a white collar occupation, by high school boys in a school context: Canada, 1965

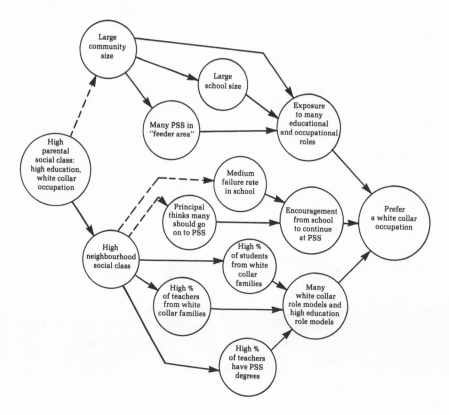

Source: Breton (1972: Chapter III-3), data rearranged

student who comes to prefer a white collar occupation will typically know what kinds of jobs (and educational training) are available: he will have been encouraged to follow his educational and occupational preferences, and will have observed white collar people frequently and perhaps intimately.

The opportunity to observe white collar roles may require the presence of white collar people in the student's school as much as white collar parents at home. Thus the presence of a high percentage of school peers and teachers from white collar families will help to strengthen the desire of a student to become a white collar adult, whatever his class of origin. This kind of "contextual" influence on aspiration (and quality of education) was discussed by Coleman et al. (1966) in his analysis of American schools; it led to the idea of racial and class intermixture of students by school busing. The percentage of teachers who hold a post-secondary school (hereafter, P.S.S.) degree is probably correlated with the percentage of teachers from white collar families. Independently of this, education in a school a high percentage of whose teachers have P.S.S. degrees increases a student's exposure to role models of high educational attainment, and this will lead indirectly into a preference for higher occupational attainment.

The exposure of a student to many occupational and educational roles is dependent upon school size, the number of P.S.S. in the vicinity of the secondary school attended, and community size. The larger the school size, the greater is the variety of curricula and courses offered and thus the greater is the opportunity and need to consider a wide variety of occupational alternatives. The larger the number of P.S.S. in the feeder area of the secondary school, the greater is the exposure to a wide variety of post-secondary training programs. The larger the community size, the greater is the division of labour in the community and the wider the variety of jobs available nearby.

Encouragement received from the secondary school to continue education in a P.S.S. is measured by only two variables in Chart 7.3: the Principal's belief about the proportion of students who should go on to P.S.S., and the level of failure in the school. The Principal's perception of the student body probably influences and is influenced by the prevailing failure rate. In those schools where the Principal feels a high proportion of students should go on to P.S.S., a higher proportion of students intends to enter white collar occupations. The Principal's belief may reflect or determine his teachers' behaviour, especially the grades and guidance counselling teachers give to encourage or discourage P.S.S. education and white collar aspiration among students.

The extent of role modelling on white collar life by students and teachers varies with the social class of the neighbourhood. A student living in a neighbourhood of predominantly white collar families will have a higher proportion of white collar peers and teachers than one living in a working class neighbourhood. Most Canadian (urban) populations are segregated by social class (as well as by ethnic group), and teachers from white collar backgrounds typically prefer to teach in middle class schools. The kind of neighbourhood a student lives in will be determined in large part by his father's socio-economic status; hence, indirectly as well as directly, father's class will determine the white collar role modelling and encouragement his child receives. The predominant social class of a neighbourhood may also determine the amount of encouragement a neighbourhood school gives its students to continue at P.S.S. Principals and teachers are at least somewhat responsive to the aspirations of the parents of children they teach. We noted earlier that parental social class also influences the community size in which a child lives, and thus indirectly influences his exposure to many educational and occupational roles.

Determinants of Educational Choice

Obviously, parental social class has a very important direct and indirect influence on the occupational aspirations of high school boys, within both the home and the school contexts. If aspirations were all that counted in the attainment of occupational status, the children of white collar parents would be greatly overrepresented in white collar occupations. They are indeed overrepresented, but not only because of differential class-based aspirations. After secondary education, the usual next step in attaining white collar status is attendance at a post-secondary educational institution. Surveys have shown that the children of high status parents were overrepresented in P.S.S. three years after the Breton survey of educational and occupational intentions (Dominion Bureau of Statistics, 1970). A much higher proportion of white collar children went on to P.S.S. than had told Breton (three years earlier) they intended to go, while a much smaller proportion of medium status children (i.e., children of skilled blue collar workers) went on to P.S.S. than had intended to go. The planned and actual attendance of low status children were roughly equal, suggesting that lower class children had never entertained impractically high ambitions while children of skilled workers had.

Table 7.1 shows the high proportion of P.S.S. students in 1968–69 who came from families in which the father was self-employed or a white collar worker. Because of the great overrepresentation of middle and upper class children in post-secondary schools, and the greater proportion of these attending P.S.S. than had indicated an intention to do so in the Breton study, we are led to suppose that income is the main determinant of P.S.S. attendance. A sufficiently high parental income allows students who wish it to attend P.S.S. (and then attain a white collar job), while a lower parental income makes aspiration to P.S.S. education and a white collar job impracticable.

In a study of Ontario university graduates, Harvey (1972) has shown that children of high status fathers are primarily dependent on parents and relatives for financial support during university studies. Children of lower status fathers are primarily dependent upon employment earnings, bursaries, and loans. Thus lower class children must expend greater effort to complete a university degree than higher class children; they must do the same academic work and also earn enough money to support themselves. It may be this added difficulty that more often prevents lower class children from realizing their aspirations than higher class children with the same aspirations. It seems likely that lower class children who graduate from university have *greater* aspiration and/or talent than higher class children who graduate in the same program with similar grades.

Not only does parental income influence the likelihood that a student will follow his aspirations to P.S.S.; it also influences the likeli-

Table 7.1

*Occupational status of fathers of post-secondary school (P.S.S.)
students: Canada, 1968–69 (per cent)*

Employment status	%	Occupational category	%
Self-employed	23.4	Professional	6.5
Works for employer	59.5	Business	15.4
Keeps home	0.2	Executive, manager	10.5
Retired	5.1	Professional, technical	9.3
Unable to work	1.8	Administrative, supervisor	11.0
Parent deceased	9.0	Clerical, secretarial, sales	6.3
No response	1.0	Service worker	5.6
		Process, assembling, machining	5.9
Total	100.0	Labouring	9.2
		Farm	8.8
N =	387,242	Other	5.4
		No response	6.3
		Total	100.2
		N =	387,242

Source: Dominion Bureau of Statistics (1970: Tables 22, 23), data recomputed

hood that a student will enter a P.S.S. program that leads to white collar
status. Canadian P.S.S. students in 1968–69 were more likely to be
college undergraduates or postgraduate students if their parent's
income was high than if it was low. As parental income declined, the
likelihood increased that a P.S.S. student was engaged in advanced
vocational training ("Other") not typically leading into a white collar
occupation. The likelihood that a student was enrolled in a nursing or

Table 7.2

*Most important source of financial support for university studies,
Ontario university graduates (1960, 1964, 1968), by father's
occupational status (per cent)*

Source of financial support	Father's occupational status	
	Low	High
Parents, relatives	25.1	52.8
Spouse	2.3	1.4
Part-time and/or summer work	42.5	31.6
Full-time work	9.5	2.3
Grants, bursaries, etc.	7.0	4.4
Loans	8.9	3.7
Savings	3.2	2.3
Total =	98.5	98.5
N =	2246	1669

Source: Harvey (1972: Table 5.26)

Table 7.3

Program of post-secondary studies, Canada 1968–69, by father's educational attainment: males only (per cent)

Program of study	Father's educational attainment				
	2 or more univ. degrees	1 univ. degree	H.S. grad.	Some H.S.	Some elementary school
University post-graduate	12.7	12.2	11.2	8.3	7.0
University under-graduate	78.2	76.8	69.5	67.3	57.9
Nursing	0.0	0.0	0.0	0.1	0.2
Teacher training	0.7	1.0	1.9	2.4	3.8
Other	8.3	10.1	17.5	21.9	31.1
Total	99.9	100.1	100.0	100.0	100.0
N =	14664	20668	32834	52360	55042

Source: Dominion Bureau of Statistics (1970: Table 24), data recomputed

teacher training course also increased. Nursing and public school teaching are two semi-professional occupations that are most readily achieved by lower income children aspiring to white collar status.

But income is not the prime determinant of which course is taken in P.S.S. The education attained by a student's father appears in Table 7.3 to exert a much greater influence than parental income. This suggests that although student aspirations cannot be *easily* realized if there is insufficient family income, they can be realized if the aspiration is sufficiently strong. The high educational attainment of a student's father may strengthen that aspiration much more than a high parental income, which merely makes the aspiration feasible.

A Digression on the Inheritance of Advantage

We noted in Chapter Two that in most industrial societies, and even more certainly in pre-industrial societies, a majority of people inherit or remain in their father's social class. For example, only about 30% of sons cross the dividing line between manual (blue collar) and non-manual (white collar) work in our society; the remaining 70% don the same coloured collar as their fathers. This majority experience is sometimes called *status ascription* and this book has argued, like others, that status ascription decreases with industrialization. In industrial societies a new and typically higher social status can be achieved through educational achievement; ascribed social statuses—which include sex, race, birthplace or ethnicity as well as social class of origin—are expected to count for less in the attainment of success than talent and ambition.

Even so, members of the Canadian economic and other élites tend to be drawn in disproportionate numbers from among sons of upper class persons, indicating that ascribed status or inherited advantage continues to have importance in an industrial society. Porter (1965) has provided the data in Table 7.4 to illustrate this point; and a recently published study by Clement (1975) has shown that the inheritance of élite status remains important in Canadian society. Not only élite positions, but also others of the most highly paid and respected occupations, are filled in disproportionate numbers by the sons of highly educated and well paid fathers, as we have seen in preceding sections of this chapter. Thus, studies of recruitment into the élite, and studies of more general occupational mobility, show the same result: namely, that sons of fathers with high education and high income are at an advantage in the "competition" (if we can still consider it a genuine competition) for power resources.

Table 7.4

Class origins of 611 Canadian-born members of the economic élite

Class Indicator*	No.	Cumulative No.	%	% of top 100†
Upper				
Father in economic élite	135	135	22.0	30.3
Father in other élite groups	13	148	24.0	37.0
Wife from élite family	41	189	31.0	46.6
Father in substantial business	42	231	37.8	54.5
Middle or higher				
Attended private school	75	306	50.0	67.0
Middle				
Father in middle class occupation and/or attended university	197	503	82.0	85.2
Possibly lower than middle class	108	611	100	100

*Some persons could of course be put into more than one category.
†The percentages in this column are of the 88 Canadian-born who have been classed in the top 100.
Source: Porter (1965: Table XXVIII)

However, industrial nations vary somewhat in the degree to which status is inherited, and this variation indicates the relative openness of these societies. Increased attention has been given recently to studying Canada in comparison with the United States in particular and other industrial nations in general, in hopes of discovering what is basic or unique to Canadian society and culture. Turrittin (1974) warned us against too readily accepting the Lipset and Bend esis of uniform social mobility in industrial societies.

Clearly differences in history of industrialism, econom structure, role of educational institutions, and the nature of the class structure can be shown to affect mobility in important ways and these factors deserve as much attention as the search for similarities among industrial societies. Canada is a case in point, for while highly industrialized, it has several unique features which must affect social mobility. These include an economy heavily dependent on primary production and which is largely foreign-owned or controlled, where secondary manufacturing is done by branch-plants so that many firms compete for a small market with consequent small production runs and little incentive for research and development activity, where there has been a net export of capital, where until recently educational opportunity was limited, where great geographical distances separating populations have sustained important regional sub-societies (Quebec being a special case, a regional sub-society based on language and cultural uniqueness), where immigration continues to be an important source of labour supply, and where, until recently, there was heavy outmigration of population to the United States (Turrittin, 1974: 2, 3).

Turrittin's survey of intergenerational mobility in Ontario is somewhat inconclusive in demonstrating this Canadian uniqueness, for it leads to different conclusions depending on the way the same data are analyzed. "The standard outflow percentages and the summary measures of mobility for Ontario show a present pattern of mobility almost identical to the U.S. pattern in 1962 . . . The path analysis data, however, do seem consistent with the hypothesis of Lipset (1963) of a stronger élite tradition of Canada compared to the U.S." (*ibid.*: 28). While taking pains to point out the limitations of path analysis, Turrittin is nonetheless led by further analysis to accept the conclusion suggested by path analysis—namely that industrial Canada, as exemplified by Ontario, is less open to upward mobility than the United States.

In brief, the Ontario data indicate that low levels of education and occupational prestige go together, and that high levels of education and occupational prestige are correlated as well; for the U.S. only the latter strong relationship holds. The Ontario findings point to the self-perpetuation of, on the one hand, a small highly educated élite, and of, on the other hand, a large working class not using post-secondary education as a means for upward mobility (*ibid*: 32).

Cuneo and Curtis (1975) address the same problem with data from Canada's two largest cities, Montreal and Toronto. Their samples will

nimum of status ascription in Canada if we can
at status ascription is least where industrial
. These authors, like Turrittin, compare their
Blau and Duncan (1967) and are led to "reject
a is different from the U.S. in the direction of
(or degree of) social ascription" (Cuneo and
note later that "these comparisons also reveal
...ntal background variables (father's education and occupation) have about the same or greater influence on the children's generation in the United States as in Canada, while two out of the three direct paths in the children's generation itself indicate that respondent's education and/or first job have stronger influences on occupational outcomes in Canada than in the United States. These latter patterns might suggest the interpretation that there is greater social ascription in the United States than in Canada" (*ibid.*: 14, 15). However, they acknowledge that this finding may result from the "greater urban concentrations" of the Canadians sampled than those Americans sampled by Blau and Duncan.

It would seem premature to conclude that Canada is more closed, more "mobility deprived" (Porter, 1965), more élitist (Lipset, 1963) or more inclined to social ascription than the United States. The evidence shows that this is not so in the most developed regions of Canada (cf. Cuneo and Curtis); nor is ascription of statuses in Ontario as great among the youngest members of the work force as among the oldest (Turrittin, 1974: Table IX). These findings suggest that openness increases, and ascription declines over time, with industrialization, just as Chapter Two has argued.

Yet Cuneo and Curtis point out that what is far more striking than the difference in mobility between Canada and the United States is the similarity in importance of social ascription; in both countries ascription is very marked. In particular such ascriptive influences as father's and mother's education and father's occupation—in short, class of origin—as well as ethnicity, religion and gender have large effects on educational attainment. By influencing education, they influence occupational (and class) destinations of young Canadians. Perhaps there is a definitional problem here. Some might deny that status ascription is great if high educational attainment is the immediate and greatest determinant of occupational attainment: if educational achievement obviates any continuing direct effect of class of birth on class in adulthood. Cuneo and Curtis, however, seem to assert that the importance of ascribed statuses for educational attainment, and hence the great *indirect* importance of inherited advantage (or disability), sufficiently define a high level of social class ascription in Canada and the United States.

What cannot be disputed is that educational attainment is important in Canada for the attainment of high status occupations, and that educational attainment is greatly influenced by social background. The gross effect (i.e., Pearson correlation, r) and direct effect (i.e., path coefficient, p) of education on first job is generally large—greater than .5— and statistically significant for men and women, Francophones and Anglophones, in the Cuneo and Curtis sample. In Turrittin's Ontario sample, the effect of education on present job is likewise large; both r and p are about .65. The proportion of variance in educational attainments statistically accounted for by father's education, mother's education, father's occupation and (parental) family size is about 25% for all but Francophone women in the Cuneo and Curtis sample. The proportion of variance accounted for by father's education and occupation alone in the Turrittin Ontario sample is 30%. These are relatively large effects, by the standards of current survey analysis.

The kind of advantage or disadvantage that is inherited has already been discussed at some length. It includes aspiration level, financial support for continued studies, and social contacts. What we have learned from the surveys by Turrittin and Cuneo and Curtis may be summarized as follows: 1) Canada, like other industrial nations, places an emphasis upon educational attainment for occupational attainment; but 2) educational attainment is very much influenced by social background. It is for this reason that most sons-inherit their father's social positions: they tend to inherit his educational level as well, as Turrittin has indicated. If we are to increase upward social mobility, the problem does not lie in guaranteeing that ascribed characteristics will be unimportant to the employer selecting among people with similar educational attainment. It lies rather in ensuring that people with different social backgrounds will attain a similar educational level, if they have the talent to do so. While acknowledging that stereotyping and discrimination act to limit mobility, as we have done in Chapter Six, we must now recognize that they limit mobility less than low educational attainment.

Occupational Aspiration and Occupational Attainment

Let us suppose that a student has mustered sufficient aspiration in high school to graduate with good grades and proceed on to studies in a university. This level of aspiration will have been somewhat higher among students suffering the disabilities of low parental income, which requires the student to "work his way through college". The student will, upon graduation, seek the job to which he has been aspiring: the white collar status that has motivated him at least since he chose to enter the academic stream in high school.

When we examine how university graduates actually find jobs, we realize that individual aspiration has quite limited importance. In a study of managers in the United States, Granovetter (1974) concluded that personal contacts are the key to finding jobs in management. These personal contacts are often indirect: a friend of mine may hear of a job in another city from a friend of his, and pass my name along. Three, four, five or more people may intervene, all without my knowledge, before I hear about the job or the company personnel manager hears about me. Granovetter's point is that "weak ties" are very important in matching people to job vacancies. (See also Granovetter, 1973). Each of us may be "weakly tied" to thousands of other people, generally without our knowledge. Our number of weak ties determines the number of jobs we will eventually hear about (or that will "hear about" us); it is therefore useful to have many weak ties.

However, we cannot readily influence this except in a negative way. If we avoid making the acquaintance of people outside our immediate circle of family and friends, and if our circle of family and friends is a *clique* (each member of which is strongly tied to each other), we shall receive a lot of social support but little information or other assistance from outside the circle. We should therefore try to make the acquaintance (as opposed to strong friendships) of a large number of people and, further, hope that these acquaintances are making the acquaintance of many others and are not monopolized by us or our friends. In this way, weak ties increase outwardly and (potential) job opportunities increase in number.

The significance of weak ties is intensified by Granovetter's finding that managers received their *best* jobs through such networks of weak ties. The worst jobs were obtained by answering advertisements or using other universalistic methods, such as job placement services. It appears that jobs are widely advertised when recruiters have been unable to find suitable candidates through the search of networks containing weakly tied individuals.

University graduates rarely find their jobs through advertisements or other universalistic agencies, and they find them decreasingly in this manner after they have entered the job market and made business contacts. Once they have established some weak ties in their first job or two, universalistic methods of finding jobs are largely unnecessary. Male and female university graduates get jobs and change jobs in similar ways, although women get fewer new jobs by promotion and make slightly greater use of universalistic methods than do males (Harvey, 1972). This suggests that job information networks are sex-specific or discriminate against females, although it may mean instead that these networks are highly job-specific and women are usually in jobs about which less information travels through networks—for example, lower status occupations.

Yet for both male and female graduates, advertisements and agencies play only a small part in finding jobs. The largest single method of finding a job is by "contacting future employers on own"; desire and perseverance are apparently rewarded. We cannot tell from this whether graduates are more likely to contact prospective employers who they know (directly or indirectly) or have heard (through a network of acquaintances) would be receptive to their approach. If these *are* employers who are known about through personal networks, aspiration once again appears to have relatively slight importance. Some aspiration is necessary to find jobs through a network of weak ties, but it is far from sufficient.

The largely uncontrollable nature of a job search is further suggested by data in Table 7.5. Male university graduates used methods of finding jobs which differed according to the year they graduated. Later cohorts (graduating in 1964 and 1968) made greater use of government and private agencies, and university placement services than 1960 graduates. They also made somewhat less use of business and personal contacts. In part this change is attributable to the tightening of the job market in the late 1960s. While there was little variation in the number of job offers a new graduate received—regardless of his date of graduation, it averaged about two—those who graduated in 1968 were the most likely to have been dissatisfied with their first job, to have been laid off from it, to have been unemployed at some point, and to have perceived a need for further education to get a good job. Those who graduated in 1964, at the height of the job boom, were least likely to have experienced these difficulties.

The change in the job market cannot be held wholly responsible for changes in the approach taken to job finding noted in Table 7.5, for the latter changed smoothly over time while the job market got better, then worse, in the 1960s. The increase in universalistic job finding reflected a change in the class composition of the graduating student body. During the 1960s, enrollment in Ontario universities increased rapidly and a progressively higher proportion of students was drawn from working class and lower middle class families. Data in Table 7.6 indicate that the median occupational prestige of university graduates' fathers declined from a score of 56 to 50 (out of 99) between 1960 and 1968.

All other things (such as ethnicity, region of residence, size of community, and religion) being equal, people of higher social class have larger and better job-finding networks than people of lower social class. At the least, networks of high status people include a larger proportion of other high status people. Also, they are probably more heterogeneous in class composition than are lower class networks. We noted earlier a relationship between social status, and the location and

Table 7.5

Methods by which Ontario male university graduates obtained their first, second and third jobs after graduation, by year of graduation (per cent)

Method of obtaining job	Job/	1960 1	1960 2	1960 3	1964 1	1964 2	1964 3	1968 1	1968 2	1968 3
Advertisements		21.0	20.3	11.8	19.4	20.6	19.2	18.4	18.2	20.0
Government agency		1.3	1.0	0.6	1.1	1.2	0.8	2.8	2.5	6.2
Private agency		0.8	3.1	1.2	2.0	2.7	5.6	3.1	4.1	1.5
University placement service		9.8	2.8	1.2	10.5	2.9	0.8	14.6	2.5	1.5
Contact future employers on own		32.3	36.7	31.7	35.6	33.0	27.2	34.5	43.0	41.5
Business contacts		19.2	17.5	19.3	16.2	17.7	13.6	8.9	6.2	10.8
Promotion		1.0	10.5	24.2	3.9	13.0	26.4	5.8	15.7	13.8
Personal contacts		8.1	3.5	4.3	5.9	3.5	4.0	8.0	6.2	0.0
Other		6.6	4.5	5.6	5.4	5.3	2.4	3.9	1.7	4.6
Total		100.1	99.9	99.9	100.0	99.9	100.0	100.0	100.1	99.9
N =		396	286	161	648	339	125	721	242	65

Source: Harvey (1972: Tables 6.18, 6.25, 6.26), data rearranged

Table 7.6

Measures of job changing and cohort status mobility, by year of graduation: Ontario university graduates (male and female)

	Year of graduation		
	1960	1964	1968
Job changing:			
Percentage in sample taking a job after graduation	88.8	89.2	77.6
Percentage of job takers who move to a second job	77.2	63.3	39.8
Percentage of second-job holders who took a third job	55.6	46.2	29.7
*Job prestige:**			
Father's occupation	56.0	54.0	50.0
Job 1	62.1	63.1	60.2
Job 2	63.4	63.5	58.0
Job 3	63.1	62.5	56.4
Low prestige† first jobs as percentage of low prestige father's jobs	20.6	13.8	32.9
High prestige‡ first jobs as percentage of high prestige father's jobs	51.9	73.4	23.7

*Median occupational prestige, as calculated on the 99-point Porter-Pineo Occupational Prestige Scale.
†Low prestige = scores of 1-29 points
‡High prestige = scores of 70-99 points
Source: Harvey (1972: Tables 6.18, 6.25, 6.26, 6.15, 6.21, 6.22, 3.17), data recomputed

size of community of residence; there is also a correlation between ethnicity (and religion) and social class (Porter, 1965). Middle class Protestants or Jews living in large cities in central Canada will probably have more heterogeneous, larger networks, containing a higher proportion of white collar people, than will Canadians with other characteristics.

Just as father's social class is outside the control of a job-seeking graduate, so is the size and quality of the graduate's job network. Thus the increased use of universalistic methods for finding jobs in the late 1960s suggests an increase in the proportion of university graduates who were dependent upon either poor quality personal networks or universalistic methods of finding a job.

Actual and Intended Mobility

The majority of university graduates in Harvey's sample entered the job market upon graduation and, as data in Table 7.6 show, achieved a higher mean status in their first and subsequent jobs than their fathers enjoyed. Using the Porter-Pineo Occupational Prestige Scale, the mean prestige scores of the three cohorts' first jobs were found to be 10.9%, 16.9% and 20.4% higher than the mean fathers' occupational prestige for cohorts 1960, 1964, and 1968 respectively. Mobility increased despite a decrease in the average prestige of jobs attained by the 1968 cohort in the worsened job market.

It is difficult to judge the career mobility of university graduates from these data since few of the students sampled had been in the work force long enough to have taken a third job (or more). Few in the 1968 cohort had changed jobs twice, and those who did had done so as a result of pushes rather than pulls to better jobs. Given this limitation, movement of university graduates from a first to a second or a second to a third job did not imply much of a gain or loss in occupational status. Second and third jobs were always substantially more prestigious than father's job, although third jobs were generally less prestigious than second (and sometimes first) jobs. People changing jobs in a short period after graduation and within a tight job market appear to lose some of the advantage gained from a university degree.

The data provided by Harvey in Table 7.6 force us to compare cohorts and father's generation as groups. Yet there is an observable regression to the mean in occupational prestige of graduate's jobs, just as there is in the inheritance of intelligence, for example (Burt, 1961). The variation in job prestige of graduates is not as wide as the variation in prestige of father's jobs. Relatively fewer university graduates than cohort fathers held low prestige or high prestige jobs. As a group, the graduates rose slightly in occupational prestige as compared with their fathers, and they became less varied in occupational prestige. The goodness of the job market in the mid-1960s is reflected in the experience of the 1964 cohort, which achieved a lower proportion of "poor" jobs and a higher proportion of "good" jobs, in comparison with their fathers, than the preceding or succeeding cohorts.

These findings are not surprising, for if it were not already known that university graduation promoted upward mobility, fewer students would attend university than do at present. Yet the cohorts of university graduates who achieved such upward mobility and, typically, white collar jobs, represent but a small proportion of high school students who aspired to white collar jobs. At least five or six years may have passed from aspiration to realization. These years would have required high school graduation, P.S.S. attendance (supported by parents in various ways), P.S.S. graduation, and a favourable job market and job-finding network.

How well would the aspirations of Breton's high school boys have been realized by now? This question can be answered through reference to Breton's data (1972) and estimates of "success" drawn from the data produced by a computer simulation of intergenerational mobility described in Chapter Two. These latter estimates are used because no more general (or reliable) estimates exist for the Canadian population, and the simulated data have shown a close similarity to observed mobility rates where we have been able to make comparisons.

The aspirations of high school boys for upward mobility from blue collar origins into white collar occupations are twice as high as are presently realizable, and actual downward movement from a white collar origin into the blue collar class is about fifty percent higher than Canadian high school boys would wish. The desire for inheritance of white collar status by boys of white collar origin is higher than obtains at present, and the actual inheritance of blue collar status by boys of blue collar origin is twice what these boys would like. Such comparisons suggest a bad fit between current aspirations and the pattern of mobility prevailing in Canada at this time. In short, many young men are certain to have their aspirations disappointed.

Frustration and disappointment result from both the high aspiration level of Canadian boys and the relatively few white collar jobs to be filled in their generation. Let us suppose however that the occupational structure of Canada were directly and wholly responsive to boys' aspirations. That is, if a boy wanted a white collar job, a white collar job would be made for him. How many white collar jobs would be needed? This question is answerable through the use of matrix algebra, if we assume that present aspirations (as measured in Breton's study) will be maintained by future generations.

The "fixed point" of an occupational mobility table at equilibrium is found in a way well known to those familiar with matrix algebra (Kemeny and Snell, 1960; Kemeny, Snell and Thompson, 1957). After one or two generations, the occupational structure would come to contain 3 times as many white collar as blue collar jobs. Ignoring farming, which already contains only a small part of the Canadian work force, 75% of all males would hold white collar jobs and 25% would hold blue collar jobs if the occupational structure were determined by high school aspirations alone. It is conceivable that the occupational structure will, through automation, take on this character in another 50 to 100 years. However, no human society either past or present is known to have this occupational structure. In Canada today, there are only .7 white collar jobs to each blue collar job, not 3 to each one as present aspirations would require.

For this reason many young people will have to give up hopes of a white collar job and/or upward occupational mobility. Their aspirations fit the prevailing occupational structure badly. But how do aspirations that are inappropriate get adjusted to the realities of social organization? How do people deal with failure and disappointment?

Adaptations to Failure

A large proportion of boys who aspire to a white collar occupation in their first year of high school will have changed their aspiration, or recognized its futility, within three or four years—that is, long before they confront post-secondary education or the white collar job market. Various kinds of barriers are erected in the schools to change aspirations or prevent their realization. Students with lower mental ability and/or students with lower incomes are streamed into non-academic programs that train them for a trade and leave no easy access to P.S.S. Streaming of students on the basis of their IQ is described by Young in his plausible piece of science fiction, *The Rise of the Meritocracy* (1967). The more subtle ways of discouraging lower income children have been described at length by Kozol and others (Kozol, 1968; Schrag, 1968; Jones and Selby, 1972). Just as school principals can encourage their students with school policies implemented through guidance counselling, "easy" grading by teachers, and low rates of failure, they can discourage their students by reversing these policies.

Parents exert an important influence on the forming of occupational aspirations and their maintenance over time. Breton shows that lack of support from "significant others" leads to self-doubt, which in turn leads to vocational indecision (*op. cit.*: 331 *et passim*). It is crucial that students aspiring to white collar jobs receive support for their post-secondary school intentions, and Breton has shown that students of low mental ability and low social origins receive less support from their parents than students with an IQ or class origin that is high or medium. Aside from psychological support, parents may not be able and willing to provide financial support for P.S.S. studies. The absence of such support demands that a student aspire more strongly, work harder and (possibly) be brighter to proceed through P.S.S. to a white collar job than if he were receiving income support. The unavailability of support will serve to reduce the number of students going on to realize their occupational aspirations.

Some have inferred that the "fittest" survive this winnowing process to reach their aspired white collar positions: that success is itself proof of their fitness. However the evidence indicates that capable children from poor families are led to aspire less highly and receive less support and encouragement for high aspirations. They may suffer the disadvantages of lower class birth at least until the completion of post-secondary school and possibly beyond that, if job networks are as important as the foregoing has suggested. Somehow all of the white collar vacancies get filled, and in that sense the needs of society are satisfied. Yet we are far from the meritocracy Young has supposed we are moving towards, and the dysfunctions of social inequality are at least as great as the functions (Tumin, 1967).

Many whose aspirations are disappointed will be capable people stuck with a job they did not want and do not find equal to their capabilities. How do people disappointed by the discontinuity between socially induced aspirations and socially determined barriers to success deal with this disappointment? Robert Merton (1965) has presented a typology of responses that is suggestive although perhaps not exhaustive.

Some people will not be disappointed by a bad fit between "culture goals" and "institutionalized means" for attaining these goals. They will have been trained to aspire to those goals, in this case the popular goal of a white collar occupation, and trained to those means, in our society the supposedly open competition based on merit and effort, our culture defines as proper. Once they are successful, they may continue as conformists to the prevailing system, endorsing the dominant cultural goals and proper social means for upward mobility.

Those who are frustrated—who do not achieve a white collar occupation, or upward mobility of any kind—may respond to their frustration through "innovation", "ritualism", "retreatism" or "rebellion", as Merton has named these alternative adaptations (op. cit.: 140 et passim). The innovator will retain his original aspirations but seek to satisfy them in ways other than those commonly thought proper; he will reject the prevailing institutionalized means. The professional criminal may exemplify this, as Bell (1960) has argued and Talese (1971) has implied in his biography of Mafia boss Joe Bonanno. Ethnic minorities discriminated against by educational and business institutions have sometimes resorted to organized crime and then deserted it when the institutionalized means for upward mobility opened up to them (Bell, op. cit.).

The ritualist will, by contrast, give up his or her desire for the cultural goal, but will keep faith in the very institutionalized means that have proven fruitless. Such a person's aspirations may be transferred to the next generation, which is encouraged to aspire to the same heights in the same way as the parents did. This may be interpreted as optimism by some or as evidence of brainwashing or false consciousness by others. Merton sees this as "ritualism" because it has made an instrumental behaviour into a goal in itself. Merton notes that in formal organizations and elsewhere, means often become goals regardless of their efficacy in practice; this tendency is related to what Merton has called a development of the "bureaucratic personality" (op. cit.: Chapter VI).

The retreatist adjusts to his frustration by rejecting both the goals he once held and the means he used to seek these goals. Some retreatists are social drop-outs: skid row alcoholics, for example. There has been some debate as to whether beatniks and hippies represent a type of retreatist in the sense defined here, or something quite different. The debate revolves around whether "alienated" behaviour is typically retreatist or rebellious.

A rebel in Merton's typology is someone who has rejected the prevailing cultural goals and institutionalized means and has substituted new ones for reasons of principle, not expediency. As with any new value system, a sect or social movement may be established to provide members with social support and to persuade others into adopting these values. The "Jesus Freaks" and Scientologists are rebels in this sense, as are political activists of a revolutionary persuasion (e.g., S.D.S. members).

Merton's typology no more than suggests a range of adaptations to thwarted aspirations. However it is important to note that criminal behaviour is not always an innovative response to frustrations, and ritualistic behaviour may reflect innate conservatism, fear or uncertainty as much as personal frustration. Alcoholic or other retreat from a competitive social life need not follow from the denial of high aspirations. And, most important, rebellious behaviour may often or even generally proceed from a sense of social injustice that is independent of the rebel's own experiences. Indeed the prevalence of children of white collar families in current rebellious movements suggests that an alternative life style may be sought after despite great opportunities for "success" by the usual means.

There is, then, in Canada as in other industrial societies, a bad fit between culturally induced aspirations—such as the predominant aspirations for high status jobs that are in short supply—and the potential for realizing these aspirations in socially approved ways. There are various adaptations to the sense of failure and frustration felt on being denied one's goals. The frequency with which one or another adaptation is selected varies from society to society, and varies over time. An individual may even try many adaptations in his lifetime. The denial of aspirations and attendant sense of failure are widespread in Canadian society and may continue so into the foreseeable future. In this respect, failure and the psychological and social adaptations to it represent a major problem in our society.

Success as a Social Problem

The Individual's Goals

Merton's discussion of adaptation refers to the _anomie_ sensed by those who discover a discontinuity between cultural goals and the institutional means for attaining these goals. He has borrowed the term anomie from Durkheim who sometimes, as in _The Division of Labor in Society_ (1964), meant roughly what Merton takes him to mean—a kind of structural disorganization—and in other places, as in *Suicide* (1951), means something quite different. The term is used in *Suicide* to imply psychological disorientation that results from rapid changes in social structure and expectations (cf. Seeman, 1959). Durkheim believed that people could feel as "anomic" (and hence, driven to suicide) under rapidly improving conditions as under rapidly deteriorating conditions: it is the rapidity of change that is critical for psychological stability.

"Futurologists" such as Alvin Toffler (1971) and Arthur Clarke (1964) often assert that no period in human history has seen as much technological and cultural–ethical change as our present century; and further, that the rate of change is constantly increasing. If these assertions are correct, Durkheim would predict that some analysts will have become more concerned about the anomie associated with rapidly improving conditions (and success) that with disappointed people and deteriorating conditions.

Many feel that a major problem in the most developed countries is affluence itself. Sorokin (1941) argued several decades ago that industrial societies were entering a period of social and moral crisis that would end in a rejection of the present "sensate" culture. Sorokin and the futurologists differ mainly in their perception of human history: the futurologists imply that historical development is evolutionary and more or less one-directional, while Sorokin believes that history repeats itself, or is cyclical.

Yet there is agreement that success, affluence and unbounded opportunity are not without problems, both for the successful individual and for society as a whole. William Simon[2] has suggested that an analysis of anomie in developed, affluent countries like Canada could be constructed following Merton's typology of adaptations to frustrated hopes. Simon would consider, not the acceptance, rejection, or change of cultural goals and institutionalized means for attaining these goals, but rather the acceptance, rejection, or change of current social relations, *in toto*. He argues that many can take the attainability of cultural goals for granted; what is problematic is the general lack of *commitment* towards achieving those goals and the lack of *gratification* people may feel after attaining them. Anomie is, for Simon, a kind of existential nausea of the kind implied in Kierkegaard's philosophy and the existentialist novels of Sartre and Gide.[3]

Following this line of thought, Simon finds one current adaptation to anomie in the "ritualistic" behaviour of people who maintain a commitment to goals whose attainment affords no gratification. The "innovator" is one who enjoys the gratification of success and affluence, devours them gluttonously when they are available, but feels no deep conviction in their value or commitment to their attainment through effort. Affluent anomie may provoke a "retreat", an indifference to the gratifications brought by purposeful activity, and hence a rejection of commitment to these activities and gratifications. "Retreatism" is, as with Merton, a determination to stay uninvolved. Finally, "rebellion" implies a substitution of goals that give gratification and a commitment to these goals, but perhaps a commitment of a new kind. The Jesus Freaks represent the kind of rebels Simon has in mind. They have substituted spiritual gratification for material gratification, as Sorokin would have predicted; and they commit their personalities and resources to this enterprise in a way that far surpasses the commitment of most people to material rewards.

Are these adaptations to rapid change and "future shock"? Are they part of a cyclical return to spiritual concerns after four centuries of secular materialism? Or are they only the consequence of permissive child-rearing and inadequate socialization by the followers of Dr. Spock's child care manuals? The same phenomena can be analyzed on various levels of abstraction, giving slightly different conclusions and predictions for the future. At this point we know only that success has become for many as problematic as failure.

Society's Goals

Greater opportunity for success through upward mobility has produced societal as well as personal problems that are still at an early stage of development and not fully visible. Peter and Hull (1970) have enunciated the now famous "Peter Principle" that "in a hierarchy every employee tends to rise to his level of incompetence" (op. cit.: 7). This assertion, set out in a joking manner, has a certain ring of truth to it. Someone of proven capability is promoted from a lower level, and if that person proves capable at the new level, there is another promotion still. Promotions cease only after the employee has failed at a new level: this level is clearly that employee's "level of incompetence". Since there is almost never downward mobility (demotion) in formal organizations, the employee finishes his or her career as an incompetent. It follows from this that the greater the mobility in a hierarchy, the more fully it will be staffed with "incompetents", i.e., people who have quickly reached their level of incompetence and remain stuck there.

Another theory about the problems caused by mobility observes that societies are becoming more meritocratic and that as opportunity increases, competent people are being moved up the hierarchy with greater speed and frequency. Meritocratic theorists such as Young (1967) and Herrnstein (1973) fear that the lower classes will be depleted of talented people because the best people (and the best genes) are being allowed to move upwards. This assumes an increasing correlation between social class and IQ (or other measures of innate ability). If a reduction in marriage across class lines occurs, the gene pools and ability levels of different classes will become increasingly distinct.

Huxley's "brave new world" will be reached through social rather than chemical means, and without major social engineering.

Halsey (1972) recognizes that increased opportunities for social mobility are more likely to make the gene pools more distinct in a "class" society, where there is both mobility and across-class marriage, than in a "caste" society where there is neither. Yet he argues from a mathematical model of genetic change that:

> The class distributions continue to overlap, the majority of people with high intelligence still remaining in the low class. Only after seven generations would low intelligence be bred out of the high class. High intelligence would never be bred out of the low class (*op. cit.*: 205).

This does not argue that a contest system of mobility based on ability will have no problems; it simply states that great opportunity is unlikely to deplete the lower classes of intelligence. Yet Halsey has assumed that only 10% of the "high" class is replaced by talented lower class people in each generation. The actual rate of replacement may be much higher than this; data in Chapter Two showed roughly 30% of white collar and blue collar sons moving across the manual–nonmanual line in each generation. Hence the rate of depletion of talent is probably much greater than Halsey has allowed, and we shall need to examine whether such depletion is excessive under these circumstances.

Combining the concerns of the Peter Principle with those of the meritocratic theorists, we would conclude that easy upward mobility determined by ability alone may diminish the proportion of talented people in the lower classes and will move talented people of all class origins into positions of greatest inutility (i.e., their level of incompetence). This suggests that mobility is very much to the disadvantage of society: somehow everyone will end up in the wrong place.

Yet there are many questionable assumptions in this theoretical exercise. Does the Peter Principle describe a general phenomenon or a perverse and relatively infrequent one? Is that principle even valid? Is "talent" measurable for the purposes of streaming into channels of upward mobility, and if so, is it adequately measured by the IQ test? How much is talent inherited and how much is it environmentally determined? And finally, does the class position of highly talented persons really make any difference to society? Societies have a way of surviving under less than optimal conditions: the caste system is an example of this. I do not mean to dismiss these problems involved in the mobility of talent; they should be raised for debate, as we are far from defining the issues adequately, much less providing a solution.

Perhaps the greatest and most evident problem of increased opportunity, one that was suggested in the first chapter, is the tendency for mobility and success to maintain the status quo. People who become successful through their own efforts endorse the status quo most strongly and provide least sympathy for people who have not succeeded. They often attribute the failure of others to inadequate effort or talent and deny that inequality erects barriers to mobility for those in the lower classes. Yet such barriers do exist. We have also noted that our culture induces aspirations that are largely unrealizable: there cannot be as many white collar jobs as high school boys would require, for example. This is a fact of life which the success of a few does not invalidate.

The problem of conformity to inappropriate values has two aspects and can be solved in two ways, excluding the unlikely possibility of a society that is not hierarchical. First, such conformity prevents the establishment of equal opportunity through the removal of class barriers to success. Opportunity could be increased, if not fully equalized, by measures such as free post-secondary education and a living allowance for all P.S.S. students who needed it. These measures alone would not ensure equality of opportunity, because real equality depends on the cultural resources and encouragement lower class children receive at home. The direct equalization of home environments would be a major social undertaking, but reducing the financial barriers to P.S.S. education might indirectly promote parental encouragement. If P.S.S. education required no personal or parental expense, more lower class parents would probably encourage their children to strive for white collar occupations and P.S.S. education.

Conformity in Merton's terms also maintains an invalid world view somewhat like the belief in unlimited natural resources. As with timber and oil, there are not enough white collar jobs to provide for all who want them. The encouragement of all students to seek white collar jobs may, once class barriers have been removed, increase the likelihood that the most talented children will enter these occupations; but it also ensures that the hopes of a substantial part of the population will be disappointed. While some disappointment is an inevitable part of the human condition, we should still try to minimize it whenever possible. If we hold that the filling of white collar positions with talented people has the highest priority, perhaps we should be also training ourselves and our children to deal more effectively with disappointment. Some part of such training might include teaching children that manual work is not intrinsically mean, debasing, dull, or trivial, let alone unremunerative.

We may need a different view of life, in which success in its current meaning plays a smaller part. By seeing ourselves as separate from the roles we play and the power we hold over other people, we can hope to transcend the disappointment and anomie that are current in our society. Transcendence should not serve as an alternative to social change any more than the conservation of natural resources should be used to mask a preference for pre-industrial conditions. The present resurgence of religious and mystical interest indicates a search, however misguided, for this kind of transcendence and should be praised as such.

Let us change what can and should be changed in the organization of our society, for that will be to everyone's advantage in the long run. As sociologists we should learn how changing the social structure increases the total sum of human happiness and well-being; changes that do not contribute to this are wasteful or pernicious. Insight and courage are needed to make those changes that are beneficial and to transcend what cannot be changed.

Chapter 7 Notes

[1] Perhaps even this underestimates the real level of preference for white collar jobs among young people and reflects their recognition that the attainability of such jobs is limited.

[2] The remarks attributed to Professor William Simon were made at a colloquium in February, 1974 at the University of Toronto.

[3] Sorokin (1964) has formulated a "dissociative hypothesis" linking social mobility to diminished intimacy, rootlessness, and increased isolation and loneliness. This hypothesis has received some support from research by Ellis and Lane (1967). Perhaps the affluent anomie observed by Simon is in fact the result of increased and widespread social mobility in North America.

BIBLIOGRAPHY

Anderson, Grace M.: *Networks of Contact: The Portuguese in Toronto*, Waterloo, Ontario: Wilfrid Laurier University Press, 1974.

Ariès, Philippe: *Centuries of Childhood*, New York: Vintage Books, 1962.

Armstrong, Donald E.: *Education and Achievement*, Studies of the Royal Commission on Bilingualism and Biculturalism, No. 7, Ottawa: Queen's Printer, 1970.

Baltzell, E. Digby: *Philadephia Gentlemen: The Making of a National Upper Class*, New York: Free Press, 1958.

Baltzell, E. Digby: *The Protestant Establishment: Aristocracy and Caste in America*, New York: Vintage Books, 1964.

Banks, J.A.: *Prosperity and Parenthood: A Study of Family Planning among the Victorian Middle Classes*, London: Routledge and Kegan Paul, 1954.

Barber, Bernard and Elinor G. Barber (ed.): *European Social Class: Stability and Change*, New York: Macmillan, 1965.

Barclay, George W.: *Techniques of Population Analysis*, New York: John Wiley, 1958.

Bartholomew, David J.: *Stochastic Models for Social Processes*, London: John Wiley, 1967.

Bartlett, M.S.: *Stochastic Population Models in Ecology and Epidemiology*, London: Methuen, 1960.

Becker, Howard S.: *Outsiders: Studies in the Sociology of Deviance*, New York: Free Press, 1963.

Bell, Daniel: "Crime as an American way of life," Reprinted in Daniel Bell, *The End of Ideology*, New York: Free Press, 1960.

Belshaw, Cyril: *Traditional Exchange and Modern Markets*, Englewood Cliffs, N.J.: Prentice-Hall, 1965.

Bhat, U. Narayan: *Elements of Applied Stochastic Processes*, New York: John Wiley, 1972.

Blau, Peter and O.D. Duncan: *The American Occupational Structure*, New York: John Wiley, 1967.

Blau, Peter and Richard Schoenherr: *The Structure of Organizations*, New York: Basic Books, 1971.

Blishen, Bernard R.: "Social class and opportunity in Canada," *Canadian Review of Sociology and Anthropology*, 7(2), 1970, 110-127.

Boorstin, Daniel J.: *The Image: A Guide to Pseudo-events in America*, New York: Harper and Row, 1964.

Bossen, Marianne: *The Patterns of Manpower Utilization in Canadian Department Stores*, Studies of the Royal Commission on the Status of Women in Canada, No. 3, Ottawa: Queen's Printer, 1971a.

Bossen, Marianne: *Manpower Utilization in Canadian Chartered Banks*, Studies of the Royal Commission on the Status of Women in Canada, No. 4, Ottawa: Queen's Printer, 1971b.

Breton, Raymond: *Social and Academic Factors in the Career Decisions of Canadian Youth*, Ottawa: Department of Manpower and Immigration, Queen's Printer, 1972.

Breton, Raymond and Howard Roseborough: "Ethnic differences in status", in Bernard Blishen, Frank Jones *et al.*, (eds.), *Canadian Society*, Toronto: Macmillan of Canada, 1971.

Bruyère, Jean de la: *Characters*, Translated with an Introduction by Jean Stewart, Harmondsworth: Penguin Books, 1970.

Bryan, James H.: "Apprenticeships in prostitution", in Marcello Truzzi (ed.), *Sociology and Everday Life*, Englewood Cliffs, N.J.: Prentice-Hall, 1968.

Bryson, Lyman: "Notes on a theory of advice", in Robert K. Merton *et al.*, *Reader in Bureaucracy*, New York: Free Press, 1951.

Burnham, James: *The Managerial Revolution*, Harmondsworth, England: Penguin Books, 1962.

Burt, C.: "Intelligence and Social Mobility," *British Journal of Statistical Psychology*, 14, 1961, 3-25.

Butler, Samuel: *Erewhon, or Over the Range*, New York: Signet Classics, New American Library, 1960.

Caplow, Theodore: The Sociology of Work, Minneapolis: University of Minneapolis Press, 1954.

Caplow, Theodore and Reece J. McGee: The Academic Marketplace, New York: Basic Books, 1958.

Chamberlain, Neil W.: Beyond Malthus: Population and Power, New York: Basic Books, 1970.

Clarke, Arthur C.: Profiles of the Future, New York: Bantam Books, 1964.

Clement, Wallace: The Canadian Corporate Elite, Toronto, McClelland and Stewart, 1975.

Coale, Ansley: The Growth and Structure of Human Populations, Princeton, N.J.: Princeton University Press, 1972.

Coleman, James S.: Introduction to Mathematical Sociology, New York: Free Press, 1964.

Coleman, James S. et al: Equality of Educational Opportunity, Washington, D.C.: Office of Education, U.S. Department of Health, Education and Welfare, U.S. Government Printing Office, 1966.

Cox, D.R. and W.L. Smith: Queues, London: Chapman and Hall, 1961.

Cuneo, Carl and James Curtis: "Social ascription in the educational and occupational status attainment of urban Canadians", Canadian Review of Sociology and Anthropology, 12(1), 1975.

Dalton, Melville: "Informal factors in career achievement", American Journal of Sociology, 56 (March), 1951, 407-415.

Davis, Kingsley: "The world demographic transition," The Annals of the American Academy of Political and Social Science, 237 (January), 1945.

Denton, Frank T. and Sylvia Ostry: Working-Life Tables for Canadian Males, Ottawa: Dominion Bureau of Statistics, 1969.

Department of Labour: Occupational Histories (of married women working for pay in eight Canadian cities), Ottawa: Queen's Printer, 1960.

Dhalla, Nariman K.: These Canadians: A Sourcebook of Marketing and Socio-economic Facts, Toronto: McGraw-Hill, 1966.

Dofny, Jacques and Muriel Garon-Audy: "Mobilités professionelles au Québec," Sociologie et Sociétés, 1 (Nov.), 1969, 277-301.

Dominion Bureau of Statistics: Post-Secondary Student Population Survey, 1968-69, Ottawa: Education Division, Queen's Printer, 1970.

Dumont, Arsène: Dépopulation et Civilisation: Etudes demographiques, Paris: Lecrosnier et Babe, 1890.

Durkheim, Emile: Suicide, Translated by John A. Spaulding and George Simpson, New York: Free Press, 1951.

Durkheim, Emile: The Division of Labor in Society, Translated by George Simpson, New York: Free Press, 1964.

Eliot, T.S.: The Complete Poems and Plays, 1909-1950, New York: Harcourt, Brace and Company, 1968.

Ellis, Robert A. and W. Clayton Lane: "Social mobility and social isolation: a test of Sorokin's dissociative hypotheses", American Sociological Review, 32 (April), 1967, 237-253.

Engels, Friedrich: The Origin of the Family, Private Property and the State, Reprinted in Volume II of Selected Works in Two Volumes, Moscow: Foreign Languages Publishing House, 1962.

Etzioni, Amitai: A Comparative Analysis of Complex Organizations, New York: Free Press, 1961.

Feller, William: Introduction to Probability Theory and Its Applications, Volume 1, Third Edition, New York: John Wiley, 1968.

Friedrich, Otto: Decline and Fall, New York: Ballantine Books, 1971.

Galbraith, John Kenneth: The New Industrial State, Boston: Houghton Mifflin, 1967.

Geoffroy, Renée and Paule Sainte-Marie; Attitudes of Union Workers to Women in Industry, Studies of the Royal Commission on the Status of Women in Canada, No. 9, Ottawa: Queen's Printer, 1971.

Gerth, Hans H. and C. Wright Mills (ed.): From Max Weber: Essays in Sociology, New York: Galaxy Books, Oxford University Press, 1964.

Glaser, Barney G. (ed.): Organizational Careers: A Sourcebook for Theory, Chicago: Aldine, 1968.

Glazer, Nathan and Daniel Patrick Moynihan: Beyond the Melting Pot, Cambridge, Mass.: M.I.T. Press, 1963.

Goffman, Erving: "Symbols of class status," Reprinted in Marcello Truzzi, *Sociology and Everyday Life*, Englewood Cliffs, N.J.: Prentice-Hall, 1968.

Goldner, Fred H.: "Demotion in industrial management," *American Sociological Review*, 30(5), 1965, 714-724.

Goldthorpe, John H.: "Social stratification in industrial society", in R. Bendix and S.M. Lipset (eds.), *Class, Status and Power*, 2nd edition, New York: Free Press, 1966.

Gouldner, Alvin W.: *Patterns of Industrial Bureaucracy*, New York: Free Press, 1954.

Granovetter, Mark: "The strength of weak ties," *American Journal of Sociology*, 78(6), 1973, 1360-1380.

Granovetter, Mark: *Getting a Job: A Study of Contacts and Careers*, Cambridge, Mass.: Harvard University Press, 1974.

Gray, James H.: *Booze: The Impact of Whisky on the Prairie West*, Toronto: Macmillan, 1972.

Haggett, Peter and Richard J. Chorley: *Network Analysis in Geography*, London: Edward Arnold, 1969.

Hajnal, John: "Age at marriage and proportion marrying," *Population Studies*, 7(2), 1953, 111-132.

Hall, Oswald: "Informal organization of the medical profession," *Canadian Journal of Economics and Political Science*, 12 (February), 1946, 31-44.

Halsey, A.H.: "Social mobility," in G.A. Harrison and A.J. Boyce (ed.), *The Structure of Human Populations*, London: Oxford University Press, 1972.

Harris, Theodore E.: *The Theory of Branching Processes*, Englewood Cliffs, N.J.: Prentice-Hall, 1963.

Harvey, Edward B.: *Education and Employment of Arts and Science Graduates: The Last Decade in Ontario*, Commission on Post-Secondary Education in Ontario, Toronto: Queen's Printer, 1972.

Havel, J.E.: "Some effects of the introduction of a policy of bilingualism into the polyglot community of Sudbury," *Canadian Review of Sociology and Anthropology*, 9(1), 1972, 57-71.

Heap, James L. (ed.): *Everybody's Canada: The Vertical Mosaic Reviewed and Re-examined*, Toronto: Burns and MacEachern, 1974.

Hecht, J. Jean: "Social mobility among the servant class of 18th century England," in Bernard Barber and Elinor G. Barber (ed.), *European Social Class: Stability and Change*, New York: Macmillan, 1965.

Herrnstein, R.J.: *I.Q. in the Meritocracy*, Boston: Little, Brown, 1973.

Hodge, Robert W. et al: "A comparative study of occupational prestige," in Reinhard Bendix and S.M. Lipset, (eds.) *Class, Status, and Power*, Second Edition, New York: Free Press, 1966.

Holmes, Jeffrey: "Demography affects employment, promotion," *University Affairs*, March, 1974.

Homans, George C.: *Social Behavior: Its Elementary Forms*, Revised Edition, New York: Harcourt Brace Jovanovich, 1974.

Horowitz, Irving L.: "The Vertical Mosaic: a review" in James L. Heap (ed.), *Everybody's Canada*, Toronto: Burns and MacEachern, 1974.

House, J. Douglas: "Entrepreneurial career patterns of residential real estate agents in Montreal," *Canadian Review of Sociology and Anthropology*, 11(2), 1974, 110-124.

Howard, Leslie and Jack Wayne: "Ethnicity in Canada: a social structural view", *Journal of Comparative Sociology*, forthcoming, 1974.

Hughes, Everett C.: *Men and Their Work*, Glencoe, Ill.: Free Press, 1958.

Hutton, J.H.: *Caste in India*, Cambridge: The University Press, 1946.

Hutson, Susan: "Social ranking in a French Alpine Community," in F.G. Bailey (ed.), *Gifts and Poison: The Politics of Reputation*, Toronto: Copp Clark, 1971.

Janowitz, Morris: *The Professional Soldier*, New York: Free Press of Glencoe, 1960.

Johnson, Samuel: *Letter to Lord Chesterfield*, quoted from F.L. Lucas, *Style*, New York: Collier Books, 1962.

Johnstone, John C.: *Young Peoples' Images of Canadian Society*, Studies of the Royal Commission on Bilingualism and Biculturalism, No. 2., Ottawa: Queen's Printer, 1969.

Jones, F. Lancaster: "Social mobility and industrial society: a thesis re-examined," *The Sociological Quarterly*, Summer, 1969, 292-305.

Jones, Frank: "Some social consequences of immigration for Canada," in Bernard Blishen, Frank Jones et al. (eds.), *Canadian Society*, Toronto: Macmillan of Canada, 1971.

Jones, Frank and John Selby: "School performance and social class," in Thomas J. Ryan (ed.), *Poverty and the Child: A Canadian Study*, Toronto: McGraw-Hill Ryerson, 1972.

Jones, Gavin W.: "Effect of population change on the attainment of educational goals in the developing countries," in National Academy of Sciences, *Rapid Population Growth, Volume 2*, Baltimore: The Johns Hopkins Press, 1972.

Kahl, Joseph A.: *The American Class Structure*, New York: Holt, Rinehart and Winston, 1957.

Kalbach, Warren E.: *The Impact of Immigration on Canada's Population*, Ottawa: Dominion Bureau of Statistics, Queen's Printer, 1970.

Kalbach, Warren E. and Wayne McVey: *The Demographic Bases of Canadian Society*, Toronto: McGraw-Hill Ryerson, 1971.

Kantner, Andrew et al: "Canada", *Country Profiles*, New York: The Population Council, September, 1974.

Kaufmann, Arnold: *The Science of Decision-making*, New York: McGraw-Hill, World University Library, 1968.

Kemeny, John G., J. Laurie Snell, and Gerald L. Thompson: *Introduction to Finite Mathematics*, Englewood Cliffs, N.J.: Prentice-Hall, 1957.

Kemeny, John and J.L. Snell: *Finite Markov Chains*, Princeton N.J.: D. Van Nostrand, 1960.

Keyfitz, Nathan: "The growth of the Canadian population," *Population Studies*, 4, 1950, 47-63.

Keyfitz, Nathan: *Introduction to the Mathematics of Population*, Reading Mass.: Addison-Wesley, 1968.

Keyfitz, Nathan and Wilhelm Flieger: *Population: Facts and Methods of Demography*, San Francisco: W.H. Freeman and Company, 1971.

Kitagawa, Evelyn and Philip M. Hauser: *Differential Mortality in the United States: A Study of Socioeconomic Epidemiology*, Cambridge, Mass.: Harvard University Press, 1973.

Klein, William: "Recruitment of the Canadian Judiciary, 1905-1970," Toronto: unpublished doctoral dissertation, University of Toronto, 1975.

Kornhauser, William: *Scientists in Industry*, Berkeley: University of California Press, 1962.

Koestler, Arthur: *The Case of the Midwife Toad*, New York: Vintage Books, 1973.

Kozol, Jonathan: *Death at an Early Age*, New York: Bantam Books, 1968.

Kubat, Daniel and David Thornton: *A Statistical Profile of Canadian Society*, Toronto: McGraw-Hill Ryerson, 1974.

Kuznets, Simon: *Modern Economic Growth*, New Haven: Yale University Press, 1966.

Lambert, Ronald: *Sex Role Imagery in Children: The Social Origins of Mind*, Studies of the Royal Commission on the Status of Women in Canada, No. 6, Ottawa: Queen's Printer, 1969.

Lanphier, C.M. and R.N. Morris: "Structural aspects of differences in income between Anglophones and Francophones," *Canadian Review of Sociology and Anthropology*, 11(1), 1974, 53-66.

Laslett, Peter: *The World We Have Lost*, London, Methuen and Company, 1965.

Lawrence, J.R. (ed.): *Operational Research and the Social Sciences*, London: Tavistock Publications, 1966.

Lenski, Gerhard E. "Status crystallization: a non-vertical dimension of social status," *American Sociological Review*, 19, 1954, 405-413.

Lenski, Gerhard E. *Power and Privilege: A Theory of Social Stratification*, New York: McGraw-Hill, 1966.

Lerner, Daniel: *The Passing of Traditional Society*, New York: Free Press, 1964.

Levine, Joel: "A two parameter model of interaction in father–son status mobility," *Behavioral Science* (17), 1972, 455-465.

Levy, Reuben: *The Social Structure of Islam*, Cambridge: Cambridge University Press, 1965.

Lipset, Seymour Martin: *The First New Nation*, New York: Basic Books, 1963.

Lipset, S.M. and Reinhard Bendix: *Social Mobility in Industrial Society*, Berkeley, California: University of California Press, 1959.

Lucas, Rex: *Minetown, Milltown, Railtown*, Toronto: University of Toronto Press, 1972.

Mackinnon, Colonel David: *The Origin and Services of the Coldstream Guards*, Two volumes, London: Richard Bentley, 1833.

Maine, Henry Sumner: *Ancient Law*, Boston: Beacon Press, 1963.

Malthus, Thomas R.: *An Essay on the Principle of Population*, 2 volumes, London: Everyman's Library, Dent. and Sons, 1958.

Marcson, Simon: *The Scientist in American Industry*, Industrial Relations Section, Princeton University: Harper and Row, 1960.

Marshall, T.H.: *Citizenship and Social Class*, London: Cambridge University Press, 1950.

Martin, Norman H. and Anselm L. Strauss: "Patterns of mobility within industrial organizations," *Journal of Business*, 29(2), 1956, 101-110.

Marx, Karl and Frederick Engels: *Manifesto of the Communist Party*, Reprinted in Volume 1 of *Selected Works in Two Volumes*, Moscow: Foreign Languages Publishing House, 1962.

McClelland, David C.: *The Achieving Society*, Princeton, N.J.: Van Nostrand, 1961.

Mead, George Herbert: *Mind, Self, and Society*, Chicago: University of Chicago Press, 1934.

Meadows, Donella H. *et al*: *The Limits to Growth*, New York: Universe Books, 1972.

Medvedev, Zhores A.: *The Rise and Fall of T.D. Lysenko*, New York: Doubleday Anchor Books, 1971.

Merton, Robert K.: *Social Theory and Social Structure*, Revised edition, New York: Free Press, 1965.

Miller, S.M.: "Comparative social mobility: a trend report and bibliography", *Current Sociology*, 9, 1960, 1-89.

Mills, C. Wright: *White Collar*, New York: Oxford University Press, 1951.

Mitamura, Taisuke: *Chinese Eunuchs: The Structure of Intimate Politics*, Rutland, Vt.: Charles E. Tuttle Company, 1970.

Mizruchi, Ephraim H.: *Success and Opportunity*, New York: Free Press, 1964.

Moore, Barrington: *Social Origins of Dictatorship and Democracy*, Boston: Beacon Press, 1966.

Moore, Wilbert E.: *The Impact of Industry*, Englewood Cliffs, N.J.: Prentice-Hall, 1965.

More, Douglas M. "Demotion," *Social Problems*, 9(3), 1962, 213-221.

Morton, Frederick: *The Rothschilds: A Family Portrait*, New York: Fawcett World Library, 1963.

Mosteller, Frederick: "Association and estimation in contingency tables," *Journal of the American Statistical Association*, 63 (March), 1968, 1-28.

Moyer, M.S. and G. Snyder: *Trends in Canadian Marketing*, Ottawa: Dominion Bureau of Statistics, 1967.

Myrdal, Gunnar: *Asian Drama, Volume 3: Economic Realities*, New York: Patheon, 1968.

Nadel, S.F.: *The Theory of Social Structure*, London: Cohen and West, 1965.

Nosanchuk, Terrance A.: "A note on the correlation coefficient for assessing the similarity of occupation rankings," *Canadian Review of Sociology and Anthropology*, 9(4), 1972, 357-365.

Ostry, Sylvia: *Unemployment in Canada*, Ottawa: Dominion Bureau of Statistics, 1968.

Parai, Louis: *Immigration and Emigration of Professional and Skilled Manpower During the Post-War Period*, Special study No 1, Ottawa: The Queen's Printer, for the Economic Council of Canada, 1965.

Parsons, Talcott: *The Structure of Social Action*, New York: Free Press, 1964.

Parsons, Talcott: "On the concept of political power," in Reinhard Bendix and S.M. Lipset (eds.), *Class, Status and Power*, Second Edition, New York: Free Press, 1966.

Pereyra, Simon: *Curanta Anos en el Lecho del Ganges, 1708*, Excerpted in Jorge Luis Borges and Aldolfo Bioy Casares, *Extraordinary Tales*, New York: Herder and Herder, 1971.

Peter, Laurence J. and Raymond Hull: *The Peter Principle*, New York: Bantam Books, 1970.

Podoluk, Jenny R.: *Incomes of Canadians*, Ottawa: Dominion Bureau of Statistics, 1968.

Podhoretz, Norman: *Making It*, New York: Bantam Books, 1969.

Porter, John: *The Vertical Mosaic*, Toronto: University of Toronto Press, 1965.

Porter, John: *Canadian Social Structure: A Statistical Profile*, Toronto: McClelland and Stewart, 1967.

Reitz, Jeffrey: "Analysis of changing group inequalities in a changing occupational structure", Presented at the Annual Meetings of the Canadian Sociology and Anthropology Association, Toronto, August 21-24, 1974.

Renner, Karl: *The Institutions of Private Law and their Social Functions*, London: Routledge and Kegan Paul, 1949.

Richer, Stephen and Raymond Breton: "School organization and student differences: some views of Canadian educators", *Canadian Education and Research Digest*, (March), 1968, 20-37.

Richmond, Anthony H.: "Social mobility of immigrants in Canada," in Bernard Blishen, Frank Jones et al (ed.), *Canadian Society*, Toronto: Macmillan of Canada, 1971.

Robson, R.A.H. and Mireille Lapointe: *A Comparison of Men's and Women's Salaries and Employment Fringe Benefits in the Academic Profession*, Studies of the Royal Commission on the Status of Women in Canada, No. 1, Ottawa: Queen's Printer, 1971.

Rogoff, Natalie: *Recent Trends in Occupational Mobility*, Glencoe, Ill.: Free Press, 1953.

Roseborough, Howard and Raymond Breton: "Perceptions of the relative economic and political advantages of ethnic groups in Canada," in Bernard Blishen, Frank Jones et al. (ed.), *Canadian Society*, Toronto: Macmillan of Canada, 1971.

Roth, Julius A.: *Timetables*, Indianapolis: Bobbs-Merrill, 1963.

Royal Commission on the Status of Women in Canada: *Report*, Ottawa: Queen's Printer, 1970.

Russett, Bruce et al: *World Handbook of Political and Social Indicators*, New Haven: Yale University Press, 1964.

Sauvy, Alfred: *Fertility and Survival*, New York: Collier Books, 1963.

Schachter, Stanley, *The Psychology of Affiliation*, Stanford California: Stanford University Press, 1959.

Schrag, Peter: *Village School Downtown*, Boston: Beacon Press, 1968.

Schultz, T. Paul: "An economic perspective on population growth," in National Academy of Sciences, *Rapid Population Growth, Volume 2*, Baltimore: The John Hopkins Press, 1972.

Seeman, Melvin: "On the meaning of alientation," *American Sociological Review*, 24 (December), 1959, 738-791.

Smigel, Erwin O.: "Selecting law partners," in Barney G. Glaser (ed.), *Organizational Careers: A Sourcebook for Theory*, Chicago: Aldine, 1968.

Smith, David and Lorne Tepperman: "Changes in the Canadian business and legal elites, 1870-1970," *Canadian Review of Sociology and Anthroplogy*, 11(2), 1974, 97-109.

Soares, Glaucio: "Economic development and class structure," in Reinhard Bendix and S.M. Lipset (eds.), *Class, Status and Power*, Second Edition, New York: Free Press, 1966.

Sorokin, Pitrim A.' *The Crisis of Our Age: The Social and Cultural Outlook*, New York: E.P. Dutton and Company, 1941.

Sorokin, Pitrim A.: *Social and Cultural Mobility*, New York: Free Press, 1964.

Spellman, A.B. *Four Lives in the Bebop Business*, New York: Random House, 1966.

Stouffer, Samuel A.: "Intervening opportunities: a theory relating mobility and distance," and "Intervening opportunities and competing migrants," Reprinted in his *Research to Test Ideas*, Chicago: University of Chicago Press, 1963.

Sutherland, Edwin H.: *The Professional Thief*, Chicago, University of Chicago Press, 1937.

Talese, Gay: *Honor Thy Father*, Greenwich, Conn.: Fawcett Crest Book, 1971.

Taylor, Norman W.: "The French-Canadian industrial entrepreneur, and his social environment," in Marcel Rioux and Yves Martin (ed.), *French Canadian Society*, Volume 1, Toronto: McClelland and Stewart, 1964.

Tepperman, Lorne: "The natural disruption of dynasties," *Canadian Review of Sociology and Anthropology*, 9(2), 1972, 111-133.

Tepperman, Lorne: "The multiplication of opportunities: a model of sponsored mobility, Coventry, England, 1420-1450," *Canadian Review of Sociology and Anthropology*, 10(1), 1973, 1-19.

Tepperman, Lorne: "Demographic aspects of career mobility," *Canadian Review of Sociology and Anthropology*, 12(2), 1975(a), 163-177.

Tepperman, Lorne: "A simulation of social mobility in industrial societies," *Canadian Review of Sociology and Anthropology*, forthcoming, 1975(b).

Tepperman, Lorne and Barry Tepperman: "Dynasty formation in eight imaginary societies," *Canadian Review of Sociology and Anthropology*, 8(3), 1971, 121-141.

Thrupp, Sylvia: *The Merchant Class of Medieval London*, Ann Arbor, Michigan: University of Michigan Press, 1962.

Toffler, Alvin: *Future Shock*, New York: Bantam Books, 1971.

Tumin, Melvin M.: *Social Stratification: The Forms and Functions of Inequality*, Foundations of Modern Sociology Series, Englewood Cliffs, N.J.: Prentice-Hall, 1967.

Turner, Ralph H.: "Sponsored and contest mobility and the school system," in Celia Heller (ed.), *Structured Social Inequality*, Toronto: Collier Macmillan Canada, 1970.

Turrittin, A.H.: "Intergenerational occupational mobility in Ontario: a secondary analysis of 1968 sample survey data," Presented at the Annual Meeting of the Canadian Sociological and Anthropological Association, Winnipeg, 1970.

Turrittin, A.H. "Social mobility in Canada: a comparison of three provincial studies and some methodological questions," Presented at the Eighth World Congress of Sociology, Toronto, 1974.

United Nations, Department of Economic and Social Affairs: *Manual IV: Methods of Estimating Basic Demographic Measures from Incomplete Data*, New York: Population Studies, No. 42, ST/SOA/Series A/42, 1967.

Urquhart, M.C. (ed.), *Historical Statistics of Canada*, Toronto: The Macmillan Company of Canada, 1965.

Valentine, Charles A.: *Culture and Poverty: Critique and Counter-proposals*, Chicago: University of Chicago Press, 1968.

Veblen, Thorstein: *The Theory of the Leisure Class*, New York: Viking, 1912.

Warner, W. Lloyd and James C. Abegglen: "Organization career patterns of business leaders," in Barney G. Glaser (ed.), *Organizational Careers: A Sourcebook for Theory*, Chicago: Aldine, 1968.

Weber, Max: *The City*, New York: Free Press, 1958.

Weiner, Myron (ed.), *Modernization: The Dynamics of Growth*, Voice of America Forum Lectures, 1966.

White, Harrison: *Chains of Opportunity: System Models of Mobility in Organizations*, Cambridge, Mass.: Harvard University Press, 1970.

White, Harrison and Cynthia White: *Canvases and Careers: Institutional Change in the French Painting World*, New York: John Wiley, 1965.

Wilensky, Harold L.: "Careers, life-styles, and social integration," *International Social Science*, 12(4), 1960, 553-558.

Wiley, Norbert F.: "The ethnic mobility trap and stratification theory", *Social Problems*, 15 (Fall), 1967, 147-159.

Women's Bureau, Canada Department of Labour: *Changing Patterns in Women's Employment*, Ottawa: Queen's Printer, 1966.

Wray, Joe D. "Population pressure on families: family size and child spacing," in National Academy of Sciences, *Rapid Population Growth*, Volume 2, Baltimore: The John Hopkins Press, 1972.

Wrigley, E.A.: *Population and History*, New York: McGraw-Hill World University Library, 1969.

Young, Michael: *The Rise of the Meritocracy, 1870–2033*, Baltimore: Penguin Books, 1967.

Ziegler, Phillip: *The Black Death*, Harmondsworth, England: Penguin Books, 1970.

Zipf, George K.: *Human Behavior and the Principle of Least Effort*, Cambridge, Mass.: Addison-Wesley Press, Inc., 1949.

INDEX

⌇